SCHUYLER COUNTY MISSOURI

HISTORY
AND
BIOGRAPHIES

Goodspeed

Heritage Books
2024

HERITAGE BOOKS

AN IMPRINT OF HERITAGE BOOKS, INC.

Books, CDs, and more—Worldwide

For our listing of thousands of titles see our website
at
www.HeritageBooks.com

A Facsimile Reprint
Published 2024 by
HERITAGE BOOKS, INC.
Publishing Division
5810 Ruatan Street
Berwyn Heights, MD 20740

Reprinted: 2006
Mountain Press
Signal Mountain, Tennessee

International Standard Book Number
Paperbound: 978-0-7884-9415-4

HISTORY OF SCHUYLER COUNTY.

BOUNDARY AND TOPOGRAPHY.

SCHUYLER is the third county west from the Mississippi River on the northern tier of counties in the State of Missouri. It is bounded on the north by parts of Appanoose and Davis Counties, Iowa; on the east by Scotland County; on the south by Adair, and on the west by the Chariton River, which separates it from Putnam County. In form it is nearly square, being a little longer from east to west than from north to south, and its area is about 320 square miles, or 205,000 acres. It varies in its surface features from the broken to rolling and even flat, and is about evenly divided in these characters. The broken or hilly uplands gradually descend into level lands, which pass by gradual slopes into gently rolling or undulating prairie, and this, in turn, as it nears the streams, becomes hilly and often quite broken. In the northern part of the county, the rolling character seems to predominate; the surface usually rises gently from the bottoms, gradually merging into rolling land, when it will again vary from flat to undulating prairie. An elevated plateau, known as the Grand Divide, runs quite irregularly from north to south through the county, at an average distance of five miles east of the Chariton River. It is a part of the Grand Divide between the Mississippi and Missouri Rivers, or, more properly speaking, it is the watershed between the Mississippi and Chariton Rivers. The country slopes off irregularly from this ridge or divide, becoming quite hilly on the west toward Chariton River, but level on the east. The southeastern corner of the county is broken, rising into rough ridges and hills in the vicinity of streams, and extending a considerable distance on each side of them.

Most of the broken land lies near the Chariton River. The bottoms along the streams vary in width from one-eighth of a mile or less to two miles. Lancaster is, perhaps, nearly the highest point in the county. Some points on the Grand Divide rise to a height of 180 feet above the Chariton River, and Downing, which lies about a mile west of the east line of the county, is 100 feet below Lancaster, and from fifty to sixty feet above the Chariton River bottoms. The country immediately east of Lancaster is made up of rolling prairie and low, flat ridges, with wide, shallow valleys between. It is very seldom that the streams come in immediate contact with the hills; usually a bottom is interposed between, extending on both sides of the stream. With but few exceptions, this is the case even on the Chariton River. It will be seen by the foregoing that but little of the county is so broken as to render it unfit for cultivation.

Hydrography.—The county is watered west of the Grand Divide by the Chariton River and the streams flowing into it from the east; and east of the Grand Divide it is watered by the North Fabius, Middle Fabius, South Fork of Middle Fabius, South Fabius, Salt River and their tributaries. All these streams flow in a southeasterly direction, and finally empty into the Mississippi River; while the Chariton, which carries the waters from the western part of the county, empties into the Missouri River in Chariton County. The banks of the streams are usually low, being seldom more than five feet in height, and their beds are mostly muddy, and consequently good fords are rare in wet seasons. There are no good situations on any of the streams for mills, except on the Chariton, where a few have been built and put into operation. All the other streams are, in ordinary seasons, too slow and sluggish to afford sufficient power for mill purposes. There are, however, some steam saw-mills with a grinding attachment in the western part of the county. There are but few springs, but good water in an abundant supply can easily be obtained anywhere throughout the county by digging wells. On most of the ridges it is reached at from fifteen to twenty-five feet, and at Lancaster it is obtained at from ten to forty feet; the latter being the maximum depth of the deepest wells. The most of them are much less. The stock water is, however, mostly obtained from the streams and artificial ponds, and that for family use, from wells and cisterns, the latter being in general use, and much preferred by a majority of the citizens.

It is a curious fact, worthy the attention of scientists, that when the country was first settled in Northeastern Missouri, the water lay much farther from the surface than it does at the present writing. In sections where it was formerly obtained at from thirty to eighty feet, it is now reached at from ten to fifty feet. True, at some points on the ridges it can not now be obtained at fifty feet, while at other places, especially in the ravines, it comes almost to the surface.

Geology.*—There are but few exposures of rock in the county, and these are confined to the western border along Chariton River, and are only found north of the dividing line between Townships 65 and 66. The quaternary formation effectually conceals any rocks there may be in the remainder of the county. The formations found in the county include the quaternary and coal measures. The former overlies the whole county, and is remarkably thick, when it is taken into consideration that only three of its four divisions are present. These divisions are alluvium, bottom prairie and drift. Alluvium and bottom prairie present their usual characteristics, and are found along the various streams and in the valleys. As is the case in Putnam County, and in fact in all the northern counties of the State, the drift is remarkably thick. Nearly all of the material going to make up the hills (especially in the eastern part of the county) may be referred to this formation. Also the gravel, some of the sand-beds, etc., along the creeks. Clays enter largely in the formation. No exact measurement of this formation has been made, but it undoubtedly reaches the thickness of 100 feet or more. Boulders of syenite, granite, diorite, rosy quartzite, fragments of hornblendic rock, chloritic schist, etc., have been observed in this formation. Some of the boulders are rounded on one side, while the other is planed off smooth, with occasionally parallel grooves or scratches. This is evidently due to glacial action.

The coal measures are believed to underlie the entire surface of the county, with a possible exception of a small portion in the southeast corner, although the exposures are confined almost entirely to the western part along the Chariton River. The following is a general vertical section of this division of Schuyler County:

---

*Adapted to this work from State Geological Report.

No.		Feet.	Inches.
1.	Red and green clay	3	6
2.	Hard blue and gray limestone	1	0
3.	Buff calcareous shale	0	6
4.	Hard, thick-bedded limestone	4	0
5.	Blue calcareous shale	1	0
6.	Blue clay, banded with yellow	2	6
7.	Soft limestone; color variable	3	0
8.	Drab calcareous shale	1	0
9.	Limestone, occurring in several layers	2	0
10.	Buff calcareous shale	1	0
11.	Drab argillaceous shale	6	0
12.	Bituminous shale	1	0
13.	Bituminous coal (Coal A of Putnam County)	3	0
14.	Under clay	2	0
15.	Hard, mottled, ashy-white limestone	1	0
16.	Limestone, variable in color and consistency	4	6
17.	Limestone, compact, ash-colored hydraulic (?)	2	0
18.	Bluish white clay	2	6
19.	Dark-bluish, argillo-sandy shale	17	0
20.	Drab, sandy shale	5	0
21.	Limestone, dark, earthy, pyritiferous	0	2
22.	Dark semi-bituminous shale	3	0
23.	Bituminous slate	3	0

In many instances the foregoing section corresponds with that of Putnam County. The limestones overlying and underlying the coal, however, are not so compact, and differ in a few other points. These limestones appear to become more argillaceous as they enter Iowa, occurring in thinner individual layers, but with a total thickness greater than in Missouri. No. 23 of the Schuyler County section is equivalent to No. 31 of Putnam County; by examining the section of rocks in the latter county two coal beds will be found to occur below Slate No. 31, one at a depth of 69 feet, and another at a depth of 91 feet. These same coals may be looked for in Schuyler County. Carrying the general section, with the aid of that made in Putnam County, gives as No. 24, a space of 69 feet, then as No. 25, 28 inches coal, then a space of from 15 to 20 feet, and then 18 inches coal. The coal bed No. 13 of the section is the only one exposed in the county. It is believed that the Chariton River coal does not extend across Schuyler County, but that the two lower coals of Putnam County do.

For the benefit of those who may bore for the lower coals of Putnam County, the depth at which they should be reached at a few points in Schuyler is given. At Lancaster, at from 250 to 275 feet; at Downing, 150 to 175 feet; at Griffin, 210 to 230; at Glenwood, 235 to 260 feet. These calculations are based upon the belief that the two coals which occur below Slate No. 23 of the general section are co-extensive with the county.

There have been but few coal mines opened in the county, and these are in the western part. The first mines opened are said to be those of the Mock Brothers, in the northwestern part of the county, in Township 67 north, Range 16 west. Several openings have been made in this vicinity. In the northeast quarter of Section 27 in this Congressional Township a shaft has been sunk on North Polecat Creek; and Mr. William F. James works the same coal in the northwest quarter of Section 34 in the same township. His mines, as well as those of the Mock Brothers, are operated by drifts, that is, by an opening extended into the earth nearly on a level from the foot of the hill. From these mines the same coal (No. 13 of the general section), which averages 3½ feet in thickness, is worked. The dip of the coal, following a course east of south, is not quite five feet to the mile. About the year 1879 a shaft was sunk in Section 23, Township 65 north, Range 16 west, by C. W. Hight. It is now owned by Herman Herboth. The depth of this shaft is about 73 feet, and the bed of coal is 28 inches in thickness, and several feet below this is the second bed of coal.

In 1881 Ira Golston sunk a shaft 65 feet through the stratified rock in the aforesaid section of land, and there found a bed of very superior coal, 34 inches in thickness; and three feet below this he found the second bed of coal, 18 inches in thickness. Only about two-thirds of the second bed is pure coal, and that is inferior to the coal of the first bed. Another shaft with similar results to the one owned by Mr. Herboth has been sunk in the same section, and some openings have been made at other points in the county, but nowhere in the county has the coal been mined to any considerable extent. Potter's clay abounds in the western part of the county; and the clay covering many of the ridges throughout the county makes an excellent quality of brick; and the gravel found at different points along the Chariton answers well for roadbeds.

Soil.—Though not rich in mineral deposits, Schuyler county is well adapted for farming. The soil, except on some of the ridges, is deep, dark and rich, being composed of a mixture of humus, clay and sand, in such proportions as to make it very productive. The soil of the valleys, being principally alluvial, is much deeper, and consequently more productive, than that of the uplands. The entire surface of the county is underlaid with a tenacious clay subsoil, commonly called "gumbo," which is impervious to water, and consequently, in very wet seasons, the grain crops suffer on account of the excessive moisture. In ordinary seasons the soil produces abundantly, and, with proper cultivation, it also produces abundant crops of grain in very dry seasons. With a proper system of underground drainage (not yet introduced), together with deep cultivation and thorough fertilization by "green soiling," the lands of Schuyler County will produce abundantly every year. With the present system of cultivation, which consists in general of stirring only the surface soil, the grasses do well except in seasons attended with drouth.

Timber.—The greater part of the county is lightly timbered with the oak in most of its varieties, common and scaly-bark hickory, elm, black walnut, some ash, red haw, crabapple, wild cherry, hazel, sumac, etc.

For many years prior to the settlement of the county, it had been the custom of the Indians, after the frost had killed the rank growth of vegetation, especially the wild grasses, and it had become dry, to set fire to it, and thus burn over the entire surface of the ground. This annual burning destroyed the young germs of forest trees and prevented a dense growth of timber; so, when the early settlers came, they found no undergrowth of timber. The forest trees, nearly all of which had a short, scrubby growth, stood far apart, and, there being no underbrush, the forests were so open that the deer could be seen for hundreds of yards, and the pioneer could ride and drive through the timber without any difficulty. It is not so now, a gradual but distinct change having been brought about. Soon after the settlement began the annual fires ceased to occur, and as a consequence the young timber began to grow. The citizens needed the timber in the old trees, and accordingly they were felled and used, especially all the valuable ones, so that now only a few, comparatively, of the original forest trees remain. The young trees have grown up densely, and the once open forest is to-day thickly covered with the young or second growth timber. In other words, the forests of fifty years ago have been largely replenished with new trees, and the young timber, on account of its closeness on the ground, has grown much taller in proportion to its size of trunk than the old. There are not as many acres of timber as there were when the settlement began, but on account of its dense growth now, as compared to what it was then, it is believed by many that there is actually more wood.

EARLY RACES.

The Indians.—In aboriginal times the land embraced within the limits of Schuyler County belonged to the Indians known as the Sac and Fox tribes. Their title, however, was extinguished by treaty with the United States, before the settlement of the county began, but they were allowed to return and make fall hunts for a number of years thereafter. James Myers, who had settled on Bear Creek, in the then Macon County, and others made a trade with the Indians, and then refused to give up the property, in consequence of which a fight ensued on what is now Battle Creek, in the southwest part of this county. This occurred in 1835. Several Indians were killed, and the following named whites: James Myers' father, William Black and one Owenly. William Winn was wounded and left on the ground. The white men, being overpowered, fell back to Huntsville, in Randolph County, where they were reinforced, and then returned under the command of John B. Clark, Sr., only to find the charred remains of William Winn, who had been burned by the Indians. This was the only difficulty that the settlers had with the savages in this county, and it is claimed by some that it would not have occurred had not Myers fired the first gun. Afterward Myers became a great friend to the Indians, and allowed them to camp on his lands when they came to make their annual hunts. Having acquired the use of their language to some extent, it is said that he would invite the Indians to encamp on his lands even to the displeasure of some of his neighbors, who preferred that they remain away. Their principal camping ground, however, when they returned to this region of country for the purpose of hunting, was located in the forks of the North Fabius, in Scotland County, about one mile north of what is now Crawford's Station, on the Keokuk & Western Railway. They were very fond of sport, and delighted in having the settlers visit their camps and take part in the exercises. And, according to tradition, the "pioneers of the forest" made frequent visits to the Indian camps, and eagerly engaged in the sport. Horse racing and target shooting were the principal exercises indulged in. In the former the Indians would generally come out ahead, and then the chief, Keokuk, would slap his hands, dance and rejoice. In the latter exercise the whites excelled with the rifle, while the Indians excelled with the bow and arrow. Sunday was usually the day chosen to visit the Indian camps. Among the early settlers who spent much time with the Indians was Branch Miller, who lived in the western part of Scotland County, and near the Schuyler County line. William L. Mills, who settled in the northwestern part of Scotland County, and also near Schuyler, in the year 1835, says that he spent many a Sunday with Keokuk and his braves, hunting, wrestling and shooting at a mark with a rifle. At the latter sport he could beat all the braves, much to the amusement of the old chief. Mills was well acquainted with two sons of Black Hawk, Battist, the half-breed and interpreter, White Breast, Wa-pa-co-las-cock, and others. The last two named were very conspicuous braves. Keokuk, the chief, was very large and weighed about 240 pounds. There was at one time a controversy between Keokuk and his friends and a son of Black Hawk and his friends as to who should be the principal chief of the Sacs and Foxes. Knowing that Keokuk and his followers were friendly to the whites, and that the Black Hawks and their friends were rather hostile, President Jackson settled the matter in favor of Keokuk, and presented him with a large silver medal on which were engraved the words: "Keokuk, the Principal Chief of the Sacs and Foxes." This settled the matter and the Black Hawk faction acquiesced.

The old chief took great delight in showing this medal to the early settlers. After receiving it, he and his family dressed in the best style of the whites, he being attired in a suit of broadcloth, and fine boots, and a silk hat, with the silver medal always in view. He and his family then rode the finest horses obtainable, and, when thus attired and mounted, presented a formidable pageant in the wilds of the frontier. The chief, aside from his Indian physiognomy, was a noble looking specimen of the physical man, but, unfortunately for him, he was fond of the white man's "fire water," and consequently led a dissipated life. About the year 1842 he and his tribe moved westward, and finally settled down on the Indian reservation southwest of Ottawa, in Kansas, where he spent the remainder of his days. After his death, a plain marble slab, appropriately lettered, was erected over his grave, and subsequently his remains were removed to the city of Keokuk, in Iowa, which city was named in his honor, and there re-interred in the public park, where a monument has been erected to his memory. In one face of this monument is encased the original slab that stood over his remains in Kansas.

Portions of the Sac and Fox Indians made their annual hunts in Schuyler County until 1841, after which they never returned. During their visits to the county, excepting the fight on Battle Creek, they were always very friendly with the whites, and even put on an air of dignified honor.

The Mound-Builder.—A number of mounds, supposed to have been constructed by that pre-historic race of people called the Mound-Builders, are found along and near the Chariton River. They have never been explored scientifically for the purpose of discovering their contents. Some of these mounds exist on the lands of John J. Logan, about five and a half miles west of Glenwood, and a number of years ago, before the county had railroad accommodations, some parties, while taking stones from one of the mounds for the purpose of burning them into lime, came upon a skeleton of a human being, which they estimated to be larger than the average man of the white race. The skeleton, especially the teeth, was in a fair state of preservation. This, however, may have been the remains of an Indian, as it is believed that the Indians, while knowing nothing about the constructions of the mounds, sometimes buried their dead therein.

ERA OF SETTLEMENT.

Introductory and preparatory to giving an account of the actual settlement of Schuyler County, it is quite proper to begin with the exploration of Marquette and Joliet.

Exploration of Marquette and Joliet.—On the 17th of May 1673, Father Marquette and Sieur Joliet, two French missionaries, together with five men, set out from the mission of St. Ignatius, on the Straits of Mackinaw, in Michigan, in two bark canoes, in search of the "great father of rivers." Eagerly they rowed their boats through the waters of Lake Michigan and Green Bay, thence up Fox River, in Wisconsin, to a point from whence they crossed overland (carrying their canoes) to the Wisconsin River; thence down the same to the great Mississippi, which they entered with safety, on the 17th of June following. Then, filled with enthusiasm over their great discovery, they floated down the Mississippi, observing the wild animals that sported on the shores, the beautiful birds of the air, and the fishes of the river, in a land of native and solitary wildness, until at last, on the 25th of June, they perceived footprints of men by the water side, and a beaten path entering a beautiful prairie. Here, then, we let Father Marquette tell his own story: "We stopped to examine it, and, concluding that it was an Indian village, we resolved to go and reconnoitre; we accordingly left our two canoes in charge of our people, cautioning them to beware of a surprise; then M. Joliet and I undertook this rather hazardous discovery for two single men, who thus put themselves at the discretion of an unknown and barbarous people. We followed a little path in silence, and, having advanced about two leagues, we discovered a village on the banks of the river, and two others, on a hill, half a league from the former.* Then, indeed, we recommended ourselves to God with all our hearts; and, having implored His help, we passed on undiscovered, and came so near that we even heard the Indians talking. We then

---

* John C. Shea, in his valuable work, "Discovery and Exploration of the Mississippi Valley," says: "These villages are laid down on the map on the westerly side of the Mississippi, and the names of two are given, Peouarea and Moningwena, whence it is generally supposed that the river on which they lay is that now called the Des Moines." The dates and objects mentioned in Father Marquette's narrative tend to prove that these villages lay on the Des Moines, and the distance traveled from the Mississippi, where they left their canoes, leads to the conclusion that they were situated not far above its mouth—probably on the bluffs on the Iowa side, not far from St. Francisville.

deemed it time to announce ourselves, as we did by a cry, which we raised with all our strength, and then halted without advancing any further. At this cry the Indians rushed out of their cabins, and, having probably recognized us as French, especially seeing a black gown, or at least having no reason to distrust us, seeing we were but two, and had made known our coming, they deputed four old men to come and speak with us. Two carried tobacco pipes, well adorned, and trimmed with many kinds of feathers. * * * Having reached us at last, they stopped to consider us attentively. I now took courage, seeing these ceremonies, which are used by them only with friends, and still more on seeing them covered with stuffs, which made me judge them to be allies. I, therefore, spoke to them first, and asked them who they were; they answered that 'they were Illinois,' and, in token of peace, they presented their pipes to smoke. They then invited us to their village, where all the tribe awaited us with impatience. These pipes for smoking are called, in the country, calumets. * * At the door of the cabin in which we were to be received, was an old man awaiting us in a very remarkable posture, which is their usual ceremony in receiving strangers. This man was standing, perfectly naked, with his hands stretched out and raised toward the sun, as if he wished to screen himself from its rays, which, nevertheless, passed through his fingers to his face. When we came near him, he paid us this compliment: 'How beautiful is the sun, O Frenchman, when thou comest to visit us! All our town awaits thee, and thou shalt enter all our cabins in peace.' He then took us into his cabin, where there was a crowd of people, who devoured us with their eyes, but kept a profound silence. We heard, however, these words occasionally addressed to us: 'Well done, brothers, to visit us!'

"While the old men smoked their pipes after us to do honor, some came to invite us on behalf of the great sachem of all the Illinois to proceed to his town, where he wished to hold a council with us. We went with a good retinue, for all the people who had never seen a Frenchman among them could not tire looking at us. They threw themselves on the grass by the wayside; they ran ahead, then turned and walked back to see us again. All this

was done without noise, and with marks of a great respect entertained for us. Having arrived at the great sachem's town, we
espied him at his cabin door, between two old men, all three
standing naked, with their calumets turned to the sun. He
harangued us in a few words, to congratulate us on our arrival,
and then presented us his calumet and made us smoke; at the
same time we entered his cabin, where we received all their
usual greetings." A council was then held, during which the
missionaries made presents to the Indians, and told them of the
true God, in reply to which the sachem said: "I pray thee to
take pity on me and all my nation. Thou knowest the Great
Spirit who made us all; thou speakest to Him and hearest His
word; ask Him to give me life and health, and come and dwell
with us, that we may know Him." "Then," says Father Marquette, "the council was followed by a great feast, which consisted of four courses, which we had to take with all their ways;
the first course was a great wooden dish full of sagaminty, that is
to say, of Indian meal boiled in water and seasoned with grease.
The master of ceremonies, with a spoonful of sagaminty, presented
it three or four times to my mouth, as we would do with a little
child; he did the same to M. Joliet. For the second course he
brought in a second dish containing three fish; he took some
pains to remove the bones, and, having blown upon it to cool it,
put it in my mouth, as we would food to a bird; for the third
course they produced a large dog, which they had just killed,
but, learning that we did not eat it, it was withdrawn. Finally,
the fourth course was a piece of wild ox, the fattest portions of
which were put into our mouths.   *   *

"We slept in the sachem's cabin, and the next day took
leave of him, promising to pass back through his town in four
moons. He escorted us to our canoes with nearly 600 persons,
who saw us embark, evincing in every possible way the pleasure
our visit had given them."

Father Marquette and his party then descended the Mississippi, and, after going many hundred miles down the river, they
returned to the place from whence they started, by way of the
Illinois River and Lake Michigan. This brief sketch of the
explorations of Marquette and Joliet has been given to call

SCHUYLER COUNTY, MISSOURI   13

****

attention to the fact that the Indian villages mentioned, which these missionaries visited, were close to Northeastern Missouri, and the further fact that, 214 years ago, white men, Frenchmen, visited this territory, and traveled down and along the eastern boundary thereof, and perhaps landed on its soil. Other French explorations, of which no authentic accounts have been preserved, were undoubtedly afterward made. Between the dates of the exploration of Marquette and Joliet, and that of the Louisiana Purchase, the French explored the Des Moines River and made further explorations of the Mississippi, and established mission stations and trading posts at various places along both of these rivers, but did not effect any permanent settlement as high up as this tier of counties. Many places having French names were named by these early adventurers and traders. In the remains of an old habitation, near the mouth of Fox River, some metal instruments were found by the early settlers, which bore a French manufacturer's name, and the date of 1670. These instruments were undoubtedly left there by Marquette and Joliet, or some of their followers.

Pike's Discoveries, Etc.—The most authentic account of the early explorations, touching Northeastern Missouri, is that of "Pike's Voyage to the Sources of the Mississippi in the years 1805 and 1806." The journal of Maj. Pike's passage up the river says: "18th August—Sunday—embarked early; about 11 o'clock passed an Indian camp on the east side. They fired several guns, but we passed without stopping. Very hard head winds during the day. Caught six fish. Distance, twenty-three miles. August 19, Monday, embarked early and made fine way, but at 9 o'clock, in the turning point of a sand bar, our boat struck a sawyer; at the moment we did not know it had injured her, but a short time afterward discovered her to be sinking. However, by thrusting oakum into the leak, and baling, we got her to shore on a bar, where, after entirely unloading, we, with great difficulty, keeled her sufficiently to cut out the plank and put in a new one.   *   *   *   But after dark we became entangled among the sand bars, and were obliged to stop and encamp on the point of a beach. Caught two fish. Distance, fourteen miles.* August 20th, Tuesday, arrived at the rapids

* This day he passed what is now Clark County.

DeMoyen* at 7 o'clock, and, although no soul on board had ascended them, we commenced ascending them immediately. Our boat being large and moderately loaded, we found great difficulty. The river all the way is from three-fourths to a mile wide. The rapids are eleven miles long, with successive ridges and shoals extending from shore to shore.   *   *   *
We had passed the first and most difficult shoal when we were met by Mr. William Ewing (who, I understand, is an agent appointed to reside with the Sacs to teach them the science of agriculture), with a French interpreter, four chiefs and fifteen men of the Sac nation, in their canoes, bearing a flag of the United States. They came down to assist me up the rapids, and took out thirteen of my heaviest barrels, and put two of their men in the barge to pilot us up. Arrived at the house of Mr. Ewing, opposite the village,‡ at dusk.   *   *   Distance, sixteen miles."

Maj. Pike did not explore the Des Moines River, but accompanied his report to the United States Government, in whose employ he was, with a map of said river, giving the names of its tributaries, some of which were French, and also the names of forts and trading posts thereon. He also gave the location of the Sac village on the west side of the Mississippi, above the Des Moines rapids. It is supposed that he got his information pertaining to the Des Moines River from Mr. Ewing, the Indian agent.

Permanent Settlement.—Explorers, hunters and surveyors visited the territory of Schuyler County some time before its permanent settlement began. The approaches of the early settlers were from the east, southeast and south, through the already partially settled counties of Missouri, and a few came from the northeast, through the territory of Iowa. The early settlers came mostly from Kentucky and Tennessee, and from the older counties of this State; others came from Virginia, Ohio, Indiana, and Illinois, and a few from southeastern Iowa. The first settlement in this, the northern tier of counties in Missouri, began at St. Francisville, on the Des Moines River, in what is now Clark

* Opposite Keokuk (in the Mississippi River).
‡ Sac Village.

County, in the year 1829; and after that the settlements expand-
ed westward from the Des Moines and Mississippi Rivers, and
late in the fall of 1833, the families of Levi and George Rhoads
settled in the southern part of what is now Scotland County, near
the village of Sand Hill. They were followed the next spring by
George Tobin, who subsequently settled in this county, and a
number of others, prominent among whom were Jesse Stice, Moses
Stice and Tyre March. The Stices were cousins, and both had married sisters of Tyre March. These three men with their families
(perhaps the latter had no family) emigrated from Howard County,
in this State, and on the 14th day of March, 1834, they landed at
a place near where the village of Bible Grove, in Scotland County,
now stands. There they built a house for Jesse Stice, and a
short time thereafter Moses Stice settled a few miles westward,
and in the edge of Schuyler County, and is believed to have been
the first settler thereof.

Following the settlement of Stice, in the southeast corner of
the county, it seems that Samuel Eason, who settled near the
Chariton in Township 65 north, Range 16 west, was the next.
Then came David Floyd, who settled in the same township, and
Jefferson, Richard and John S. Fulcher, who settled in Township
65 north, Range 15 west, in the year 1837. Other very early
settlers were John Davis, a Mr. Taylor, Martin Parton, Robert
Bowler and Henry Downing. The latter settled where he now
resides, four miles southwest of the village of Downing, in 1837.
The following is a list of the names of early settlers in the several
parts of the county, to wit: In the central and southern part—
Austin Coffey, Price Arnold, Urial Sebree, Henry Weitzel, Jacob
Snowbarg, Nicholas Sloop, John Fugate, Harman Figge, Fred-
erick Warner, Edward K. Gibbon, Elias Fletcher, Isam B.
Fletcher, John Lesley, A. D. Farris, Samuel Tipton, Josiah
Hathaway, Elkanah Hensly, William T. London, Charles M.
London, Jesse Holt, William Barlow, Spottswood Bradford,
James M. Bryant, David Rice, Henry Mull, Thomas B. Du Bois,
John Mikel, Elias and John Brower, Moran Husley, John and
Benjamin Brown, John Johnson, Leonard Griggs, and George
Crump; in the northern part—James Custer, James H. Ford, A.
K. Cowgill, Bright Gilstrap, James Hombs, William Athel,

Hiram Reeves, George Bridewell, Morris James, Robert J.
Maize, William Maize, Jesse Grey, Henry Piercy, Stephen G.
Custer, Peter Blansett, and Mancil Garrett; in the eastern
part—James Hall, Nicholas Shope, Edward Snyder, William
Ogg, William Webster, George F. Palmer, John Lyle, Henry
Prime and Charles Cook.

Land Entries.—Further, in connection with the settlement of
the county, the following list, which comprises nearly all the
land entries made prior to the year 1850, is here given. No
lands were entered in Schuyler County prior to 1844 except
those in Range 13, which had been previously surveyed, and put
into the market. The Township and Range will first appear,
and then the name of the purchaser, year of entry and description of land, to wit:

Township 64, Range 13—J. M. Smith, 1836, east half of
southwest quarter of Section 17; E. Briggs, 1842, southwest
quarter of Section 18.

Township 65, Range 13—A. T. Hite, 1844, southwest quarter
of Section 6; Lewis Piper, 1844, east half of northwest quarter
of Section 8; G. S. Lake, 1844, west half of southeast quarter of
Section 8; William V. Rippey, 1844, northwest quarter of Section 9; G. A. Buehler, 1845, south half of northeast quarter of
Section 5; Charles Lake, 1845, west half of the northwest quarter of Section 8; A. E. Rice, 1845, southeast quarter of southeast
quarter of Section 17; Ed. F. Dingle, 1845, east half of the
northwest quarter of Section 29; Henry Rhods, 1846, west half
of the northeast quarter of Section 4; J. W. Givins, 1846, east
half of the northeast quarter of Section 33; Wesley Jackson,
1846, west half of Section 18; William George, 1847, west half
of the southeast quarter of Section 18; G. R. Thomas, 1847, east
half of the northeast quarter of Section 30.

Township 66, Range 13—Thomas Butt, 1844, southwest
quarter of Section 9; James Prime, 1844, east half of the northeast quarter of Section 32; Charles Hall, 1845, eighty acres in
Section 31; Mark and R. I. Phillips, 1846, north half of the southwest quarter of Section 6; William N. and James Phillips, 1846,
south half of northwest quarter of Section 6; Ambrose Hulen,
1846, northwest quarter of Section 19; George W. Tompkins,
1847, eighty acres in Section 5.

Township 67, Range 13—Jonathan Wright, 1849, east half of the northeast quarter of Section 28; James Morrison, 1850, fractional Sections 20 and 21; Jeremiah Buford, 1850, land in Section 30; Benjamin Tompkins, 1850, south half of the southeast quarter of Section 33; William Buford, 1850, southwest quarter of Section 32; John A. Westhoff, 1850, land in Section 28.

Township 64, Range 14—Henry P. Buford, 1842, where he now resides, aged eighty-nine; W. A. Z. Rhoden, 1845, west half of the northeast quarter of Section 14.

Township 65, Range 14—Henry Keeter, 1845, northwest quarter of Section 3; Henry Downing, 1848, south half of northwest quarter of Section 2; Caleb Martin, 1848, southwest quarter of Section 3; Milton Jacks, 1848, southeast quarter of Section 4; William Beasley, 1849, land in Section 1.

Township 66, Range 14—R. S. Neeley, 1845, southwest quarter of the southwest quarter of Section 8; John M. Fish, 1845, west half of the northwest quarter of Section 32; John Jones, 1845, southwest quarter of Section 28; John Rogers, 1845, west half of southeast quarter of Section 36; James Myers, 1846, southwest quarter of Section 20; Thomas Leedom, 1846, west half of the southwest quarter of Section 19; Mary Spears, 1846, northeast quarter of Section 31; William Cochrane, 1846, west half of the northeast quarter of Section 32; D. M. T. Brasfield, 1846, west half of the southwest quarter of Section 33; William Ingram, 1847, southeast quarter of the southwest quarter of Section 8; Y. W. Payton, 1848, northwest quarter of Section 8; P. M. Nichols, 1849, southwest quarter of Section 4; J. R. Meek, 1849, southwest quarter of Section 35.

Township 67, Range 14—E. M. Harlan, 1848, 160 acres in Section 31; Cicero Houston, 1848, southeast quarter of Section 25; G. N. Stewart, 1848, land in Section 29.

Township 64, Range 15—Oliver Towles, 1844, southeast quarter of Section 14; J. Brower, 1844, southeast quarter of the northeast quarter of Section 9; Henry Davis, 1845, west half of the southeast quarter of Section 10; Abraham Stille, 1845, west half of the northwest quarter of Section 9; J. H. Davis, 1845, southeast quarter of the southeast quarter of Section 10; Robert Fugate, 1847, west half of the southwest quarter of Section 4.

Township 65, Range 15—W. H. Rusk, 1845, east half of the southeast quarter of Section 15; John S. Fulcher, 1845, west half of the southeast quarter of Section 8; Jefferson Fulcher, 1845, east half of the southwest quarter of Section 5; Richard Fulcher, 1845, east half of the southeast quarter of Section 17; M. Garrett, 1845, east half of the northeast quarter of Section 17; D. McQuittey, 1845, east half of the northeast quarter of Section 29; David Bozarth, 1845, east half of the northeast quarter of Section 1; G. T. Naylor, 1846, south half of the northwest quarter of Section 1; Thomas J. Thrailkeld, 1847, east half of the northeast quarter of Section 4; William H. Roberts, 1848, south half of the southeast quarter of Section 3; Peter Klein, 1848, east half of the northeast quarter of Section 12; Caswell Dennis, 1849, south half of the southwest quarter of Section 21; J. C. Mitchell, 1850, south half of the northwest quarter of Section 3.

Township 66, Range 15—Isaac Mitchell, 1845, south half of the southeast quarter of Section 35; Eliza Tobin, 1845, northeast quarter of Section 2; John Sawyer, 1845, northeast quarter of Section 3; William Partin, 1846, southwest quarter of Section 7; Neal Murphy, 1847, northwest quarter of Section 18; William Searcy, 1847, north half of the southwest quarter of Section 18; Jos. Bradburn, 1847, south half of the northeast quarter of Section 18; George Nicholas, 1847, west half of the southeast quarter of Section 28; William Smith, 1848, northeast quarter of Section 12; James Hepburn, 1848, west half of the northeast quarter of Section 13; G. N. Bradley, 1848, west half of the southwest quarter of Section 35; J. Wright, 1849, southwest quarter of Section 36.

Township 67, Range 15—Alex Denny, 1847, west half of the northeast quarter of Section 26; George Combs, 1848, southeast quarter of the southeast quarter of Section 28; John Sawyer, 1850, southeast quarter of Section 34.

Township 64, Range 16—No land entered in this township by actual settlers prior to 1850.

Township 65, Range 16—Martha Eason, 1845, northeast quarter of Section 15; David Floyd, 1845, east half of the southeast quarter of Section 36; Michael Coy, 1849, northeast quarter of the southwest quarter of Section 35; John Coy, 1849, southeast quarter of the southwest quarter of Section 35.

Township 66, Range 16—Samuel B. Knox, 1845, northeast quarter of Section 1.

Township 67, Range 16—H. B. Birch, 1849, northwest quarter of Section 28; Perren Bryant, 1849, northeast quarter of the southeast quarter of Section 36.

All or nearly all persons named in the foregoing list were actual settlers on the lands therein described, but it must not be inferred that the date of entry of these lands governs the date of settlement thereon by the purchaser, as many of them settled or "squatted" upon their claims several years before the lands became subject to entry.

It will be observed that a very small proportion of the public lands of the county were entered prior to the year 1850, but from that year to 1856 (including the latter) there was a rush for the acquisition of land; and during that period about one-half or more of all the lands in the county was entered.

Customs.—As usual in all new countries, the early settlers encountered many disadvantages. They were far away from mills and blacksmith shops, which are so essentially necessary in all communities. Some of them were fortunate to have a hand mill in a neighborhood, with which to grind their corn, and some pulverized it in a mortar with a maul or iron wedge. One old pioneer has graphically described the way they fared, thus: " We made what we called a hominy mortar, so you see we had plenty of meal when we ground it, and plenty of honey when we found it, with plenty of fat hog and hominy." Wild honey was found by the early settlers in great abundance, so great indeed that honey and beeswax, as articles of commerce, were a considerable source of revenue to the industrious pioneers, who gathered the honey, and pressed it out and made the beeswax, and then conveyed both articles many miles away to market. Before the settlement of the county began, the bee hunters, especially from the older counties south of this, followed up the dividing ridge, or the Grand Divide, as it is called, through the territory of this county, and far up into Iowa Territory, in search of bee trees, which they found in great numbers. They gave the ridge the name of Bee Trace. While it is true that the old pioneers suffered many hardships, they also had many pleasures. In general they preferred corn bread rather than wheat bread, and consequently did not suffer when deprived of the latter. Their hogs fattened on the mast, and thus they acquired cheap pork. Then, with plenty of wild honey, vegetables, wild turkey, venison and pork, "and a hoe cake to sop in the gravy," they lived as rich as kings.

Judge Caywood, a resident of this county, well known to all, and also an early settler, says: " A large proportion of the early citizens of this and neighboring counties were made up of men and families of more than ordinary culture and education. This, however, is accounted for in this way: Following the hard times and general crash among all classes in the year 1837, found thousands of the best business men, including all classes, hopelessly ruined; and rather than drag out an aimless life, when they were all at the bottom round of the ladder, without hope, many of them gathered up their little remnant of a former fortune, and determined with brave hearts to start anew in life, in the far West, and there, with the class of hardy hunters that had preceded them, rebuild their ruined fortunes; and they carried with them what they found among the earlier pioneers—hearts overflowing with kindness and good feeling for their fellowmen; being all poor, with no wealthy nabobs amongst them to imitate or envy, their wants were few, and each one made it a point to contribute to the general enjoyment and happiness, and, with moderate industry, aided by the rich virgin soil, they soon gathered around their humble homes a sufficiency of property and conveniences to make them comfortable; and, as time rolled on, advanced to even the luxuries of life, and now, from among the children of this stock of hardy pioneers, have arisen and gone out into the world the best business men, and the finest talent of the country."

In evidence of the truth of the foregoing assertion, that the pioneers were poor and self-reliant, it is proper to say that only a few of the early settlers of Schuyler County brought slaves with them—so few, that in 1850 there were only fifty-seven colored people in the county. Being on the border of a free State, into which the slaves could so easily flee, slave holders preferred not to become settlers, believing, as they did, that slavery could not be made profitable here. The loss, if any, to the county by the abolition of slavery when it came, was not felt, there being only thirty-nine colored people in the county in 1860, and, as a matter of course, only a portion of those were competent to labor. Though in a slave State, the county was almost free from the influence of slavery.

COUNTY ORGANIZATION, ETC.

The Creating Act.—Two years prior to the complete organization of Schuyler County, the General Assembly of the State of Missouri passed the following act, entitled "The act to define the boundaries of Schuyler County:"

SECTION 1. All that territory lying within the following limits, to wit: Beginning at the northeast corner of Adair County, In the middle of Range 13, thence due north to the northern boundary line of the State of Missouri; thence west with said State line to the middle of the Chariton River; thence south through the middle of the main channel of said river to the northern line of Adair County; thence east with said northern line of Adair County to the place of beginning, shall be hereafter organized and known by the name of Schuyler County.

SEC. 2. Schuyler County shall be attached to the county of Adair for all civil and military purposes.

SEC. 3. The revenue levied and collected by the county of Adair, for county purposes, within the limits of the above described county of Schuyler, shall, after deducting the expenses of assessing and collecting the same, and all expenses which may arise from criminal prosecutions originating in the county of Schuyler, be reserved for the use of Schuyler County, whenever the same shall be organized.

This act shall be in force from and after its passage.

Approved February 17, 1843.

Afterward, on the 21st day of March, 1845, Gov. John C. Edwards issued to William L. Robinson, of Schuyler County, a commission in the words and figures following, to wit:

The State of Missouri to all who shall see these presents. Greeting:

Know ye, that, reposing especial trust and confidence in the integrity and ability of William L. Robinson, I, John C. Edwards, Governor of the State of Missouri, on behalf and in the name thereof, do hereby commission him a justice of the county court within and for the county of Schuyler, of the State of Missouri, and do authorize him to discharge according to law the duties of said office, and to hold and enjoy the same, together with all the powers, privileges and emoluments thereunto appertaining, until the legal termination thereof.

In testimony whereof I have hereunto set my hand, and caused the great seal of the State of Missouri to be affixed at the city of Jefferson this 21st day of March, in the year of our Lord one thousand eight hundred and forty-five, and of the independence of the United States the sixty-ninth, and of the State the twenty-fifth.   By the Governor,   JOHN C. EDWARDS.

[SEAL.]

JAMES L. MINOR, *Secretary of State.*

On the same day like commissions were issued by the same
authority to Alexander D. Farris and William Hendron, respectively, whereby they were constituted as the other two justices of
the county court. Robinson was sworn into office by William
Barlow, a justice of the peace of Schuyler County, and Farris
and Hendron, by William V. Rippey, a justice of the peace of
Adair County; and on the third Monday of April following, it
being the 21st of said month, these county court justices assembled and organized the first court ever held in Schuyler County,
as shown by the following caption at the beginning of the record
of their proceedings:

> Be it remembered that at a term of the county court of the county of
> Schuyler, of the State of Missouri, beginning and held at the house of Robert S.
> Neeley, formerly occupied by James Gates, on the third Monday in April, in the
> year of our Lord eighteen hundred and forty-five, there were present William
> L. Robinson, Alexander D. Farris and William Hendron.

This house stood in Section 7, Township 66 north, Range 14
west, near the south line of the southeast quarter thereof, and
on the place now occupied by W. R. Jones. The court organized
by choosing William L. Robinson as presiding justice, and by ap-
pointing Jonathan Riggs as elisor for its first term. Isaac N.
Ebey was appointed first clerk of the county court, and he at
once appeared and filed his official bond in the penal sum of
$5,000, which was approved by the court, and Ebey immediately
assumed the duties of his office. George Naylor was then
appointed county assessor, and G. W. Johnson, county surveyor.
These gentlemen at once appeared and filed their bonds, qualified and assumed their official duties. The county was then subdivided into municipal townships, as follows:

Fabius Township.—Beginning at the southeast corner of
Schuyler County; thence due north along the county line of the
counties of Schuyler and Scotland, sixteen and one-half miles;
thence due west six miles; thence due south to the county line of
Schuyler and Adair Counties, at the southeast corner of Section
16, Township 64 north, Range 14 west; thence east along said
county line to the place of beginning.

Independence Township.—Beginning at the northeast corner
of Fabius Township; thence north to the north line of the State;
thence due west along said northern boundary line to where the

same is intersected by a range line dividing Ranges 14 and 15; thence from the point of intersection last aforesaid, south along said range line to a point one mile south of the Indian boundary line, as run by John C. Sullivan; thence due east to the place of beginning.

Wells Township.—Beginning at the northwest corner of Independence Township; thence due west along the northern boundary line of this State to the middle of the Chariton River; thence south down along the middle of said river to a point one mile south of the Indian boundary line, as run by John C. Sullivan; thence due east to the southwest corner of Independence Township; thence north to the place of beginning.

Chariton Township.—Beginning at the southwest corner of Wells Township, in the middle of the Chariton River, to a point where the township line dividing Townships 65 and 66 crosses said river; thence east to the northeast corner of Section 4, of Township 65, of Range 15; thence north to a point one mile south of the Indian boundary line as run by John C. Sullivan; thence west to the place of beginning.

Liberty Township.—Beginning at the northwest corner of Fabius Township, thence due west to the northeast corner of Chariton Township; thence due south to the northeast corner of Section 16, of Township 65, of Range 15; thence six miles due east; thence north to the place of beginning.

Salt River Township.—Beginning at the northeast corner of Section 16, Township 65, Range 14; thence due west six miles to the northeast corner of Section 16, Township 65, Range 15; thence two miles north to the northeast corner of Section 4, Township 65, Range 15; thence west along the township line dividing Townships 65 and 66 to the middle of the Chariton River, thence down along the middle of the channel of said river to the county line dividing the counties of Schuyler and Adair; thence east along said county line to the southwest corner of Fabius Township; thence due north to the place of beginning. The first officers having been appointed and the county subdivided into municipal or civil townships, its organization was then complete.

It will be observed that, as the county was organized and

24   SCHUYLER COUNTY, MISSOURI

****

subdivided into municipal townships, the disputed territory which caused the Iowa War was all included in Wells and Independence Townships, and also a strip a mile wide south of the aforesaid Indian boundary line. Afterward, in 1848 and 1849, after it became evident that the State line would be established on said Indian boundary line, the county court of Schuyler County ordered the lines of Chariton, Liberty and Fabius Townships, to be extended northward to the Indian boundary line, and then, as the balance of Wells and Independence Townships were believed to be in the territory of Iowa, Schuyler County lost her jurisdiction over them, and they were dropped from her records.

Subsequently, at the August term, 1853, of the county court, it was "ordered that the municipal township of Fabius be and the same is hereby divided," making Bridge Creek the line through said township; the north end to retain the name of Fabius Township, and the south end to be called Independence Township. Thus a new township called Independence was organized to take the name of the original township of that name on the disputed strip of land. Afterward, in November, 1858, the boundary line between Fabius and Independence Townships was made to conform to the township line dividing congressional Townships 65 and 66 north; and, thus bounded, those two townships still remain.

Afterward the municipal townships of Glenwood and Prairie were organized, and the following are the descriptions of the boundaries of each township as they are now constituted, excepting Fabius and Independence, which have already been defined:

Liberty Township.—Beginning at the southeast corner of Section 33, Township 66 north, Range 14 west; thence north on the section line to the Iowa State line; thence west on said line to the northwest corner of Section 26, Township 67 north, Range 15 west; thence south on the section line to the southwest corner of Section 35, Township 66 north, Range 15 west; thence east to the place of beginning.

Chariton Township.—Beginning at the Chariton River between Sections 9 and 16, Township 66 north, Range 16 west; thence east on the section line to the range line between Ranges

15 and 16; thence north on said line one mile; thence east to the southeast corner of Section 3, Township 66 north, Range 15 west; thence north to the Iowa State line; thence west on said line to the Chariton River; thence following the meanders of said river to the place of beginning.

Glenwood Township.—This township is bounded on the north by Chariton Township, east by Liberty, south by the township line between Townships 65 and 66 north, and west by the Chariton River.

Prairie Township.—This township comprises all the territory in the county in Township 65 north, lying west of Independence Township.

Salt River Township.—This township comprises all the territory in the county, lying south of Prairie Township and west of Independence.

First Justices of the Peace.—The county court, after having defined the boundaries of the original municipal townships, proceeded to appoint justices of the peace for the same, as follows: William Barlow, Henry P. Beauford and Jahiel Parks, for Fabius Township; John Willis, for Independence Township; James Wells, for Wells Township; Thomas I. Bennett, William Oglesby and Thomas Partin, for Chariton Township; Thomas B. Du Bois, David A. Roberts and Samuel Ow, for Liberty Township; and A. B. Alverson, for Salt Creek Township. Jahiel Parks, John Willis, James Wells, William Oglesby, Thomas B. Du Bois, I. B. Alverson and Robert S. Neeley were then appointed districting justices for their respective townships. Jonathan Riggs then appeared and filed his bond, to the acceptance of the court, in the sum of $1,000, conditioned for the faithful collection of the State and county revenues for the year 1845; and at the same time Robert S. Neeley gave bond for the same amount, as treasurer of Schuyler County.

First Probate Business.—Then came Jesse Hall, who presented a petition for the appointment of a guardian for Joseph Jackson, an alleged insane person; whereupon the court ordered the empaneling of a jury of "six good and lawful men" to inquire into the insanity of said Hall. The jury selected were George W. Johnson, George Naylor, Burrel W. Wetherford, James Lusk,

David A. Bozarth and William Barlow. These men, after being
duly sworn to inquire, as aforesaid, and after due examination of
the matter, returned the following verdict: " We, the jury, find
Joseph Jackson to be a person of unsound mind, or insane;
George W. Johnson, foreman." And thereupon the court appointed
Jesse Hall guardian of the estate and person of the said Jackson. Here we have an account of the first jury empaneled in
the county, the first jury trial, the first verdict rendered, and the
first guardian and ward. The second term of the county court,
it being a special term, was held at the same place on June 2,
1845, and the first act of the court was the appointment of Henry
Davis, as agent for the county, to draw its portion of the road and
canal fund from the State.

Location of the County Seat.—The old town or village of Tippecanoe (the first one in the county), located in the southeast
part of Section 30, Township 66 north, Range 14 west, was, as
may be seen by reference to the map, near the center of the
county as it is now constituted. A strenuous effort was made
by John M. Fish and other property owners in the vicinity of
Tippecanoe, to secure the location of the county seat at that place;
while James Lusk, who then represented the territory of Schuyler County in the Legislature, and others opposed to the location
of the county seat at Tippecanoe, secured the passage of a law
which required the county seat to be located within one mile of
the geographical center of the county. And, inasmuch as the
nine-mile strip of disputed territory heretofore explained was
then claimed to belong to the county (and which was actually
required to make Schuyler a constitutional county), Tippecanoe
was not located near enough the geographical center thereof to
entitle it to become the county seat; and in this way Fish and
his friends were defeated in their aspirations. Two of the commissioners appointed to select the site for the location of the seat
of justice, namely, Harrison Mundy and Judge Romjeau, met at
the house of John Jones, in Tippecanoe, and, regarding the line
north of the disputed strip as the true State line, they found the
site of the present town of Lancaster to be within one mile of
the geographical center of the county, and selected it as the
place on which to establish the county seat. The land thus

selected was entered by Edwin French, with money made up by himself, Samuel Ow, James Lusk, Isaac N. Ebey, A. D. Ferris and other citizens, and donated to the county by them for the purpose of a county seat. And on May 10, 1845, the said Edwin French and Esther, his wife, conveyed said tract to Schuyler County by a deed bearing that date. The land thus conveyed was described as follows: Commencing 26 rods and 8 links north from the southeast corner of the west half of the southeast quarter of Section 13, Township 66 north, Range 15 west; thence north 100 rods; thence west 80 rods; thence south 100 rods; thence east 80 rods to the place of beginning; containing 50 acres, more or less.

The county court at its aforesaid special term, June 2, 1845, made the following entry on its record: "Ordered by the court that the seat of justice, selected by the commissioners for that purpose for the county of Schuyler, shall be known and called by the name of Lancaster."* Edwin French was then appointed commissioner of the county seat, and ordered to lay off the site into squares, blocks, lots, streets and alleys, and "to offer for sale in the town of Lancaster, on the first Monday in August, 1845, 100 lots on a credit for twelve, eighteen and twenty-four months, in installments, the purchasers giving bonds with approved securities." And the court then adjourned to term in course. At the regular July term, 1845, of said court, Edwin French appeared and reported, that, with the assistance of the county surveyor, George W. Johnson, he had laid out the town of Lancaster as directed, and filed a plat of the same, in the office of the county recorder, for record. The report was approved, and George W. Johnson was allowed the sum of thirty dollars for making the survey and plat of the town.

At the January term, 1846, of the county court, the commissioner of the county seat was ordered "to sell at private sale all unsold lots in the town of Lancaster, as follows: all lots fronting the public square at not less than $30 each, and the residue at not less than $5 each, on same terms as heretofore." At the following October term of said court, James M. Bryant was appointed commissioner of the county seat, *vice*

---

*Name was selected by James Lusk.

Edwin French, resigned, and subsequently he (Bryant) was succeeded in that office by William S. Thatcher. At the July term, 1851, of the county court, an abstract of the condition of the several funds of the county was spread upon its record, from which the following extracts are taken:

County seat fund Dr. to lots sold,

By Edwin French, first commissioner................$ 604 50
By James M. Bryant, second commissioner.......... 1,035 00
By William S. Thatcher, third commissioner......... 45 50
_____
Total..$1,685 00

This shows the full amount of funds derived from the sale of lots up to that date; and no considerable amount was ever afterward added to that fund, the valuable lots having been nearly all, if not quite all, sold.

After the county seat had been established at Lancaster, as aforesaid, the legality of the proceedings of the commissioners who selected the site for the same was questioned, especially by those opposed to the location; so, in order to settle all difficulties that were likely to grow out of this matter, the General Assembly passed the following act, entitled "an act in relation to the county seat of Schuyler County."

SECTION 1. The proceedings of the commissioners appointed by law to select and locate the seat of justice of Schuyler county are hereby declared lawful, and that Lancaster, the place selected by them, is hereby declared the seat of justice for said county.

This act to be in force from its passage.

Approved February 4, 1847.

MISCELLANEOUS SUBJECTS.

Public Lands.*—The land in this county was surveyed by Government surveyors, George B. Sargent, with John S. Sheller and Edward K. Gibbon, as assistants; with Richard B. Robinson and George Crump, chainmen; John Mitchell, flagman; and Thomas Adams, axeman, in the fall of 1842, except the west half of Range 13, which had been sectionized prior to this time. The ownership of the land had consisted in what were called "claims;" each settler as he came in would lay off a quarter section, more or less, but generally more, on any unoccupied or unclaimed tract. Difficulties would of course occasionally occur in reference

_____
* Judge Richard Caywood.

to boundaries, and these were settled by arbitrations, or committees appointed for that purpose. This mode of owning the soil was continued for several years after the land was surveyed, and claims were conformed as near as practicable to the lines of the Government survey. As the settlers were all poor, and had little or no money when the land came into market, it became necessary for the protection of their homes, and improvements against land sharks, to organize into what was called a "protective club;" the permanent settlers, of course, all joined in, including every officer in the county. Among the by-laws was one pledging themselves to use all lawful means to prevent any person from entering any recognized claim or improvement. The word lawful, however, had a peculiar and significant meaning; as all persons who violated the rules of the club by entering on the "claim" of another, soon found out that it was not healthy to remain long in the county, unless he deeded the land to the proper occupant upon payment of the entrance price, the amount of which was raised by contribution, if the owner did not have it, as was generally the case.

Prior to the admission of Missouri as a State into the Federal Union, the title to the territory of which Schuyler County now forms a part was vested in the United States Government. But when the State was admitted, Congress donated to it the sixteenth section of land in each and every congressional township therein, for the purpose of maintaining free schools; the said lands to be sold by the laws enacted by the State, and the annual interest arising from the loan of the proceeds thereof to be appropriated for the support of the schools. Hence the sixteenth section, as aforesaid, has always been known as the "school section," or "school lands." The sale of these lands, and the use of the proceeds thereof, is fully set forth in another chapter, under the head of schools. In 1850 Congress passed a law, known as the Swamp Land Act, granting to the State of Arkansas, and to all other States of the Federal Union, the swamp and overflowed lands thereof, the same to be selected and conveyed by patent deed to each State, and afterward to be sold in forty-acre tracts, under laws enacted by the State, and the proceeds thereof to be applied first to defray the expense of selecting and listing the said lands, then to the draining and reclaiming of the same, under State laws enacted for that purpose, after which the county courts were given discretionary powers as to the disposition of the balance of the fund.

Under this liberal act, many advantages were taken of the general Government; for instance if a very small spot of wet or overflowed land could be found on a forty acre tract, the whole would generally be listed as swamp or overflowed lands. In this way many tracts of good upland, containing a small basin which might be overflowed for a short time in a wet season, became classified as swamp land. After the swamp lands were confirmed to the State, Schuyler County contained, and has ever since contained, three classes of public lands, viz: " The Congressional Township or Congress Lands," which consisted of all the lands not conveyed by the general Government to the State, but which were sold to individual purchasers at the general land office for this district; and the school and swamp lands hereinbefore defined. The first action of the county court of Schuyler County in regard to the swamp lands was taken at its October term, 1851, when the clerk thereof was ordered to correspond with the Governor or Secretary of State for instructions, and Richard Caywood was appointed commissioner " to ascertain, survey, lay off and reclaim the inundated or swamp lands lying in said county, and to take such steps and perform all such acts as may be necessary to secure to said county the interest in said lands." Mr. Caywood, however, declined to act under said appointment, and there the matter seemed to rest for a time, and until John W. Minor was appointed as swamp land commissioner, and at the June term, 1853, the court accepted a proposition from said Minor to allow him to select the said lands, and also to allow him to select lands at $1.25 per acre to pay him for his services before putting the swamp lands into market.

It was then thought that only a small amount of land belonging to this class could be found in Schuyler County; but by the method of selecting swamp lands already explained, Mr. Minor succeeded in selecting and listing about 37,000 acres. Before confirming these lands, however, and after being informed that several tracts of first-class land were included in the selection, the general Government sent an agent to inspect the selection made by Mr. Minor, and he cut it down to about 23,000 acres, which were afterward confirmed and conveyed to the State; and even then, much of this class of land, on account of its superior quality, was improperly classified. Strong opposition to allowing Mr. Minor to select lands in payment for his services was afterward made by the bringing of a suit against him in the circuit court, conducted on the part of the county by Judge Richard Caywood, which finally resulted in a compromise by which he was allowed ten cents per acre for about 17,000 acres of the selection, it being payment in full for his services. At the October term, 1856, of the county court, Thomas Roberts, sheriff, was ordered to sell all the swamp lands of Schuyler County (except what might be reserved from sale) at the court-house door, the sale to commence on the first Monday of December following, and to continue from day to day until all were offered for sale. The said lands were to be sold to the highest bidders, and one-fourth of the purchase money to be paid down, and the balance to run twelve months, with interest at 10 per cent from date of sale, by the purchaser giving approved security, and no lands were to be sold for less than $2.50 per acre. Before the day of sale arrived the court changed the conditions so as to allow the purchasers to pay $5 down on each forty-acre tract purchased instead of one-fourth of the purchase money.

On December 15, 1856, Sheriff Roberts reported to the court that the proceeds of the first sale of swamp lands, made in accordance with the order of said court, amounted to $30,425. Before the sale took place, Richard Caywood was appointed "to correct the list of swamp lands for sale, by marking off and arranging the same for sale." Afterward he was appointed and served for a number of years as swamp land commissioner. A large amount of these lands remained unsold after the first sale, and many tracts then sold were afterward forfeited back to the county. No further sales took place until the first Monday of January, 1867, when the sheriff again sold a portion thereof in obedience to a previous order of the court. And at the August term, 1868, of the county court, the sheriff was ordered "to offer for sale all the swamp lands in Schuyler County remaining unsold, and all such as had been back to the forfeited county, on December 15, 1868, and to continue the sale from day to day until all were offered for sale." These lands could not all be sold at $2.50 per acre, according to the conditions of the first sale, but were sold at from $1.25 to about $6 per acre, averaging, perhaps, $2, and the aggregate amount for which they have been sold is closely estimated at $46,000.

A small portion of the swamp land in the county yet remains unsold. Of the lands selected and conveyed by the general Government to the State as belonging to this class, several tracts had previously been sold and conveyed to individual purchasers, who thus obtained priority of title. To make up this deficiency to the county, the general Government, by an arrangement with the State, has allowed Schuyler County to select and acquire title to 2,600 acres of land in Douglass and Wright counties, in this State, and all of this latter selection remains unsold.

Wild Animals and Game.—A number of years before the settlement of the territory now comprising Schuyler County began, it was infested with all the native wild animals common to this part of the country. The buffaloes, in almost countless numbers, grazed upon the open prairies, and made their trails from thence to their watering places, and sheltered themselves under the forest trees along the streams. They had nothing then to make them afraid save the Indian hunter, who seems not to have materially disturbed their peace. But when the white hunter, explorer and adventurer advanced upon them, they appeared to scent the approach of civilization, and fled to the westward, and thus kept far in advance of the permanent settler, who found nothing but the skeletons and horns of their dead when he arrived. Likewise the bears had fled for safer haunts, when the first settlers came; but the panthers lingered in limited numbers, only two of them having been killed, as it is believed, after the settlement began. Prairie wolves, wild cats and catamounts, which were very numerous, seemed not to fear the approach of civilization, but remained in their former haunts, and surrendered them only as a result of their extermination. The deer also remained, and were very numerous. Wild turkeys, too, were found in great abundance. There seemed to be a providence in

SCHUYLER COUNTY, MISSOURI 33

****

the great numbers of deer and turkeys, and the ease with which the early settlers shot and captured them for food for their families. Of the deer, nothing but the hind quarters, commonly called the "saddles," were used for food, the balance of the carcass usually being left where the animal was killed. At some seasons of the year, when the wild turkeys would trespass upon the settler's plantation to feed upon his crops, he could procure all he needed for family use without going off his premises. And sometimes it became actually necessary to guard the "patch" to prevent the turkeys from consuming all the corn.

When the first settlers came, they found but few if any foxes, and these cunning little animals were not noticed until about the year 1849 or 1850, when they appeared to a limited extent, but never became numerous. Rabbits, on account of their destruction by the wildcats, did not become numerous until the latter animals were mostly extinct. Raccoons, squirrels and some other small animals are now and have always been common, and at times quite abundant. All the savage wild animals have become extinct, and the deer have also disappeared. The turkeys remain in sufficient quantities to make it amusing, and sometimes quite profitable, to the sportsman. After the settlement began, some of the hogs belonging to the pioneers strayed away, and became lost in the forests, subsisted on the mast, increased, and grew almost as wild and savage as the native animals. Those having lost hogs in this way were said to have "wild hog claims," and the persons having such claims would form into clubs, in the late fall and early winter season, and go into the forest in a body to hunt and kill wild hogs; and the number killed that were fat enough for pork were divided among the hunters, and the others were thrown away. None were allowed to kill wild hogs but those having claims as aforesaid. This condition of things did not exist after the county became more thickly settled.

Agriculture and Stock Raising.—With the exception of the limited supply of coal which has been mined, and the manufactures common to all rural counties, Schuyler may be said to be exclusively an agricultural and stock raising county. The soil, as has been mentioned in a former chapter, is very productive, and has always remunerated the husbandman liberally, in spite of the bad manner in which it has been cultivated. No artificial fertilizer worthy of mention has ever been applied to the lands of Schuyler County. But little clover, the greatest of fertilizers, has ever been raised, and "turned under," to pulverize, make friable and enrich the soil. When the early settlers commenced their farming operations in this county, or rather in the territory out of which the county was afterward formed, they found the ground covered with the tall, wild prairie grass, which had caused the entire surface, except in some of the densely timbered portions, to contain a stiff sod, which they subdued with turning plows drawn by from two to four yoke of oxen. This grass grew so tall that the old settlers claim they could hide themselves in it while on horseback. As soon as they began to subdue the native grass, the blue-grass took hold and grew spontaneously in its stead, and consequently the former, on lands that had not been disturbed with the plow, as well as that that had been broken, began to give place to the encroaching blue-grass, and finally the native grasses have almost become extinct, and the entire surface has become covered with the blue-grass. In fact, the latter has become so completely established, that when land is allowed to lie idle after taking a crop from it, it will soon become covered again by the spontaneous growth of the blue-grass.

During the settlement of the county the markets were so far away, and so inaccessible, that there was no encouragement to the farmers to raise a surplus over that needed for home consumption, as it would cost more than it would bring to convey it to market. Consequently, they raised and spun flax, and wove it into cloth, made and wove homespun clothing, and spent a considerable portion of their time in hunting, making occasional trips to towns in the older counties for the purpose of obtaining groceries and such necessary things as they could not manufacture. And in this way they plodded along without producing and obtaining much wealth, until, with the increase and improvements of the settlements in their rear, the markets drew nearer, and thus furnished them a means for disposing of their surplus productions. In 1855, ten years after the county was organized, and nineteen years after the first settler built his humble cabin within its limits, there were only 743 taxable polls therein, and, although a large amount of land had been taken up or entered, much of it remained unpatented to the purchasers, and was therefore not taxable. The aggregate of the taxable property assessed for that year was as follows:

```
91,330 acres of land assessed at................. ......$316,984
167 town lots assessed at... ................... ....... 16,664
53 slaves assessed at.................................. 24,760
Money at interest.................................... 46,225
Other personal property............................. 118,820
                                                       _____
     Total assessment of taxable property..............$523,253
```

The 743 polls were also taxable per capita.

Passing on to the year 1860, there were found to be 1,116 taxable polls, and taxable property as follows:

```
160,657 acres of land assessed at......................$681,575
416 town lots assessed at ........................... 39,816
46 slaves assessed at................................. 25,000
Money at interest........ ......................... ... 94,583
Other personal property............................. 190,768
                                                       _____
     Total assessment of taxable property...........$1,031,782·
```

These statistics are introduced here to show the advancement the county was making in obtaining wealth. By comparison the reader will observe that the assessed value of the county had more than doubled during the five years from 1855 to 1860. This was due partly to the fact that during that time there was a large influx of settlers who brought some property with them, and partly to the increased advantages afforded the farmers in the way of disposing of their surplus productions, and also to the further fact that more than double the number of acres of land had become taxable. The day of railroads had also come, and Schuyler County was happy in the anticipation of securing one at no distant day; although a decade or more passed away before she realized what she so fondly anticipated. The principal productions of Schuyler County have always been Indian corn, oats, wheat, rye, hay, and various kinds of vegetables; however, since the Civil War, the raising of live stock has become a leading wealth-producing factor.

The following table shows the farm productions in grain, hay, vegetables, and tobacco for the years 1869 and 1879, as shown by the United States census reports of 1870 and 1880:

	1869.	1870.
Indian corn....	279,460 bush.	1,087,370 bush.
Oats............................	125,442 "	230,508 "
Wheat........................	49,725 "	38,058 "
Rye...........	10,399 "	10,674 "
Irish potatoes.................	28,155 "	30,340 "
Sweet potatoes....	125 "	1,911 "
Tobacco......................	22,194 lbs.	32,252 lbs.
Hay..........................	not given	16,900 tons.

These figures show an increase in the ten years of nearly four times the amount of Indian corn produced, and nearly twice the amount of oats, a decrease in the production of wheat, and a moderate increase in the production of all the other enumerated articles. The raising of Indian corn, oats, hay, and live stock has mostly absorbed the attention of the farmers for many years. Wheat has not been considered a sure crop, and, consequently, its production has been neglected. It is believed, however, by good farmers, that if the ground was put into proper condition, and the proper attention was given to the production of this cereal, the yield would generally be abundant. The yield of wheat per acre in Schuyler County, for the last year (1887), without the best of husbandry—that of having the land enriched and pulverized to a sufficient depth—has been enormous; and it is to be regretted that the aggregate production for the year is not obtainable. Many fields have averaged from thirty to forty bushels per acre, and that is much greater than in many portions of the country, where wheat is the staple product.

Live Stock.—A few farmers have made a specialty of raising live stock in Schuyler County from a comparatively early day in its history. The first herd of cattle, amounting to 100 head, wintered in Schuyler County, was owned by James Gates; and previous to 1850 young cattle sold at from $5 to $7.50 per head. Samuel Ow went into Pike County, Ill., purchased forty hogs for $100, and, bringing them into Schuyler County, exchanged eighteen for five young steers, and hewed logs enough to build a house 18x20 feet for the owner of the steers. From that time prices ranged as high as $15 to $20 per head.* The following table shows the number of head of live stock in Schuyler County for the years noted:

* Extra from chronicles published in *The Excelsior*.

	1870.	1880.	1885.
Horses	3,686	4,684	5,021
Mules and asses	1,002	405	424
Cattle	3,450	12,667	16,193
Sheep	15,961	13,055	24,309
Hogs	11,928	32,319	17,347

The foregoing indicates a gradual increase in the number of horses, while the number of mules decreased about 60 per cent from 1870 to 1880, and then slightly increased for the next five years. The number of cattle, as shown for the year 1870, only includes milch cows and working oxen, the others not being given in the census reports. The figures for 1870 and 1880 are taken from the United States census reports, and those for 1885 from the assessor's book; hence it must not be inferred that the apparent decrease in hogs was real. The census gives the highest number owned in the year, while the assessor's book only shows what is owned at the time the taxes accrue, and it is a characteristic of people everywhere to always own the least property at that season of the year when the tax assessor makes his annual visit.

Fruit.—Fruit growing has never been extensively practiced in Schuyler County, although the orchard products, as given by the census of 1880, compare very favorably with the best fruit-growing counties in the State, when its area is taken into consideration.

There are but few manufactories in the county, and they are mentioned in connection with the history of the towns where they are located. Schuyler will undoubtedly continue to be, as it always has been, one of the best agricultural counties in the State. Its soil is susceptible of being raised to the highest degree of production, and its railroad facilities to the best city markets, in all directions, are excellent. In general, the farms are too large; they should be divided. New farmers should be encouraged to come in; none should move out. Less acres should be cultivated by the individual, and a better and more thorough system of farming should be inaugurated, and, consequently, much more produced.

The Schuyler County Agricultural and Mechanical Society.—On the 7th of February, 1859, John Fugate, Benjamin Brown,

G. W. Gatlin, and sixty-two other citizens of the county, filed a petition with the county court of Schuyler County, praying for an order to incorporate them into a society to be styled "The Schuyler County Agricultural and Mechanical Society, for the improvement of agriculture and the mechanical arts." And the court being satisfied that there were at least fifty petitioners who had signed the petition, as required by law, and that they were all freeholders of the State, ordered and declared the said petitioners incorporated for the purpose specified in their petition, as a body politic and corporate, by the name and style of "The Schuyler County Agricultural Society," and that by that name they and their successors should be known in law, have perpetual succession, sue and be sued, plead and be impleaded, defend and be defended, and have all the powers granted by law to similar associations.

Elias Brown, the owner of the northwest quarter of the northwest quarter of Section 10, Township 64 north, Range 15 west, leased to the society a part of the land just described for a "fair ground," to be used as such by the society so long as desired. About six acres were enclosed, and a floral hall and other temporary buildings and sheds were erected thereon. The floral hall has since been removed, and is now used by Judge Payton as a barn.

The first fair or exhibition on this ground was held by the society in the fall of 1859, and the next in 1860. The Civil War then coming on, no more fairs were held until 1865, and the last one was held in 1867. The shares to the capital stock of the society were only $5 each, and this admitted the shareholder's family, his hired help, and all his stock entered for exhibition, to the fair free. This, of course, passed so many through the gate free that it was impossible for the society to raise sufficient funds to defray its running expenses, and consequently it was disbanded. The fair ground was located near Green Top, and also near the line between Schuyler and Adair Counties, and it was really a union fair of the two counties, although incorporated in Schuyler. At one of the exhibitions of this society, William Gargis was killed by a horse which ran against him.

In the year 1872 another society was organized under the

name and style of "The Schuyler County Agricultural and Mechanical Association," to have perpetual succession by that name, with power to sue and be sued in all the courts of law and equity. Its object, as stated in its constitution, was "to develop the agricultural and mineral resources of the county, the encouragement of mechanical arts, and the improvement of domestic animals." And the method through which this object was to be accomplished was by the holding of annual fairs. The capital stock was made to consist of $50 shares, and the original stock subscribed amounted to $1,550, and each share entitled the holder thereof to one vote, and the constitution provided that the capital stock should not be increased without the consent of two-thirds of the stockholders. The business of the society was to be transacted by five directors, to be elected by ballot on the last day of each annual fair, and none were eligible to serve as directors but stockholders. The directors thus elected were to choose from their own body a president, secretary and treasurer. The following is a list of the original stockholders, and the amount subscribed by each: William Hombs, $100; George Reeves, $150; W. S. Lancaster, $50; Joseph Knott, $50: W. D. Sizemore $50; L. Schmidt, $100; W. B. Hays, $100; R. Blurton, $50; William Niblack, $100; A. G. Moore, $100; John Baker, $50; Thomas Russell, $50; DeN. Jewett, $50; F. T. Hughes, $50; William A. Coffey, $50; Matthew Coffey, $50; Spencer Greer, $50; J. R. Rippey, $150; R. K. Grant, $50; Henry Miller, $50; W. L. Munsell, $50; Thomas Lewis, $50; total, $1,550.

After being fully organized, the association purchased from Edwin French and James Raley, as trustees of the Lancaster Real Estate Company, for the consideration of $2,750, the following described tract of land: Commencing at the northeast corner of Downing's addition to Lancaster, and running west 2,540 feet to the Missouri, Iowa & Nebraska Railroad; thence along the northeast line of said railway to a point parallel with the north side of alley in Blocks 17, 18 and 19; thence on and along the north side of said alley to the middle of Fifth Street; thence along Fifth Street to the place of beginning; containing fifty-five acres, and procured a deed for the same dated December 12, 1872.

The following year this land was enclosed and fitted up for the fair ground of the association, with a floral hall, ticket office, music stand, stalls for stock, etc., and the first fair was held in the fall of that year, and they continued to be held until the fall of 1880, when the last one was held. A fair for the fall of 1881 was fully advertised, and the people assembled at the ground on the first day thereof, when, on account of the financial trouble that the association was then laboring under, the fair was dismissed, and the ground closed against the society. Thus ended the second agricultural and mechanical society of Schuyler County, and none has since been organized. A mortgage had been given on the grounds when purchased to secure the deferred payments, and the association did not become able to make all of said payments. Meanwhile Louis Schmidt became the owner, by purchase, of the major part of the capital stock, and the mortgage was finally foreclosed, and the land was sold by the sheriff to satisfy the judgment to said Schmidt, who has since removed the buildings, and now uses the fair ground for a pasture.

Early Highways.—The first public road established in Schuyler County, after its organization, was the State road leading from Kirksville, in Adair County, to the northern boundary line of the State of Missouri, in the direction of Iowa City, by the way of William Naylor's and James Gates'. The report of the commissioners who laid out and established this road was received and approved by the county court at its July term, 1845. Isaac N. Ebey, William L. Robinson and Henry Davis were the commissioners to lay out said road, and each were allowed the sum of $9 for his services as such. George W. Johnson was the surveyor of the road, and was allowed $18 for his services as such. Peter Kline and Thomas S. Davis were the chain carriers, and were allowed $4.50 each for their services, and James Davis was allowed $12 for his services as wagoner on said survey.

Overseers of county roads were then appointed as follows: Jefferson Meek and Warren Hunt, for the one commencing at the township line of Fabius and Liberty Townships; thence east to the range line dividing Ranges 13 and 14, to be opened and kept in repair thirty feet in width. George Lake, overseer for the road commencing at range line dividing Ranges 13 and 14; thence east by way of William V. Rippeys' to the Scotland County line, to be opened and kept in repair thirty feet in width. James Hill, overseer of the road commencing at the range line dividing Ranges 13 and 14; thence east to the Scotland County line. Alfred Adams, overseer of the road commencing at the township line dividing Fabius and Liberty Townships; thence northeast to the Fabius Creek. Edwin Snyder, overseer of the road commencing at the Fabius Creek; thence east to the Scotland County line. James Varner, overseer of the road commencing at Tippecanoe; thence east by the way of Hall's blacksmith shop to the township line of Fabius and Liberty Townships. John W. Lesley, overseer of the road commencing at Tippecanoe; thence southeast to the township line dividing Fabius and Liberty Townships. John Jones, overseer of the road commencing at Tippecanoe; thence east by the way of John Jones' to the township line dividing Fabius and Liberty Townships.

Then at the same time, July, 1845, overseers of State roads were appointed as follows: George Naylor, overseer of Division No. 1 of State road, commencing at the township line of Liberty and Salt River Townships; thence north to William L. Robinson's, to be opened and kept in repair thirty feet in width. Stephen D. Ruddle, overseer of Division No. 2, of the same road, commencing at William L. Robinson's; thence north to the Fabius Creek, near B. H. Wetherford's, to be opened and kept in repair forty feet in width. Meridith J. Norman, overseer of Division No. 3, of said State road, commencing at the Fabius Creek near B. H. Wetherford's; thence north to the township line dividing Liberty and Independence Townships, to be opened and kept in repair thirty feet in width. George W. Johnson, overseer of State road, commencing at the township line of Liberty and Chariton Townships, near Bradley's; thence east to Tippecanoe, to be opened and kept in repair thirty feet in width. Benjamin Schloop, overseer of State road commencing at Tippecanoe; thence south to the township line of Liberty and Salt River Townships. Jefferson Saling, overseer of State road commencing at the township line dividing Liberty and Independence Townships; thence north to a point opposite William Russel's. James Ray, overseer of said State road, commencing at a point opposite William Russel's; thence north to the northern boundary line of the State.

The width of all the foregoing roads, not otherwise specified, was established at thirty feet. Afterward, at the October term, 1845, of the county court, that portion of the State road in Schuyler county, which had been established from Kirksville in Adair County to Tippecanoe in this county, commencing at the Adair County line, and running thence by the way of William Roberts' old place, to a point opposite the Chilley Grove, was vacated; and at the same time a plat of the State road, from Tippecanoe to Alexandria in Clark County, was filed and accepted by the county court; and Joseph R. Webster and William V. Rippey were appointed overseers of that part of it lying in Schuyler, and ordered to open it and keep it in repair to the width of thirty feet.

Nearly all of the foregoing roads were established before Schuyler County was organized, and are mentioned here to show the reader what roads were then in process of construction, and also to give the names of the first road overseers appointed in Schuyler County. It should be observed that the descriptions given of the early roads were so indefinite that several roads might have been made to suit the same description. At the July term, 1849, of the county court, Thomas Hope, Josiah Hargis and Henry Davis, commissioners appointed by the Legislature to lay out a State road from Hargraves' mill, in Putnam County, to Lancaster, in Schuyler County, reported said road extended on to near Hope's mill in Scotland County; and Jahiel Parks was appointed to act conjointly with a commissioner, to be appointed in Putnam County, to locate, let and superintend the building of a bridge across the Chariton River, at or near Hargraves' mill, on the aforesaid State road. The first roads of the county were laid out on the nearest and most available route from point to point without regard for section lines. Many of them have been vacated, and latterly the highways have been vacated, so far as the contour of the grounds would admit, on the section lines, or parallel therewith.

County Officers.—The following is a list of the names of the county officers, together with the time served by each, from the organization of the county to the date of the present writing (November, 1887), excepting the county court justices, and the judges of the probate and circuit courts, and prosecuting attorneys, whose names will be given in full under the head of "Courts."

Representatives.—James Lusk, representative of Adair County, to which Schuyler was attached for civil and military purposes, continued to represent the latter until after the election in Schuyler County in 1846, since which time the county has been represented in the Legislature as follows: Edwin French, 1846–50; John W. Minor, 1850–54; Thomas Roberts, 1854–56; Don C. Roberts, 1856–62; John McGoldrick, 1862–66; Seth Hathaway, 1866–68; Andrew J. Baker, 1868–70; John Sharp, 1870–72; Jesse Carter, 1872–78; M. B. Patterson, 1878–80; John R. Rippey, 1880–82; P. C. Berry, 1882–84; Nat. M. Shelton, present incumbent, elected in 1884, and re-elected in 1886.

County Court Clerks.—Isaac N. Ebey, 1845–51; Jahiel Parks, 1851–52; B. H. Wetherford, 1852–53; I. B. Alverson, 1853–62; Jared O. Jewitt, 1862–64; Geo. W. Gatlin, 1864–66; Andrew J. Baker, 1866–67; Alex. M. Felton, 1867–70; Daniel T. Truitt, 1870–74; Daniel D. Smith, 1874–86; Charles W. Bunch, present incumbent, elected in 1886.

Circuit Court Clerks.—Isaac N. Ebey, 1845–51; Jahiel Parks, 1851–52; Burrel H. Wetherford, 1852–53; Iverson B. Alverson, 1853–62; * Edwin French, 1862–66; William McAfee, 1866–67; John Baker, 1867–75; Ward L. Munsell, 1875–78; De N. Jewett, present incumbent, elected first in 1878—present term continues to 1890.

Recorders.—The office of recorder has always been connected with that of the circuit court clerk; hence the circuit court clerk has always been the recorder.

Sheriffs.—Jonathan Riggs, 1845–46; B. H. Wetherford, 1846–50; L. H. Conklin, 1850–54; Thomas Roberts, 1854–58; L. H. Conklin, 1858–63; John Baker, 1863–67; A. K. Cowgill, 1867–69; F. M. Wilcox, 1869–71; Jacob Miller, 1871–73; Armstrong G. Moore, 1873–79; N. T. Roberts, 1879–83; Nicholas Sloop, 1883–85; George Bush, 1885–87; re-elected in 1886.

---

* The county court clerk was also clerk of the circuit court from organization of county to 1862.

Treasurers.—Robert S. Neeley, 1845–47; James Hepburn, 1847–55; William S. Thatcher, 1855–56; William Lindsay, 1856–58; Edwin French, 1858–62; John Gildard, 1862–68; Moses Baker, 1868–72; William B. Hays, 1872–76; Samuel A. Dysart, 1876–78; Charles W. Bunch, 1878–82; Henry A. Miller, 1882–84; Jared O. Jewett, 1884–86; Fielden C. Hulen, present incumbent, elected in 1886.

Collectors.—William A. Coffee, 1872–78; Thomas P. Leedom, 1878, September to November; Frank A. Irvin, 1878–82; Thomas P. Leedom, 1882–86; Nicholas T. Roberts, present incumbent, elected in 1886.

Surveyors.—George W. Johnson, 1845–47; John S. Sheller, 1847–51; Richard Caywood, 1851–56; Stephen Caywood, 1856–60; Jesse K. Beard, 1860–61; Ira Roberts, 1861–68; Joseph T. Casper, 1868–72; Thomas D. Brown, 1872–76; George P. Martin, 1876–80; John H. Davis, 1880–84; Henry D. Satterfield, present incumbent, elected in 1884.

School Commissioners.—D. T. Truitt, 1875–77; D. B. Nichols, 1877–79; C. C. Fogle, 1879–83; Edwin F. Payton, 1883–85; George E. Davis, 1885–86; Thomas J. Cleeton, 1886–87; James T. Fugate, 1887, present incumbent.

Elections.—The first elections in Schuyler County were held on the first Monday in August, 1845, at the following places: Independence Township, at the house of Joseph Carter; Wells Township, at the house of Theophilus Rials; Chariton Township, at the house of Norman Lampieurs; Liberty Township, at the house of James Cochrane; Fabius Township, at the Fabius meeting-house; Salt River Township, at the house of Andrew Mc-Quitties.

The judges of these elections were Isaac Newland, Wilkins Hewlet and William Hewlin, for Fabius Township; Samuel Riggs, John Willis and Joseph Carter, for Independence Township; Morgan Hensley, Elijah Horn and John S. Johnson, for Wells Township; Thomas I. Bennett, George Hull and Edward Hughes, for Chariton Township; Stephen B. Ruddle, Thomas B. Du Bois and Samuel Ow, for Liberty Township, and Henry Davis, William A. Hamilton and John Mikel, for Salt River Township. The officers elected at this election were the county officers, who were serving in their respective offices under appointment of the county court at its first session, and whose names have been mentioned therewith, and are also mentioned under the head of county officers.

The following shows the number of votes cast in Schuyler County for each presidential candidate at the several presidential elections, beginning with the year 1848, that being the first election for that purpose after the county was organized, to wit:

1848—Zachary Taylor, Whig, 204 votes; Lewis Cass, Democrat, 192.

1852—Franklin Pierce, Democrat, 222 votes; Winfield Scott, Whig, 177.

1856—James Buchanan, Democrat, 472 votes; John C. Fremont, Republican, 287.

1860—Stephen A. Douglas, Democrat, 455 votes; John C. Breckinridge, Democrat, 251; John Bell, American, 267; Abraham Lincoln, Republican, 14.

1864—Abraham Lincoln, Republican, 546 votes; George B. McClellan, Democrat, 191.

1868—Ulysses S. Grant, Republican, 508 votes; Horatio Seymour, Democrat, 241.

1872—Ulysses S. Grant, Republican, 792 votes; Horace Greeley, Democrat, 788.

1876—Samuel J. Tilden, Democrat, 1,117 votes; Rutherford B. Hayes, Republican, 909; Peter Cooper, National, 17.

1880—Winfield S. Hancock, Democrat, 1,065 votes; James A. Garfield, Republican, 570; Gen. Weaver, National, 457.

1884—Grover Cleveland, Democrat, 1,203 votes; James G. Blaine, Republican, 1,009; John P. St. John, Prohibition, 13.

The foregoing figures have been kindly furnished by Missouri's able Secretary of State, Michael K. McGrath. By reference to the votes cast for each of the presidential candidates, as shown by the foregoing, the political complexion of the county (excepting the years 1864 and 1868, when Southern sympathizers were disfranchised), can readily be discerned. At the August election in 1853, Claiborne F. Jackson, Democrat, received 293 votes in Schuyler County, for congressman, against 230 received by James J. Lindley, Whig, for the same office.

And in 1856, Trusten Polk, Democrat, received 511 votes in
Schuyler County; Robert C. Ewing, Whig, 271, and Thomas H.
Benton, 22, for the office of Governor of the State. Coming down
to more modern dates, it is seen that in 1868, William H.
Hatch received, in Schuyler County, 877 votes for the office of
congressman, while his competitors for the office received votes
as follows: John M. London, 824; Henry Clay, Democrat, 2, and
John M. Glover, 1.   At the same time M. B. Patterson received
949 votes for the office of representative in the Legislature, and
his opponent, Adam Kuhn, received 910.   The vote for Governor
of the State in 1870, in the several voting precincts of the county,
was as follows:

	DEMOCRAT.	REPUBLICAN.
	B. Gratz Brown.	J. W. McClurg.
Liberty	133	96
Glenwood	65	111
Prairie	141	99
Fabius	94	21
Independence	91	28
Salt River	76	30
Chariton	61	14
Totals	661	399

Majority for Brown, 262.

The same year (1870) James G. Blair, Democrat, received in
Schuyler County 635 votes for the office of congressman, and his
opponent, J. T. K. Hayward, Republican, received 416; and Robert
H. Brown, Democrat, received 672 votes for the office of State
senator, and his opponent, John B. Glaze, Republican, 370; and
John Sharp, Democrat, received 672 votes for the office of representative in the State Legislature, and his opponent, Edward
Higbee, Republican, 382.   At the presidential election in 1872
the vote of the county by precincts was as follows:

	REPUBLICAN.	DEMOCRAT.
	Grant.	Greeley
Liberty	143	133
Glenwood	174	81
Prairie	177	123
Fabius	72	152
Independence	80	125
Salt River	101	83
Chariton	45	91
Totals	792	788

The same year John B. Henderson, Democrat, received 792 votes for the office of Governor of the State, and his opponent, Silas Woodson, Republican, 812.

In 1876 John S. Phelps, Democrat, received 1,116 votes in Schuyler County for the office of Governor of the State, while his opponents received votes as follows: Gus A. Finkelnburg, Republican, 912, and Jesse P. Alexander, National, 15; and for congressman John M. Glover, Democrat, received 1,110 votes, and his opponent as follows: J. T. K. Hayward, Republican, 902, and John M. London, National, 17; and for representative in the Legislature, Jesse Carter, Democrat, received 1,105, and John Scovern, Republican, 920. At the November election in 1880 the vote of the county, by precincts, for the office of Governor, was as follows:

	DEMOCRAT. T. J. Crittenden.	REPUBLICAN. D. P. Dyer.	NATIONAL. L. A. Brown.
Liberty	184	102	77
Fabius	241	39	51
Glenwood	92	111	83
Chariton	94	36	27
Prairie	186	170	106
Salt River	92	75	58
Independence	179	48	58
Total	1,068	581	460

By comparison it will be seen that these aggregates nearly agree with the votes cast at that election for the presidential candidates. At the election in 1882 William H. Hatch, Democrat, received 1,031 votes in Schuyler County, for the office of congressman, while his opponents, John M. Glover, also a Democrat, received 949, and F. A. Leavitt, National, 19 votes; and at the same time W. C. Berry, Democrat, received 1,039 votes for the office of representative in the Legislature, and his opponent, F. M. Rose, Republican, 1,019. At the November election in 1884 William H. Hatch received 1,231 votes in the county, for the office of congressman, and his opponent, Abram L. Gray, 990; and at the same time W. M. Vancleve, Democrat, received 1,211 votes for the office of State senator, and his opponent, Morris Tuttle, Republican, received 1,016 votes; and Nathan M. Shelton received 1,253 votes in the county for the office of representative in the Legislature, and Frank A. Irvin 967 for the same office.

In 1886 William H. Hatch received 1,290 votes in the county for the office of congressman, and his opponent, William P. Harrison, 973. William H. Sears, Democrat, received 1,271 votes for the office of State senator, and his opponent, Thomas Moody, Republican, 983; and Nat. M. Shelton, 1,327 votes for representative in the Legislature, and his opponent, H. F. Minium, 930.

Population.—The following table, which has been compiled from the United States Census Reports, shows the population of Schuyler County for the years noted, commencing with the year 1850, at which time the first census was taken after the county was organized. The table shows by the column headings the number of white and colored inhabitants, and the aggregate, together with the number of native and foreign born. The latter are principally Germans.

Year.	White.	Colored.	Total.	Native.	Foreign.
1850	3,230	57	3,287	*3,174	*113
1860	6,658	39	6,697	6,480	217
1870	8,806	14	8,820	8,500	320
1880	10,461*	9	10,470	10,132	338

*Estimated.

According to this table, the reader will observe that from 1850 to 1860 the population of the county more than doubled, and this is owing to the fact that during that decade there was a much greater influx of settlers than at any other period of its existence. Supposing the increase of the population to have been the same since 1880 that it had been for the ten years prior thereto, it would now be about 11,200.

The population of the minor civil divisions of the county for the year 1880, which is the last reliable enumeration of its inhabitants, was as follows:

Chariton Township, including Coatsville............ 765
Town of Coatsville..................................... 98
Fabius Township......................................1,826
Glenwood Township....................................1,316
Independence Township................................1,496
Liberty Township, including Lancaster.................1,729
Town of Lancaster...................................... 528
Prairie Township, including Queen City................2,227
Town of Queen City.................................... 357
Salt River Township, including Green Top..............1,111
Town of Green Top..................................... 220

****

Finances.—As soon as the government of the county of Schuyler was fully established, it became necessary to provide for the accumulation of a revenue to support it; and for that purpose the county court, at its special July term, 1845, made the following entry: "Ordered that the amount of county revenue levied and collected for county purposes for the year 1845 shall be as follows: upon all licenses for groceries and dramshops there shall be levied and collected for county purposes 100 per cent upon the amount levied and collected for State purposes; on all merchants' license there shall be levied and collected for county purposes, 150 per cent upon the amount levied and collected for State purposes; and upon all other objects of taxation 200 per cent upon the amount levied and collected for State purposes." This was the first levy on property and privileges after the county was organized, and a similar levy with the necessary changes has been annually made ever since. At the following January term of said court the clerk was ordered to certify to the auditor of public accounts that George Naylor, the first assessor of Schuyler County, had occupied twenty-two days to assess the taxable property of the county, and that the State was bound to pay said assessor $22 for such services for the year 1845. The assessor was allowed $44 for twenty-two days' work, and the law required the State to pay one-half, and the county the other. There is a striking contrast between the time it took and what it cost then to assess the county, and the time it now takes and what it costs to assess the county. But then the county was in its infancy, and there were only a few persons and but little property to assess. The following year, 1846, there were only 576 names assessed on the tax list, and the amount certified for the State to pay the assessor, Mr. Naylor, was $36, being one-half the amount for his services.

At the July term, 1846, of the county court, Josiah N. Hargis, court-house commissioner, was allowed $6 for six months' services as such commissioner, and James Hepburn, treasurer of the county, was allowed $1 per month out of each fund for his services as treasurer from the date of his bond. The county court failed to make an exhibit on its record of the annual receipts and expenditures of funds until 1851, when it caused such an exhibit to be made to include all the back years with the current one, so as to show the amounts then on hand. The following is the exhibit:

Date.	Sources of Revenue.	Amount.
1845	Amount of tax book	$ 346 46
1845	Amount of tax on licenses	205 78
1846	Amount of tax book	413 34
1846	Amount of tax on licenses	42 90
1847	Amount of tax book	426 00
1847	Amount of tax on licenses	59 14
1848	Amount of tax book	419 10
1848	Amount of tax on licenses	34 16
1849	Amount of tax book	358 09
1849	Amount of tax on licenses	57 18
1850	Amount of tax book	484 90
1850	Amount of tax on licenses	97 38
1851	Amount of tax book	642 34
1851	Amount of tax on licenses	93 91

Total...$3,680 68
Amount of delinquent list allowed from 1845 to 1850.. 683 50

Amount of net revenue collected from 1845 to 1850....$2,997 18

The exhibit of the road and canal fund drawn from the State treasury by the several commissioners appointed to receive the same from 1845 to 1851 was as follows: Total amount drawn, $3,425.16; amount expended, $1,952.63; amount in the treasury, $1,472.53. The exhibit of the State school money was as follows: Amount received from 1845 to July 1, 1851, $1,493.64; amount disbursed, $1,332.64; leaving $160.99 on hand. The county seat fund derived from the sale of town lots was as follows: Received on lots sold by Edwin French, first commissioner, $604.50; from James M. Bryant, second commissioner, $1,035; and from William S. Thatcher, third commissioner, $45.50, making a total of $1,685; expended, $1,668.37, leaving a balance of $16.63 in the treasury.

The following table shows the comparative value of the taxable property of the county at the end of different periods, beginning with the year 1855:

YEAR.	Value of Taxable Property.	State Tax.	All other Taxes.	Total Tax.
1855	$ 523,253 00	$ 1,325 51	$ 2,374 12	$ 3,699 63
1860	1,031,782 00	2,482 06	5,987 72	8,469 78
1870	1,936,249 00	9,829 32	34,312 68	44,142 00
1880	1,714,271 00	....	....	....
1887	2,252,491 00	9,012 20	34,584 39	43,596 59

By reference to this table, there seems to be an inconsistency which needs explanation. For instance, the taxable property in 1870 was assessed much higher than it was in 1880, ten years later, and nearly as high as it is at the present time. This is accounted for by the fact that at that time property retained its inflated value caused by the Civil War. To illustrate, the assessment on the North Missouri Railroad, now the Wabash, St. Louis & Pacific, was placed in 1870 at $325,600, whereas it is now assessed at only $143,445, or less than one-half the former assessment. Again, the taxes levied for 1870 seem unreasonably high, but, in the amount assessed, provision was made for the payment of $19,658.67 of the county bonds. The items composing the total amount of taxable property in the county, as shown by the foregoing table for the year 1887, are as follows:

Real estate	$1,161,378
Personal property	844,283
Wabash, St. Louis & Pacific Railroad	143,445
Keokuk & Western Railroad	99,500
Western Union Telegraph Company	3,885
Total assessed value	$2,252,491

To ascertain the real value or wealth of a county, it is generally safe to double its assessed value. This would make the true value or wealth of Schuyler County, $4,504,982.

Railroads.—The building of railroads in the east, and the completion of the Southern Michigan & Northern Indiana Railroad to Chicago in 1851, created a railroad fever, which spread like an epidemic throughout the west. Individuals and public officials began to look about to conceive plans and to devise means for the building of railroads here and there and everywhere. The North Missouri Railroad Company, having been chartered by an act of the General Assembly of the State of Missouri, approved March 3, 1851, with authority to " survey, mark, locate and construct a railroad from the city of St. Charles, in the county of St. Charles, passing up the divide between the tributaries of the Mississippi and Missouri Rivers, as near as may be to the northern boundary line of the State," and the county of Schuyler being directly on the route thus described, the people thereof hoped that they would soon have a railroad. And, in order to hasten its construction, the county court of Schuyler County, at its June term, 1853, made an order on its record to set aside the net proceeds arising from the sale of the "swamp lands" belonging to Schuyler County, to be used in extending the North Missouri Railroad from the point where it might cross the line between Adair and Schuyler Counties, on to Lancaster. In making this order, the intention of the court was good; fortunately, however, none of this fund was so appropriated, but, instead thereof, the major part of it eventually found its way into the permanent school fund, where it has done the most good.

Afterward the county court ordered that an election be held at each of the several voting places in the county on the first Monday in February, 1854, to decide whether the county should subscribe $30,000 to the capital stock of the North Missouri Railroad Company, and also whether the money should be raised by issuing bonds, or by a direct tax in four annual installments, commencing one year after the location of said road. The elections were accordingly held on the first Monday in February, 1854, and 292 votes were cast in favor of making the proposed subscription to the capital stock of said company, and 152 votes were cast against it, making a majority of 140 in its favor; and 287 votes were cast in favor of raising the money by taxation, and five were cast for raising it by issuing bonds. Then, on the 3d of April following, the county court made the following entry upon its record:

Ordered by the court, that the county of Schuyler subscribe to the capital stock of the North Missouri Railroad Company the sum of $30,000, to be paid by taxation, upon the following express conditions, to wit:

First. Said road to be permanently located through the county of Schuyler.

Second. The whole amount of said $30,000 subscribed is to be expended in the actual construction of said road north of the Hannibal & St. Joseph Railroad.

Third. The whole amount hereby subscribed is to be paid in four equal annual installments, the first installment not to be paid prior to the time of collecting the revenue for the State for the year 1855, nor until the money is actually needed for the use of the construction of said road as aforesaid, north of the Hannibal & St. Joseph Railroad. And the court doth further order and appoint William S. Thatcher, agent, to represent the county of Schuyler, to vote or transfer its stock, give its votes and receive its dividends, and to do any and all things necessary for the interest of said county in the premises.

Afterward, at the December special term, 1854, of the county court, it was "ordered that the county of Schuyler, in its corporate capacity, subscribe to the capital stock of the North Missouri Railroad Company 500 shares, or $50,000, to be paid as called for by order of the board of directors of said company by taxation, provided said road is located on or near the present survey, and, in compliance with the present charter, through Schuyler County, as has been surveyed. This subscription is to be in lieu of all others heretofore made by order of said county court." At the same time James S. Rollins, of Boone County, was appointed agent for Schuyler County, with authority to subscribe the full amount of the aforesaid stock to the said railroad company on the foregoing expressed conditions. Justice William Barlow dissented from the foregoing order subscribing the $50,000 to the capital stock of said company. This latter subscription was made to and accepted by the said railroad company in lieu of the former subscription made by the county, and nothing more of importance in the matter occurred until November 5, 1859, when the directors of the company called on the county court for 30 per cent of the aforesaid subscription of $50,000.* Not having the funds in the treasury with which to pay this amount, the court on the 7th of said November, ordered " that for the purpose of paying the first installment of Schuyler County's subscription to the capital stock of the North Missouri Railroad Company, fifteen $1,000 bonds of said county be issued, numbering from one to fifteen, payable in the city of St. Louis on the 1st day of March, 1860; that said bonds be signed by the president of this court, and attested by the clerk thereof, and that the following form be observed:"

$1,000.   No.— $1,000.

The county of Schuyler in the State of Missouri will pay to the North Missouri Railroad Company, or bearer, at their office in St. Louis, on the 1st day of March, 1860, $1,000.

By order of county court.

Given at Lancaster this 7th day of November, 1859.

CHARLES HALE,

ATTEST: *Presiding Justice Schuyler County Court.*

I. B. ALVERSON, *Clerk.*

---

* How the first installment became 30 per cent of the $50,000 cannot be learned from the records.

In order to provide for the payment of these bonds, a tax of $1.50 on each $100 of the taxable property of the county was ordered to be levied and collected for the year 1859. Then the fifteen bonds as aforesaid were issued in open court, and delivered to John W. Minor, to be by him placed to the credit of the county, on her said subscription to the said railroad company. And at the February term, 1860, of said court, John W. Minor was appointed agent for the county of Schuyler, to cast her vote for directors of said railroad company for the year 1860; and at the same time the county court clerk was ordered not to levy and compute the railroad tax, as ordered at the previous November term, until ordered again to do so.

No further action of the county court pertaining to this railroad, and the subscription thereto, is recorded until February, 1863, when Isaac H. Sturgeon was appointed agent for the county to cast his vote on any litigation that might take place in regard to the North Missouri Railroad Company, and also to vote its stock for directors of the same at the election to be held in April of that year. He was reappointed yearly until February, 1867, when he was reappointed to serve until his power was revoked. After the aforesaid bonds became due and payable, and the county failed to pay the same, they went into litigation, and were by the courts held to be valid. No assessments were made on the taxable property for the payment of the bonds until some years after the war closed, at which time it was ascertained that the county was liable. Then the raising of taxes for the payment of the bonds began, and payments were made accordingly. On the 11th of May, 1872, the county court appointed William B. Hays as agent for the county, to make final payment and settlement with the holders of said bonds, which he did, and the writer is informed by Mr. Hays that the payment of the principal of said bonds, together with the accrued interest thereon, the cost of the litigation, and attorneys' fees, required nearly $30,000 of the people's money.

No other bonds having been issued on the subscription of the $50,000 made to the capital stock of this railroad company, no effort was made on the part of the company to collect the balance of the said subscription, and the amount that is required to redeem the aforesaid bonds, being nearly $30,000, is all that that railroad has cost the people. After this amount had all been paid, there remained in the fund raised for that purpose a small balance, which was disposed of in accordance with the following preamble and order of the county court, made June 9, 1873:

WHEREAS, the debt by Schuyler County to the North Missouri Railroad Company has been paid in full, and,

WHEREAS, there is a small surplus of money collected for the payment of said debt.

Therefore, it is ordered that said money collected for said purpose, be transferred to the building fund of said county.

This company commenced paying taxes on its railroad property in the county soon after its road was completed, and the following shows the amount annually paid into the county treasury for the last seven years: 1881, $2,438.28; 1882, $1,327.98; 1883, $2,954.64; 1884, $2,448.20; 1885, $2,447.06; 1886, $2,150.46; 1887, $2,108.86.

For these years the average assessed value of this railroad in Schuyler County has been $124,008, and the average amount of taxes annually received has been $2,267.92. The annual interest on $30,000, the amount the people have invested in said railroad, at 7 per cent, is $2,100. Thus it will be seen that the taxes paid by the company each year is a fraction over 7 per cent on the amount the people have invested.

The Mississippi & Missouri River Air Line Railroad.—On the 7th of November, 1860, the county court of Schuyler County, on petition of a number of her citizens, ordered the holding of elections at the several voting places in the county on the 15th of December, 1860, "to test the sense of the voters of said county on the proposition of the county subscribing the sum of $100,000 to the capital stock of the Mississippi & Missouri River Railroad Company." The elections were accordingly held, and 519 votes were cast in favor of, and 417 against, the proposition. The majority not being sufficient, the project was defeated. Again on Tuesday after the first Monday of November, in 1869, another election was held at the several voting places in the county on the proposition to subscribe $50,000 to the capital stock of said railroad, and this proposition was also rejected. Then, on the 7th of June, 1870, another election was held, this time on the proposition to subscribe $75,000 to the capital stock of the railroad, as it was then called the Mississippi & Missouri River Air Line Railroad, and this time the proposition was carried by the necessary majority. But afterward it became apparent to the people and to the court that there was much more prospect of the completion of the Missouri, Iowa & Nebraska Railway, and for that reason the court refused to subscribe to the capital stock of the Mississippi & Missouri River Air Line Railroad Company; and so it was, for that road never was built at all.

The Missouri, Iowa & Nebraska Railroad and Bonds.— The Alexandria & Bloomfield Railroad Company was chartered by the General Assembly of the State of Missouri in the year 1857. Its object was then to build a road from Alexandria, in Clark County, Mo., to Bloomfield, in Davis County, Iowa. In 1866 it was authorized by an act of the General Assembly to change its name to that of the Alexandria & Nebraska City Railroad Company, and to extend its line through the northern counties of Missouri in the direction of Nebraska City. By the terms of the original charter of this company, county courts of the counties through which the railroad was located were empowered to subscribe to the capital stock of said company, without submitting the question of a vote of the people. In 1870 this company and the Iowa Southern Railroad Company consolidated, and organized a new company under the name and style of the Missouri, Iowa & Nebraska Railway Company.

On May 30, 1871, a mass meeting, containing delegates from Queen City, Glenwood, Coatsville and Lancaster, convened at the court-house to hear and consider the following propositions from Henry Hill, superintendent of the Missouri, Iowa & Nebraska Railway Company. The proposition was then read by Mr. Hill, as follows:

I propose to build the main line of the Missouri, Iowa & Nebraska Railway from east to west through Schuyler County, within ten months from date, to the North Missouri Railroad in said county, for the sum of $175,000, payable in twenty years' bonds of said county at 8 per cent interest, $150,000 as a county subscription, and $25,000 as township subscriptions. The bonds to be due and delivered when said railroad is completed and cars running thereon to the said North Missouri Railroad, in said county. I propose to build, either by the way of Lancaster or Queen City, to said North Missouri Railroad, and to establish a permanent depot within the present corporate limits of the towns aforesaid through which said railroad is built. I further propose, in case the Mississippi Valley & Western Railroad is built through said county to the North Missouri Railroad within two years from the 3d day of May, 1871, and said county is compelled to pay $75,000, which is now voted to said Mississippi Valley & Western Railroad, our company is pledged to pay back to the county of Schuyler the said sum of $75,000. *Provided, however*, that said county of Schuyler shall not issue and deliver bonds in said amount of $75,000 to said Mississippi Valley & Western Railroad to be in anywise payable upon conditions otherwise than that said Mississippi Valley & Western Railroad is completed to said North Missouri Railroad, as required, within two years from the 3d day of May, 1871.

Signed,

HENRY HILL, *Superintendent.*

Then the following resolution was unanimously adopted:

Resolved, That our county court be requested by this meeting to subscribe to the capital stock of the Missouri, Iowa & Nebraska Railway Company $175,000, subject to the conditions to be adopted at a meeting to be held next Saturday, and also subject to its ratification by a majority of the voters of the county by vote or petition.

A committee of three from each township was then appointed to confer and arrange for further business. At the afternoon session this committee reported the following resolutions: "First, this committee accepts Mr. Hill's proposition as to points designated just as stated by Mr. Hill. Second, this committee recommends to the meeting to be held on Saturday, that the county subscribe $125,000, and the townships through which the road runs $50,000, to make up the $175,000 called for by Mr. Hill. Third, This committee pledges itself, individually and collectively, to support the proposed railroad tax." The report of the committee was adopted by the meeting, and an invitation extended to the members of the county court to meet with the people on the following Saturday, and report what course they were willing to pursue. The announced mass meeting was held, and the course that the county court was willing to pursue is plainly set forth in the following order, made on the 5th day of June, 1871, upon a petition therefor signed by many prominent citizens, and which was filed and recorded:

The county court of Schuyler County, Missouri, for and in behalf of said county, hereby subscribes to the capital stock of the Missouri, Iowa & Nebraska Railroad Company the sum of $125,000, to be paid in bonds of the county running twenty years at 8 per cent interest, to be issued and delivered when the main line of said road shall be completed to and intersecting the North Missouri Railroad in said county, and the cars running thereon, as hereinafter set forth, and subject to the following express conditions, to wit: The main line of said railroad shall be completed from east to west through said county, as aforesaid, within ten months from the date of this order, and regular daily trains operated thereon, and shall be built either by the way of the town of Lancaster or of the town of Queen City, and permanent freight and passenger depots, built and established within the present corporate limit of said towns through which said railroad may be built. In case the Mississippi Valley & Western Railway shall be built to the North Missouri Railroad in said county, in compliance with the terms of the vote of the people of this county, for a subscription of $75,000 to the capital stock of the Mississippi & Missouri River Air Line Railroad Company, and our said county shall be required to pay said sum of $75,000, or any part thereof, to said company, said Missouri, Iowa & Nebraska Railroad Company shall be bounden to repay to our said county the amount so required of our county to be paid to said Mississippi Valley & Western Railway Company, provided that our county shall not issue any bonds to said Mississippi Valley & Western Railway Company, to be in anywise payable upon conditions otherwise than contained in the terms of the vote for such subscription aforesaid.

And provided, further, That our said county shall not issue any bonds to said Missouri, Iowa & Nebraska Railroad Company until said company shall execute and deliver a good and sufficient bond, with securities, to be approved by the county court of this county, for the repayment of any and all sums that this county may be required to pay to said Mississippi Valley & Western Railway Company, together with all interest and costs. The county court hereby appoints Edwin French, of our county, commissioner, to subscribe the stock aforesaid upon the books of said railroad company, and to vote the stock of this county at its meetings, and in all things to represent the interests of this county at the meetings of said company, subject to the order of this court, who may be removed and another appointed in his place at any regular term of this court. The foregoing subscription subject to ratification of a majority of the resident tax payers of this county by petition, if not so ratified to be null and void, but if so ratified to stand absolute and irrevocable. Said petitions shall be canvassed by William B. Hays, Thomas Walker and George W. Melvin, and who shall file a written report under oath by June 30, 1871, and shall set forth whether said petitions contain the names of a majority of the taxpayers resident of this county, and if so the same, on filing with the county clerk of this county, then the foregoing subscription shall stand absolute and be irrevocable.

The court then appointed William A. Coffey and seventeen others to circulate petitions for the signatures of the tax payers and voters of the county, who were willing to ratify its action in subscribing the $125,000 to the capital stock of the Missouri, Iowa & Nebraska Railroad Company, and to return said petitions on or before the 29th of June following. Accordingly, on the said 29th of June, the court being then in session, the petitions were returned, and William B. Hays, Thomas Walker and George W. Melvin, the committee appointed to examine them, proceeded to perform that duty, after which they filed their written report under oath, to the effect that a majority of the resident tax payers of the county had signed their names to said petitions.

Afterward, at a special term of the county court, held July 3, 1871, its order to subscribe the $125,000 to the capital stock of the Missouri, Iowa & Nebraska Railroad Company was repeated or made anew; the new order to stand in lieu of the original one made on the 5th of June, it being a part of the May adjourned term of said court. This was done for the reason that, as the record stood, "the cart was before the horse," that is, that it was more proper to make the subscription after determining the fact that the majority of the resident tax payers were in favor of it than before.

The following is a copy of the order:

WHEREAS, It is made to appear by petition that a majority of the resident tax payers of Schuyler County, Mo., are in favor of the county of Schuyler, in her corporate capacity, subscribing $125,000 to the capital stock of the Missouri, Iowa & Nebraska Railway Company, a company existing under the laws of the State of Missouri and Iowa, composed by consolidation and mergement of the Iowa Southern Railway Company, of the State of Iowa, and the Alexandria & Nebraska City Railroad Company (formerly Alexandria & Bloomfield), and of the State of Missouri.

WHEREAS, By the terms of the charter of said railway company, it is made lawful for the county court of any county, in which any part of the route of said railroad may be, to subscribe to the stock of said company, and may invest its funds in the stock of said company, and issue the bonds of such county to pay the stock thus subscribed, and to take proper steps to protect the interest and credit of the county.

Therefore, The court, being advised in the premises, doth order that the county of Schuyler (in the State of Missouri), in her corporate capacity, subscribe $125,000 to the capital stock of the Missouri, Iowa & Nebraska Railway Company, to be paid in bonds of the county running twenty years, at 8 per cent interest; interest to commence at date of delivery to said railway company. Said subscription made in these following express terms: When said Missouri, Iowa & Nebraska Railway Company shall have permanently located their proposed railroad as far west from the town of Memphis, in Scotland County, as Middle Fabius post-office, in Scotland County, Mo., in the direction of the east line of this (Schuyler) County, then said bonds to be issued and placed in the hands of the county treasurer of said Schuyler County; said bonds to be delivered by the said county treasurer to the said railway company, when the main line of said railroad shall be completed to and intersecting the North Missouri Railroad in said county, and the cars running thereon, as hereinafter expressed, and subject to the following conditions: The main line of said railroad shall be completed from east to west through said county as aforesaid, within ten months from the sixth day of June, A. D., 1871, and regular daily trains operated thereon, and shall be built either by the way of the town of Lancaster, in this (Schuyler) County, or of the town of Queen City, in said county, and permanent freight and passenger depots built and established within the present corporate limits of said town, through which said railroad may be built.

And provided further, That said county treasurer shall not deliver said bonds, or any part thereof, to the said Missouri, Iowa & Nebraska Railway Company, until said company shall execute and deliver to said county treasurer their bond of indemnity, with security to be approved by the county court, in favor of said Schuyler County, conditioned, that if the Mississippi Valley & Western Railway Company, now claiming, by a vote of the people of said county of Schuyler, that they are entitled to a subscription of $75,000 in the bonds of said county, shall complete their proposed railroad, and have their cars running thereon through Schuyler County, Mo., by the way of the town of Lancaster, in said county, to the North Missouri Railroad, by the third day of May, A. D. 1873, and said county shall, by reason of said completion of said Mississippi Valley & Western Railroad, as aforesaid, have to pay to said Mississippi Valley & Western Railway Company $75,000 in bonds, or any other sum, by reason of said completion as aforesaid, they will return to said county of Schuyler $75,000, or the sum so paid by said county of the said bonds received by them (the said Missouri, Iowa & Nebraska Railway Company), or their equivalent in lawful money.

The foregoing subscription of $125,000 is made and to be accepted in lieu and to operate as a release of all former subscriptions made to said Missouri, Iowa & Nebraska Railway Company, and especially the subscription of the sum of $125,000, made by this court at its May adjourned term, A. D. 1871. The county court hereby appoints Edwin French, of this county, agent, to represent the county of Schuyler, to subscribe the stock aforesaid upon the books of the said Missouri, Iowa & Nebraska Railway Company, and to vote for it and receive its dividends, and to guard and protect the interests of the county in and to said railroad.

Then appeared Gen. F. M. Drake, president of the railroad company, and filed his written acceptance of the subscription then made, in the words and figures following:

I, F. M. Drake, president of the Missouri, Iowa & Nebraska Railway Company, hereby accept the subscription of $125,000 made by the county court of Schuyler County, at this special term (July 3, 1871), and consent to the release of the subscription made by this court at its May adjourned term, 1871, to said Missouri, Iowa & Nebraska Railway Company.

Signed,   F. M. DRAKE, *President.*

Afterward on August 9, 1871, the county court being then in session, it was ordered that the county should subscribe $25,000 additional to the capital stock of said railroad company, to be paid in bonds of $1,000 each, to run twenty years at 8 per cent, on the same conditions that the bonds for the $125,000 previously subscribed were to be issued. Provided that the said railroad was to be completed to the North Missouri Railroad in ten months from August 9, 1871; and this extension of time was also made to apply to the conditions upon which the $125,000 had been previously subscribed. Edwin French was appointed to subscribe the stock upon the company's books. Then came Gen. F. M. Drake and filed the following written instrument:

It is agreed, upon the part of Gen. F. M. Drake, president of the Missouri, Iowa & Nebraska Railway Company, if the county court of Schuyler County, Mo., will subscribe the additional sum of $25,000 to the capital stock of said Missouri, Iowa & Nebraska Railway Company, that, in consideration thereof, the said company agrees to forthwith locate their railroad through said county as prayed for in said petition asking said subscription, that they will not ask, accept or receive any other or greater sum than in the aggregate will amount to $175,000 on the county, township or town subscriptions; and that for the additional sum of $10,000 they will not defer the location and building of their said road, but will do as per agreement in their petition.

Signed,   F. M. DRAKE,
                    Pres. M., I. & N. Ry. Co.

How modest! The promise to not ask for a greater subscription than $175,000 was made to induce the court to at once subscribe another $25,000. And the modest demand for $10,000 more, sounds like two parties making a contract, and one of them then demanding of the other a bonus for his fulfillment of the same. The county having now authorized the subscription of $150,000 to the capital stock of said railway company, it remained to execute the bonds for the same. Accordingly, William Casper, the then presiding justice of the county court, executed and signed 150 county bonds of $1,000 each, numbering from 1 to 150 inclusive. These bonds were dated September 1, 1871, and were made payable twenty years after date, with interest payable annually at 8 per cent; hence there were attached to each bond twenty interest coupons for $80 each. According to the record, these bonds were not signed in open court, nor is there any record of their execution at the time they were signed. However, they were afterward delivered to the railway company, as the people have found out to their full satisfaction. Soon after being delivered, and even before the first interest coupons became due, it was rumored that they had been issued without the authority of law. It was claimed that the right granted by the Legislature to county courts to subscribe to the capital stock of the Alexandria & Bloomfield Railroad Company ceased to exist when that company, under its new name, that of the Alexan-

dria & Nebraska City Railroad Company, consolidated with
the Iowa Southern Railroad Company, and formed the new company known as the Missouri, Iowa & Nebraska Railway Company;
and that consequently the county court of Schuyler County had
no right to issue said bonds as it did without having submitted
the question to a vote of the people, which it did not do.

But, on the refusal of the county to pay interest coupons when
they became due, suits were brought from time to time in the
United States Circuit Court for the Eastern District of Missouri,
by several different parties owners of the bonds, where they (the
bonds) were held to be valid, and judgments in favor of the
plaintiffs (the bondholders) rendered accordingly.

Refunding the Debt.—Subsequently, and after fighting the
bondholders for several years without any marked success, fifty-
eight taxpayers of Schuyler County petitioned the county court,
at its August term, 1879, to order a special election to be held in
the county on the 16th of September of that year to determine
the wishes of the taxpayers in regard to funding the railroad
indebtedness of the county. The prayer of the petition was
granted, and an order issued for the holding of the election at the
several voting precincts in the county at the time specified in the
petition. The elections were accordingly held, and on the 22d
of September, 1879, the court being in session, the votes were
counted, and it was found that 653 had been cast against funding
the said indebtedness, and 445 in favor thereof, leaving a majority of 108 votes against the proposition. Thus it is shown that
the people were not ready yet for a compromise with the bondholders. But in less than a year thereafter, viz., on the 22d of
May, 1880, a large mass meeting was held at the court-house in
Lancaster, and a proposition made to compromise the debt upon
the following conditions: first, that the rate of interest on said
bonds be reduced from eight to six per cent; second, that for
all interest then due, and for all judgments on account of interest due, the county should pay one-half in the manner and times
following: The full amount of the levy of one and three-eighths
per cent for that year should be collected and paid over to the
holders of said judgments and interest due in pro rata per cent-
age; third, that the county authorities should levy and collect,

SCHUYLER COUNTY, MISSOURI   63

****

for the year 1881, a sum sufficient to pay the balance remaining due after deducting the full amount of the levy made for the year 1880. Then the mass meeting made the following entry as a part of the record of its proceedings:

WHEREAS, The notice of this mass meeting and its object and terms, has been extensively published, and a large and respectable number of representative tax payers from every part of the county is here present, Therefore.

Resolved, First, That we, the taxpayers of Schuyler County, do now instruct the honorable county court to proceed at once to accept or propose and confirm, as the case may require, a compromise of the county indebtedness on account of bonds issued to the Missouri, Iowa & Nebraska Railway Company, on the terms as set forth in the preamble, provided all the holders of the bonds, judgments and interest coupons due, agree in writing to the terms herein made, and report the same to the county court of Schuyler County, Mo., at their next term, or receive a proposition from the holders of the bonds, or so many of them as may be represented, with the number of the bonds, for the acceptance or rejection by said court.

Afterward William B. Hays was appointed as county financial agent to negotiate and compromise with the holders of the bonds. Then, after negotiations commenced, the holders of the bonds made to Mr. Hays a proposition to compromise. And the county court, at its November term, 1880, ordered that the compromise offered by the holders of said bonds be accepted on the terms proposed to William B. Hays, the financial agent.

Nothing further was accomplished in regard to this matter until June 23, 1882, when 160 taxpayers of the county petitioned the county to order a special election to vote on the proposition previously voted on and defeated, to compromise the said railroad bonds. The court granted the prayer of the petition, and made the following entry upon its record: " Wherefore it is ordered by the court, that a special election be held at the various voting precincts of Schuyler County, Mo., on Saturday, August 5, 1882, to submit to the qualified voters of said county the following proposition to compromise the indebtedness of said county on account of stock subscription to the capital stock of the Missouri, Iowa & Nebraska Railway Company, to wit: To compromise 150 bonds of $1,000 each, dated September 1, A. D. 1871, and payable in twenty years, and bearing interest at the rate of 8 per cent per annum; the accrued interest on said bonds now due amounting to about $15,000, the said bonds to be compromised by said Schuyler County giving new bonds in the name of the county of the denominations of not less than $100 nor more than $1,000 each for the $150,000 principal, dollar for dollar. To compromise and refund the accrued interest on said bonds by giving new bonds of said denomination for said amount of $15,000, 50 cents on the dollar for all of same except the $12,000 interest accruing on said bonds for the year 1881, 75 cents on the $1 for this amount. Said new bonds to bear interest at the rate of 6 per cent per annum, and to be evidenced by coupons attached; said bonds to be payable to bearer, and to run twenty years, and payable at the expiration of ten years, at the option of the county.

The elections were accordingly held, and the returns thereof were canvassed by the court in regular session on the 9th of August, 1882, and 640 votes were found to have been cast in favor of the proposed compromise, and 302 against it, thus leaving a majority of 338 in its favor. Whereupon the court ordered, " That the bonds of this county, as specified in said order, be issued and delivered to the holders of bonds, and accrued interest, to be compromised upon the surrender and cancellation of said old bonds, agreeably to the terms of said proposition, and that William B. Hays be and is hereby appointed and employed as a financial agent, to assist in carrying into effect said proposed compromise." On the 14th of the month the matter of signing and certifying said county bonds issued in compromise, coming up for consideration, the court signed and certified fifteen bonds of the denomination of one hundred each, and numbered from 1 to 15, inclusive, and seven bonds of the denomination of five hundred each, and numbered from 1 to 7, inclusive, and ninety-five bonds of the denomination of one thousand each, numbered from 1 to 95, inclusive. All new bonds necessary to complete the compromise, so far as it was completed, were afterward signed in open court.

The following is a brief statement of the compromise as it was finally consummated, at which time there stood against the county, in the United States circuit court at St. Louis, the following amounts, including interest and costs to the judgment creditors, to wit: Joseph T. Thomas, $2,118.33; William K. Findlay, $5,432.94; William Hill, $5,275.28; Henry Luddle, $4,337.76; James B. Dodge, $4,440.72; O. C. DuSouchett,

****

$4,337.76; William Hill, $23,938.53; Sophia P. Baker, $6,332.82; Joseph T. Thomas, $1,594.14; William M. Speckman, $4,341.97; all of which were canceled in the compromise. And the old eight per cent bonds, which entered into the compromise and were surrendered and canceled, were the following: Numbers 1 to 5, inclusive; 7 to 36, inclusive; 40 to 84, inclusive; 89 to 131, inclusive; 135 to 150, inclusive; making a total of 139, thus leaving eleven of the old bonds, which still remain uncompromised, and are now in litigation. At the date of the compromise, five of these bonds, Nos. 6, 85, 86, 87 and 88, were held by Clark, and the other six, Nos. 37, 38, 39, 132, 133 and 134, were held by DuBois. Omitting the many details of the compromise, it is sufficient to say that it required the issuing of the new six per cent bonds to the amount of $162,100 to cover the accumulated amount of the 139 old eight per cent bonds, which were compromised. The new bonds are all dated September 1, 1882, and made payable in twenty years from date, with interest at the rate of six per cent, payable annually. And at the time of the compromise, there were issued and delivered 154 bonds of the denomination of $1,000 each, numbered from 1 to 154, inclusive, making a total of $154,000; also of the denomination of $500, numbered from 1 to 11, inclusive, making a total of $5,500; and of $100, numbered from 1 to 26, inclusive, amounting to $2,600; making total amount of new bonds, $162,100. Deduct three new bonds of $100 each, since paid, and it leaves a total amount of new bonds outstanding of $161,800. Add the face of the five old Clark bonds, $5,000, and the six old DuBois bonds, $6,000, and we have a total bonded debt of $172,800.

The interest on the new bonds has been paid annually, and the amount of the principal thereof, the $161,800, together with the accumulating interest thereon, is an adjudicated and undisputed debt of the county; but, as the eleven old eight per cent bonds are still in litigation, it is impossible to say with certainty how much the county will have to pay to redeem them.

The Liberty Township Bonds.—At an election held in Liberty Township on the 8th of August, 1871, on the proposition of subscribing $15,000 to the capital stock of the Missouri, Iowa & Nebraska Railway Company, there were 181 votes cast in favor of the proposition, and only thirty-seven against it. Thereupon the county court ordered the said subscription to be made, and to be paid in bonds issued in the name of the county, said bonds to be of the denomination of $1,000 each, and to be numbered from 1 to 15 inclusive, the principal to be paid in twenty years from date, and all to bear 8 per cent interest, payable annually. The bonds were executed and dated September 1, 1871, and delivered by the county treasurer when the railroad was completed to Lancaster. These bonds were afterward compromised with the holder thereof by reducing the rate of interest from 8 to 6 per cent. Two of these bonds have been paid in full and canceled, consequently the bonded debt of the county on account of Liberty Township is $13,000, drawing 6 per cent interest. The interest is kept paid up promptly.

The Missouri, Iowa & Nebraska Railway was completed to Lancaster, and the construction train entered the town, May 14, 1872. The road was completed through the county in the following year. On the occasion of the arrival of the construction train on the 14th of May, 1872, a grand rally was held in Lancaster. A public dinner was given to all who celebrated the acquisition of the railroad. Congratulatory speeches were made, and all were gay and happy. Elections were held in other townships on several different occasions, on propositions to subscribe certain amounts to certain railroads, but, as no bonds other than those already mentioned were ever issued in consequence of such elections, the details are omitted for the reason that they would not interest the reader.

Public Buildings.—At the July term, 1845, of the county court, it was ordered that Lot 5, in Block 5, of the original plat of the town of Lancaster, be reserved from sale, and held as the site for a temporary court-house, and the building of one thereon was ordered, according to the following plan and specifications: A two-story frame house 20x24 feet in size, and each story to be eight feet high from floors to joists, the upper story to be divided into two rooms of equal size, with a four-foot hall between them; the house to be weatherboarded with walnut lumber; the flooring to be of oak lumber, and one chimney in the end of the house; the fireplace for the lower story to be four feet wide, and the one for the upper story two feet wide; the house to have one panel door in the end of the lower story opposite the fireplace, and one batten door in the center of each of the rooms of the upper story; four twelve-light windows, the lights to be twelve inches square, to be placed in the front end, and the same number to be placed in the front side, and one window of the same dimensions, in the rear side in the upper story opposite the hall, etc. The contract for the building of this temporary court-house was then let to Jahiel Parks, who erected the same and completed it in time for the county court to hold its first term therein in July, 1846. The county continued to use this building until the second court-house, the present one, was ready for occupancy. The old court-house and the lot on which it stood were sold at public sale on the first Monday of April, 1857, to William Buford, as shown by the report of Thomas Roberts, commissioner appointed to sell it. The building was afterward sold to Jason Brown, who moved it to the northeast corner of Block No. 5, where it was consumed by fire, together with other buildings attached to it, in April, 1887.

At the December term, 1856, of the county court, the plan of a new court-house, prepared and presented by Yelverton W. Payton, was adopted, and the sum of $10,000 appropriated for the building of the same. The contract for the erection of the building was let to William L. Shane. And on the 14th of August, 1857, the county court, upon a petition of a majority of the tax payers of the county, ordered that a sufficient sum of money to build the court-house should be borrowed from the swamp land fund. This was accordingly done, and on the 12th of August, 1858, it was reported to the county court, then in session, that the new court-house was completed, whereupon, on motion of T. P. Hall, it was received from the hands of the contractor, William L. Shane. Though $10,000 had been appropriated for its construction, it cost only about $9,000. It is a plain and substantial two-story brick building, forty-four feet square, set upon a stone foundation, and has four rooms for county offices, hall and stairs on the first floor, and the court room on the second. It has no fire-proof vaults for public records.

Jail.—In April, 1847, the county court ordered the building of a jail, and appointed John M. Bryant to superintend the same. Soon thereafter the jail, which was a small two-story log building, was erected on Lot 4 in Block 6 according to the original plat of the town, by William Buford, the contractor, for $200. It was consumed by fire in the year 1853; and it is said that one Renoah Reeves, a prisoner confined therein, set it on fire. He was charged with horse stealing, and was afterward tried, and found guilty, and sentenced to a term of service in the penitentiary. The lot on which this, the first jail of the county, stood, was afterward (1873) sold to George Melvin. From the time of the burning of the first jail until the present one was erected, the county remained without a jail. In September, 1869, the county court made an order for the building of a new jail, to be constructed of brick; to be 16x24 feet in size, and to be two stories in height, etc. F. M. Wilcox was appointed to superintend the building of the same. In accordance with this order, the new jail was constructed on the west part of the public square, where it now stands, and at the February term, 1870, of the court, the following allowances were made to the individuals named, for labor performed and material furnished for the construction of the same: George Reeves, brick work, $718.75; Pauley & Co., constructing cells, $561.16; J. J. Logan, for lumber, $62.85; R. K. Grant, carpenter work, $150.24; J. O. Jewitt, for plastering, etc., $105.24; William H. Steel, for iron work, $9.25; F. M. Wilcox, cash paid for material, $360.18; F. M. Wilcox, services as superintendent, $25.40; to sundry other persons for services rendered, $65.74; total then allowed, $2,058.81.

This amount substantially covered the cost of the present jail, though it may have cost a little more.

Poor Farm and Asylum.—The county poor farm, consisting of over 200 acres, and the only one the county has ever owned, is located on Sections 3 and 4 in Township 66 north, Range 14 west. J. B. Gamble, Esq., was appointed to superintend the building of the poorhouse or asylum thereon, and at the April term, 1873, of the county court, he submitted a contract made with Hezekiah Smallwood for the building of the structure. The contract stipulated that the contractor should erect a two-story frame building, 24x32 feet in size, according to the full specifications therein set forth, for the sum of $1,585. This contract was accepted by the court, and a bond executed by Mr. Smallwood, conditioned for the fulfillment of his part of the contract, was also accepted and approved. At the following October term of the court the building was found to be completed, and the last payment to the contractor, consisting of $528.33, was ordered to be made. From the organization of the county until the poorhouse was completed, the paupers of the county were cared for by appropriations made by the county court to individuals for keeping them; but under this system they became an expensive burden to the county. The records show that, just prior to the building of the poorhouse, there were from twenty to thirty poor persons thus cared for by the county, at an average cost of $37 per quarter year. As soon as the poorhouse was completed, the court let the farm to and entered into a contract with E. E. Barker, whereby he was to have the use of the farm and the buildings thereon, and was to take care of, feed and clothe the paupers for $8 per month for each individual. The court then required all persons depending on the county for their support to go at once to the poorhouse, or support themselves. This made a radical change; the number of paupers was reduced to about one-third of the former number, and thus a great saving of the county funds followed. Peter S. Sagerty is the superintendent of the poor farm at the present writing, and, according to his contract, he has the use of the farm and buildings thereon, and takes care of and feeds and clothes the paupers for $5 per month for each individual. Recently the average number of the inmates of the poor asylum has been twelve.

Casualties.—Among the casualties that have happened in Schuyler County, the saddest of all was the burning of the Ingram family. In the latter part of the decade of the forties, there stood a log cabin, containing only two rooms, at a point about one mile north of the present railroad depot at the town of Lancaster. In the west end of this pioneer dwelling was a fireplace and chimney. The roof was made of clapboards, held in position by weight-poles. In this house Stephen Ingram and his wife and six children were living. Early in the spring, in the hours of a certain night just preceding the dawn of day, this house, from some unknown cause, became on fire, and, if the story of the only survivor is to be believed, the fire had so far advanced before being discovered, as to render escape through the door impossible, consequently the father and husband cut his way through the roof and made his escape, and ran to the house of Jahiel Parks, less than half a mile away, and called for clothes and for help. Clothes were quickly furnished him, and, after putting them on, he and Parks, and perhaps others, went to the rescue of the perishing mother and children. But, alas! Too late! Too late forever! The roof had fallen in, and the wife and mother, and her six dear children, the eldest of whom was a young lady just approaching womanhood, were all in the flames, and of that family of eight persons, only one, the husband and father, remained. Nothing of the other seven was left, except their charred remains, which were found the next morning.

Ingram's lamentations were great, but from him the people soon withdrew their sympathy, believing that something on his part was wrong. "There was a mystery too great to be explained away by Ingram's loud grief and louder assertions that the flames bewildered, and the smoke so blinded him, that he could only call to his wife to pass three children through the roof, upon which he had climbed." The people did not believe Ingram's story about his efforts to save his family, and, receiving no sympathy, he sought relief by going to another land, and none regretted his going.

Another sad casualty occurred on Saturday morning, April 28, 1877. A Mrs. Cochran, with an infant in her arms, and a Miss Foglesong, aged about eighteen, who was leading a little boy of three years, of Mrs. Cochran, and a boy aged about fifteen, brother of the young lady, attempted to cross the Fabius, three miles east of Lancaster, on their way to Mr. George Foglesong's. The stream was swollen, and, when about the middle thereof, the young lady and little boy fell from the log into the water. She was rescued by her brother, and the little boy was drowned. His body was afterward found and given burial.

Temperance.—On the question of temperance as applied to the use and sale of intoxicating liquors, the people of Schuyler

****

County have had their share of public excitement. In the early
history of the county the places where liquors were sold as
a beverage were called dramshops, and, in the statutes made
and provided to regulate the sale of intoxicants, that name is
still continued; but the modern and more popular name now in
use is saloon, a word of French origin, and which Webster defines
as " a spacious and elegant apartment for the reception of company, etc." But in the popular sense it means a place for the
reception of such company as drink intoxicating liquors as a
beverage. The question as to the best way to regulate the
sale of liquors in Schuyler County has long been a theme of
animated public discussion, as will appear by the following sug-
gestion or recommendation of one of its grand juries:

We, the undersigned grand jurors, empaneled at the May term of the circuit court of Schuyler County for 1871, would respectfully represent that, in our
opinion, the present system of vending liquors in Schuyler County is altogether
wrong. Whilst we as a body are opposed to the traffic, yet, as its sale can not be
stopped, we think license should be granted by the county court for many
reasons. Under the present system, no revenue is derived from it, whilst, if
license were granted, our school fund would be greater by some $2,000 without
in the least increasing the amount of liquor sold; besides, the venders would be
under bonds by which they could be reached upon any violation of the laws
and other regulations applying to them, from which a drug store is exempt.
No indictment against the proprietors of a drug store has been successfully
prosecuted, whilst the taxpayers of the county have to foot the bill.

Signed,

> GEORGE W. MELVIN, *Foreman.*
> JOHN N. CASS.
> NICHOLAS SLOOP.
> STACY POOLE.
> Y. W. PAYTON.
> F. M. SHELTON.
> G. D. GRAY.
> THOMAS McGOLDRICK.
> SPENCER GREER.
> JOHN W. EVANS.
> R. K. GRANT.
> ROBERT MAIZE.
> WM. WELCH.
> JESSE CARTER.

The foregoing was the recommendation of fourteen of the
representative men of the county who were chosen by the proper
authority, on account of their sterling qualities, to perform their
duties as grand jurors. This occurred at a time when the

county court was not granting licenses to sell intoxicating liquors, and when some of the drug store merchants, seemingly under no restraint, were selling liquors promiscuously as a beverage. Thus the question has been agitated, and sometimes licenses authorizing the sale of intoxicants have been withheld from parties desirous of engaging in the traffic. Under the present law authorizing the electors of a county to decide by a majority vote as to whether intoxicating liquors shall or shall not be sold within the county, an election was held at the several voting places in Schuyler County on the second Tuesday in October, 1887, it being the 11th of that month, to decide for and against the sale of intoxicating liquors in said county. The vote was canvassed on the 14th of said month by C. W. Bunch, clerk of the county court, and Thomas D. Brown and John W. Milligan, two justices of the peace, and the number of votes cast in each of the several townships of the county "for selling intoxicating liquors," was found to be as follows: Liberty, 159; Glenwood, 108; Prairie, 214; Chariton, 64; Salt River, 105; Fabius, 165; Independence, 157; total, 972; and the number of votes cast in each of said townships "against the sale of intoxicating liquors" was found to be as follows: Liberty, 168; Glenwood, 122; Prairie, 153; Chariton, 60; Salt River, 48; Fabius, 77; Independence, 42; total, 670. Therefore the majority of votes cast in favor of the sale of intoxicating liquors in the county was 302. The total number of votes cast was 1,642, while the whole number of legal voters in the county amounts to 2,300, or thereabouts, thus showing that only a little over two-thirds of the voters attended the polls.

THE COURTS.

County Court.—The organization of this court has been given with the organization of the county. It continued to hold its sessions at the house of Robert S. Neeley, which stood about one and a half miles northeast of the site of Lancaster, up to and including the regular term in July, 1845, after which it adjourned to the house of James Cochrane, the site of which is in the southeast part of Lancaster, and held its first term there (it being a special term) in the latter part of the same month. Notable

****

among its orders at this term was the following: "that no compensation shall be paid to grand jurors of this county." In October following the court again met at the house of James Cochrane, and immediately adjourned to the house of C. H. Kent, in Lancaster, which house stood where the livery stable of Stretch Bros. now stands, on the north side of the street leading west from the southwest corner of the public square. At this term the attention of the court was called to the arrest of its sheriff, by the district court of the Territory of Iowa, for the county of Davis, for exercising the duties of his office on the strip of disputed territory. The action of the court on this occasion will be mentioned in connection with the Iowa War.

The court continued to meet at the house of Mr. Kent until April, 1846, when it returned to the house of Cochrane, where it continued to hold its sessions until July, 1846, when it met for the first time in the partially completed "temporary court-house," continuing to hold its sessions there until it occupied the court-house which is now standing. At this term the newly elected county court justices presented their commissions from Gov. John C. Edwards, dated August 31, 1846, and they were sworn into office by Clerk Isaac N. Ebey. John Jones was then elected as presiding justice.

The county court continued to consist of three county court justices until August, 1849, and then in obedience to an act of the General Assembly of the State, approved March 8, 1849, it was made to consist of all of the justices of the peace within the county. This form of government soon became unpopular, as it should, for the reason that three competent men can dispatch the people's business much more rapidly, and at much less expense, than a crowd of a dozen men can. A good story is related about the court as it was then organized with so many members, which is, that the bench was usually full in the early morning; then, as the surplus members became thirsty, they would retire one by one for something to quench their thirst, until only three or four were left; and those that were left were the men upon whom the transaction of the business generally depended. A body large enough for a Legislature is certainly an unnecessary and unwieldy thing as a county court. This form of county government continued less than two years, and until the aforesaid law creating it was repealed by an act of the Legislature approved February 10, 1851, by which act the county court was made to consist, as it formerly had, of three county court justices; and thus it continued to exist until after the April term in 1861, and the beginning of the Civil War.

An act of the General Assembly of the State, entitled, "An act districting the county of Schuyler, and for other purposes," approved December 13, 1855, provided that the county of Schuyler should be divided into three districts for the purpose of electing county court justices. And the act further provided that the First District should consist of the townships of Independence and Fabius, the Second District of the township of Liberty, and the Third District of the townships of Salt River and Chariton. This comprised all of the county as it was then subdivided into civil townships. The act also provided that the qualified voters of each district should vote for three candidates, and the one receiving the highest number of votes should be declared elected. This same act authorized the county court to provide for the sale of the swamp or overflowed lands as it deemed best. [See swamp lands.]

From 1861 to 1866 the county court was presided over by a sole judge. At the April term, 1866, the county court was again composed of three justices, and it has ever since and still continues to be composed of three members.

In 1877 a law was passed containing this provision, viz.: "The county court shall be composed of three members, to be styled judges of the county court, and each county shall be districted by the county court thereof into two districts of contiguous territory, as nearly equal in population as practicable without dividing municipal townships." This law was complied with, as soon as it became effective, by the county court of Schuyler County, and the districts as they are now formed are designated the Northern and Southern. The former is composed of the townships of Fabius, Liberty, Chariton and Glenwood, and the latter of Independence, Prairie and Salt River.

Under the law each district elects a judge of the county court, and one is elected by the county at large. The latter, by virtue of his election, is the presiding officer of the court. As the court is now composed, Judge William Logan is the presiding officer, and Judge T. G. Neeley represents the Northern District, and Judge Nicholas Sloop, the Southern. After the close of the Civil War, and until the present law took effect, the county court justices were elected from the county at large.

The following is a list of the county court justices and judges, together with the date of their services, from the organization of the county to the present writing, to wit: William L. Robinson, William Hendron and Alexander D. Farris, 1845–46; Thomas Partin and John Jones, 1846–48; James Wells, 1846–49; William Hendron, 1848–49; William Oglesby and Benjamin Tompkins, 1849 (a few months). Then, during the two years that the county was under township organization, the court consisted of justices of the peace, Thomas B. Du Bois, George F. Palmer, William Barlow, David A. Roberts, William Hulon, Samuel Nelson, John Fugate, Josiah H. Hathaway, Wesley Burks, George Nichols, William Casper, C. W. Stewart, William Rowland, Dennis M. T. Brasfield, Joseph W. Buchanan, Elisha Baldwin, Reuben Wright, George Naylor and H. P. Buford. Then, township organization being abolished, and the court of three justices being again established, which continued as such until 1861, the justices' names and terms of service were as follows: William Barlow, 1851–52; Charles Hale, 1851–54; Caswell Dennis, 1851–56; M. D. Lamb, 1852–56; William Barlow, 1854–56; William Casper, 1856–58; Charles Hale, 1856–60; David A. Roberts, 1856–61; James Gates, 1858–61; William A. Coffee, 1860–61. Sole judges: James H. Kerfoot, 1861–63; William Casper, 1863–66. Then the three justices again as follows: Harrison Davis and D. H. Roberts, 1866–70; David Baker, 1866–68; F. M. Wilcox, 1868–69; W. B. Newman, 1869–75; Sovern Tarr, 1870–76; William Casper, 1870–72; W. D. Gray, 1872–73; William Lindsey, 1873–78; James T. Dowis, 1875–78; Yelverton W. Payton, 1876–78; Bennet Kratzer, James K. Singleton and A. M. Lind, 1878–80; Hawley Cone, John N. Cass and John B. Glaze, 1880–82; Thomas Russell and Jacob Whittmer, 1882–84; Paul T. McCloskey, 1882–86; Gottlieb Deirling, 1884–86; William Logan, 1884; Nicholas Sloop and Timothy G. Neeley, 1886. The last three justices compose the county court at the present writing, December, 1887.

Jurisdiction.—Originally the county court had jurisdiction over the public finances, county seat, public buildings, highways, probate business, and all other general county business. During the two years, from 1849 to 1851, when the county was under township organization, there was a separate probate court, to which the probate business was transferred. That court was abolished in 1851, and the county court again resumed jurisdiction of the probate business, which it held until the probate court was permanently established in 1861. The records of this court have generally been well written up, and an unusually good index of the same has been made, and all are in a good state of preservation.

Probate Court.—A probate court was established in Schuyler County and its jurisdiction defined in 1849, by the same act which made the county court to consist of all the justices of the peace within the county, and it was abolished in 1851 by the same law which repealed the aforesaid act of 1849. During this short period of its existence, it was presided over by Judge Thomas Roberts, who was elected to the office at the August election in 1849. A permanent probate court of Schuyler County was established by law in 1861, and the sole judge of the county court was made judge thereof. Then, when the county court was made, in 1866, to consist of three justices, a separate judge was and has ever since been elected to hold the office of probate judge. The jurisdiction of this court covers all matters pertaining to probate business, the granting letters testamentary and of administration, the appointment of guardians and curators of minors and persons of unsound mind, settling the accounts of executors, administrators, curators and guardians, and over all matters relating to apprentices. Under the present law the probate judge holds his office for four years.

The following is a list of the names of the judges who have presided over the probate court of Schuyler County, together with the date of their term of service: Thomas Roberts, 1849–51; J. H. Kerfoot, 1861–62; William Casper, 1862–65; Harrison Davis, one term, in 1866; A. J. Baker, 1866–67; J. N

Shelton, 1867–71; Thomas Walker, 1871–74; Enoch Crim, 1874–82; Richard Caywood, the present incumbent, ever since 1882.

The Circuit Court.—As soon as Schuyler County was organized it became a part of the Fourth Judicial Circuit of the State, in accordance with an act of the General Assembly thereof, approved March 15, 1845. By this act the Fourth Judicial Circuit was made to consist of the counties of Monroe, Shelby, Lewis, Clark, Knox, Scotland, Adair and Schuyler. Thus composed it remained until the passage of another act of the General Assembly, approved December 12, 1855, which made it to consist of the counties of Lewis, Clark, Scotland, Knox, Adair and Schuyler; and with this latter combination it continued to exist until the passage of the present law, approved April 28, 1877, which made it to consist of the counties of Lewis, Clark, Scotland and Knox. Thus the county of Schuyler was dropped out of the old Fourth Judicial Circuit. By this latter law the Twenty-seventh Judicial Circuit was formed to consist of the counties of Macon, Putnam, Schuyler and Adair, and thus the circuit of which Schuyler County forms a part has since been and at present remains.

The following is the caption of the record of proceedings of the first term of the Schuyler County circuit court:

STATE OF MISSOURI,   } ss. Fourth Judicial Circuit.
COUNTY OF SCHUYLER.   }

Be it remembered that on this 9th day of April, 1846, at a term of the circuit court begun and held at the court-house in the town of Lancaster, in and for the county of Schuyler, and State of Missouri, in the Fourth Judicial Circuit, present the Hon. Addison Reese, judge of said circuit; James R. Abernathy, circuit attorney for said circuit; I. N. Ebey, clerk, and Jonathan Riggs, sheriff of the county aforesaid, the following proceedings were had, to wit: By the order of said judge, Jonathan Riggs, sheriff, opened court by making proclamation at the court-house door.*

Then follows, first of record, a copy of Judge Reese's commission, dated April 7, 1845, executed and signed by John C. Edwards, at that time Governor of the State of Missouri, and attested by James L. Minor, the then secretary of State. This finished the record of the first day's proceedings, simply the con-

*By reading this caption, all persons familiar with law, and the keeping of court records, will at once recognize the good ability of the first clerk of Schuyler County—the date, time, place and all officers of the court being mentioned.

78   SCHUYLER COUNTY, MISSOURI

****

vening and organization of the court. The first business the next morning was the permission granted on motion of James S. Green, to David Rorer and James H. Cowles, members of the Iowa bar, to sign the roll as practicing attorneys of the court. And then, by leave of court, the following named gentlemen signed the roll of attorneys for the court: James R. Abernathy, Thomas S. Richardson, James S. Green, James Ellison, Levi J. Wagner, S. C. Thompson, Joseph Wilson, William R. Jones, Samuel S. Fox and Clare Oxley.

The first grand jury of Schuyler County, consisting of the following named gentlemen, was then elected, tried and sworn, to diligently inquire and true presentment make of all offenses against the State committed or triable within the county, to wit: Leven Tucker, James Hall, Henry Powell, William Barlow, Richard Griggs, David A. Roberts, Thomas Mills, John D. Marney, John Bradburn, James M. Arnet, Aderson Willis, William T. London, Henry Rhoads, Stephen Hulet and James Myers. William Barlow was appointed foreman.

The first and only indictment found at this, the first term of court, was against Samuel Riggs, sheriff of Davis County, in the Territory of Iowa " for taking upon himself the office of sheriff " on the disputed territory, as explained elsewhere in this work. The first case docketed was that of Alex. Walker *vs.* William Ogg, on appeal from a justice court. In this case the plaintiff failed to appear and prosecute, and consequently his appeal was dismissed at his expense. Then followed a number of cases on appeal and for debt, of little note except to the parties interested, which being disposed of, the court adjourned to term in course. At the next term of this court, held in September, 1846, Benjamin Hewlet was indicted for disturbing a religious meeting, and William Parks was indicted " for keeping a dramshop without a license." The first case was disposed of by quashing the indictment, and the latter was continued.

Important Trials.—Like all other counties, Schuyler has had its share of trials, in which the people in general take a considerable interest, and which usually produce a great deal of excitement. The first trial for murder was that of the State of Missouri *vs.* David Grigsby, on a change of venue from Adair County.

The indictment charged on the first count that on the 1st of August, 1844, one James Trewett, in the county of Adair, in the State of Missouri, with a rifle loaded with powder and ball, etc., shot one Robert Reid in the right side of his body, from the effects of which he, the said Reid, died on the 1st of October of that year, and that the defendant Grigsby " was present, aiding, helping, abetting, comforting, assisting and maintaining the said Trewett " in committing the aforesaid murder, etc. The second count charged the same facts, except that the name of David Grigsby was mentioned first, thus making him the principal and Trewett the aider, abettor, etc. The trial was called at the September term, 1847, of the court, and the prisoner entered a plea of " not guilty," whereupon the following-named jurymen: Charles M. H. London, David B. Dixon, Henry Whitlow, Stephen D. Ruddle, Isaac Burgen, James Davis, Theophilus Ryals, Charles Cook, Adam Grossclose, Emanuel Richardson, William Oglesby and John M. Sill, were duly elected, tried and sworn to try the issues; and, after hearing the evidence and arguments of counsel, and, after retiring to consider of their verdict, the jury returned the following: " We the jury find the defendant not guilty. D. B. Dixon, Foreman." This was the first trial for murder, and the jury was the first trial jury empaneled in the Schuyler circuit court. The murder of Robert Reid, however, must not be charged to the category of crime in Schuyler County, but to that of Adair, where it occurred.

State of Missouri vs. James Sexton.—In this case the defendant was indicted at the April term, 1848, of the court, for grand larceny; the charge being for the stealing of a horse from Reuben Lee, who lived about three miles south of Lancaster. He was arrested and arraigned for trial, but on application was granted a change of venue to the Monroe County circuit court, where he was afterward tried, found guilty, and sentenced to serve a term in the penitentiary. He had settled in the southern part of Scotland County as early as 1835 or 1836, and there stole a horse from the Indians, while they were encamped on the lands of the old pioneer, George Forrister, who is still living. The Indians, with the assistance of Forrister, found their horse where Sexton had hid it, in the forest near his house. He was the first horse-thief in Scotland County, and seems also to have been the first one, or at least the first one apprehended, in Schuyler County. He was said to be a "hard case" in general.

State of Missouri vs. Renoah Reeves.—The defendant in this case was indicted at the November term of court in 1848, for the crime of grand larceny, the charge being that he stole a horse from a citizen of Schuyler, by the name of Cooksey. He was tried, found guilty, and sentenced to serve a three-years' term in the penitentiary. On his way to that institution he escaped from the sheriff, stole another horse, and pair of shoes from the owner, and then fled to a retreat under an old house in the backwoods, where he was subsequently found and rearrested. This is the offender who was charged with setting the first county jail on fire while he was confined therein awaiting his trial.

The Killing of Joel Taylor.—In the winter of 1852 or 1853, four men, including Joel Taylor, were playing a game of cards in a saloon, on the east side of the public square, in the town of Lancaster. A crowd of spectators, such as usually loaf about or frequent such places, gathered around them. The players commenced quarreling, and their friends among the spectators, more or less, took sides while looking on, and one of the latter, with a knife in hand, reached over and stabbed Taylor with the same, the blade of the knife entering the front part of the neck, just above the frontal bone of the breast, and extending downward. Taylor lived a few days, and then died from the effect of this wound. Albert Morris, one of the spectators mentioned, was arrested for the killing of Taylor, and given a preliminary examination before Howel Brewer, a justice of the peace, by whom he was released on the ground that the State failed to prove that he was the identical man who plunged the knife into the body of Taylor. Strange though it be, it is always hard for the State to prove what occurs in a drinking saloon, or dramshop, such as they were then designated by the law. They were, however, in the early settlement of this western country, more commonly called "groceries," but the groceries sold therein were always wet. After being released, Albert Morris left the county, and has never returned to it, so far as the people are informed. It has always been considered, however, that he was the guilty party. His conduct in immediately fleeing from the county, after being released upon preliminary examination, tended to lead to that conclusion.

The Killing of Alexander Page.—Alexander Page was the step-father of Ferdinand D. Lloyd, and both lived at different places, in the southeastern part of the county, and for a long time a feud had existed between them. It appears from evidence on file that Page was not a very acceptable stepfather to Lloyd, and other members of the family; and that members of the family, when oppressed, would go to the residence of Lloyd for his protection; that on one occasion, May 31, 1855, when a daughter of Page, and a half-sister to Lloyd, was at the house of the latter, Page armed himself with a butcher knife, and started for the house of Lloyd; that on nearing the latter place, and when about to enter the house yard, Lloyd, who stood in or near his door, with a rifle gun in hand, ordered Page not to enter the yard. Not heeding this order, he opened the gate and passed in, and just then was shot by Lloyd, the contents of the gun entering his back. He then walked out into the road, and went a short distance and fell. Soon thereafter John L. Jones passed by, saw the man lying in the road, but went on to the residence of William Ogg, whose farm joined that of Lloyd, and there reported what he had seen. Mr. Ogg then got some assistants, and took Page to his house, and then went out to get some help, and on returning found him dead. When Ogg and his party went after Page, the butcher knife was found lying on the ground near his body.

Lloyd was arrested, and given a preliminary examination before Howel Brewer and John Drury, two justices of the peace, by whom he was caused to be held for the action of the grand jury. Accordingly, at the October term, 1855, of the Schuyler circuit court, he (Lloyd) was indicted for the murder of the said Alexander Page. He was prosecuted by the circuit attorney, and defended by Thomas S. Richardson, of Memphis, and Richard Caywood, of Lancaster. The case was continued until the October term, 1856, of the court, and then *nolle prosequied*. It seems that Lloyd was generally sustained and justified by the people best acquainted with the parties, and that the case was dismissed on the ground that, in shooting Page, he was acting in self-defense. But here was a query, a circumstance that seemed to argue against self-defense. How could a man, acting in self-defense, shoot his assailant in the back? The explanation was that Page had turned around to close the gate, thus placing his back toward the house, when Lloyd shot him.

Manslaughter by Milton S. Locket.—George W. Olds and his family, and a family by the name of Locket, lived in a neighborhood about seven miles east of the town of Lancaster, in Schuyler County. The Locket boys were said to have been the source of much annoyance to Mr. Olds and his family and property. On the 26th of December, 1865, they went to a place near his house, armed with rifles, and began the sport of shooting at a mark. The sons of Olds were, at the same time, engaged in breaking a colt or young horse to drive. The shooting frightened the animal, and thus became very annoying, in consequence of which George W. Olds went out from his house and ordered the Locket boys to leave, but, instead of so doing, Milton S. Locket, a lad about sixteen years of age, raised his rifle and shot Mr. Olds in the left breast, and killed him instantly.

Locket was arrested, and given a preliminary trial before Squire Thomas Walker, who caused him to be held to await the action of the grand jury at the next term of the circuit court. Accordingly, at the May term, 1866, of said court, Milton S. Locket was indicted for the murder of George W. Olds. On application, he was granted a change of venue to the Adair circuit court, where he was afterward tried, and found guilty of manslaughter in the third degree, and his punishment was fixed by the jury at two years' service in the penitentiary. However, he was not thus sentenced; but, by some endeavor, the penalty as fixed by the jury was set aside, and the defendant was sentenced to serve six months in the Kirksville jail instead.

The prisoner was prosecuted, on the part of the State, by William C. Hilles, the circuit attorney, and was defended by William Burch, of Memphis; A. J. Baker and John McGoldrick, of Lancaster, and James G. Blair, of Lewis County.

The Murder of Roger McDonnough.—During the construction of the North Branch of the St. Louis, Kansas City & Northern Railway, there were two Irish shanties or boarding houses

****

on the line of that road, about a quarter of a mile north of Jules-burg, in Schuyler County. Roger McDonnough, Mike Ryan and others belonged to one shanty, and Daniel Kervick was an inmate of the other. On the 20th of August, 1868, McDonnough and Ryan went to Lancaster, and obtained a supply of whisky, and then returned home under the influence of the "beverage." After reaching home and while the whisky was holding sway, they went to the other shanty to "clean it out," and, while engaged in the fracas, McDonnough was killed by Daniel Kervick (or Kiverick). The next day a warrant was issued, by Squire W. H. Steele, for the arrest of Kervick. He was arrested, and taken before J. N. Shelton, judge of the probate court at Lancaster, where he was given a preliminary examination, and then committed to jail. At a special term of the Schuyler circuit court, held January 12, 1869, Judge E. W. Wilson presiding, Kervick ,being arraigned for trial under the charge of murder in the second degree, plead guilty of manslaughter in the third degree, and received a sentence for three years' service in the penitentiary.

The Killing of Lucien Ashford.—Lucien Ashford and "Bush" Lane resided about ten miles east of Lancaster, in Schuyler County. Ashford was at the house of Samuel Gates, where he was working. Between him and Lane a feud had existed for a short time, and Lane had challenged him to fight. On the 5th of June, 1869, Lane went to the place of Gates, and, remaining in the road in front of the house, challenged Ashford to come out and fight. The latter then went out into the yard, and, seeing that Lane had his hand on something which he supposed to be a revolver, threw a piece of brick over the fence at Lane and knocked him down. He (Ashford) then jumped over the bars and caught Lane as he was about to rise, and at this juncture Lane, who had a butcher knife in hand, instead of a revolver, stabbed Ashford in the stomach. The latter then caught up a block of wood, while Lane ran into the yard and called on Mr. Gates for protection. Ashford then threw the block of wood at Lane, and instantly fell. He was carried into the house, where he languished until the next day, and then died from the effects of his wound. Lane ran away, and has never been apprehended.

The Burning of Patterson's Barn.—In the year 1870, E. L. Patterson, a farmer living near Queen City, in Schuyler County, erected for himself a barn 40x60 feet in size, at a point about 100 feet from his residence, and about twenty-five feet from his old dwelling house. On the night of the 22d of July, 1871, this barn and the old dwelling house were consumed by fire, together with the contents of both. The barn had in it at the time three horses, two cows, three calves, six hogs, about four tons of straw, eight or nine tons of hay, 400 to 600 bushels of old corn, harness, saddles, wagon, buggy, etc. The old dwelling house contained the farming tools. The next morning Mr. Patterson discovered the tracks of two men at a point about 150 yards from the barn. These tracks indicated that one man wore boots or shoes, and that the other was barefoot. These tracks led eastward in the direction of the place where Samuel McCormack lived. Mr. Patterson and some neighbors followed the tracks some distance, but lost them before they led to any habitation. Suspicion immediately rested upon McCormack for the burning of the barn, and, accordingly, on the 26th of said month, Samuel McCormack, William McCormack and Theodore McCormack were arrested and taken before Harrison Davis, justice of the peace, and Mark B. Patterson, associate justice, and there given a preliminary examination, which resulted in holding Samuel McCormack for the action of the grand jury, at the next term of the circuit court.

At the October term, 1871, of the Schuyler circuit court, Samuel McCormack was indicted for the crime of arson; being charged with setting fire to Patterson's barn on the night when it was burned. The trial caused a great deal of excitement, but the State was unable to fully prove the charge, and accordingly the defendant was acquitted. In the estimation of the people, however, he was held "guilty." McCormack then moved to Putnam County, where he was subsequently sent to the penitentiary two years for the commitment of some other crime.

The Killing of Daniel Hamilton.—Daniel Hamilton was a watchmaker at Lancaster, and J. B. Simmons was a citizen of Coatsville. It was alleged that for some months Hamilton had held criminal relations with the wife of Simmons, and that

Simmons was cognizant of the fact, but continued to live with his wife, hoping that she would reform. Finding, however, that she did not, he left her, and about two weeks thereafter, it being on Saturday night, March 4, 1876, he entered the saloon of L. Schmidt, at Lancaster, and there found Hamilton playing pool. The latter asked Simmons to drink, an altercation ensued, Simmons commenced firing on Hamilton, who retreated through the door and fell, face downward, on the sidewalk, and was dead. Four shots had been fired, all of which took effect, and two of them penetrated the heart. Hamilton was then carried to his room in the hotel, and there examined by Drs. Potter and Rockwell. Three revolvers were found on his body. A. D. Farris, the coroner, then summoned a jury and held an inquest over the body. The verdict of the jury was in accordance with the foregoing fact. After Hamilton was killed, Simmons was arrested by Sheriff Moore, and his preliminary examination was held before Squire L. N. Melvin, who held him for the action of the grand jury. In a few days thereafter, the matter came up before the grand jury, and that body refused to indict Simmons for the killing of Hamilton. Simmons claimed the act was justifiable, and it appears that the jury took the same view of the matter.

The Killing of Easton.—In January, 1877, four men, named Easton, Corbin, Mundow and Phelps, played a game of cards at Green Top, and then discussed the game, and got into an altercation about it. Corbin struck Easton on the head with a knife, the point of which broke off leaving a piece about three-eighths of an inch long imbedded in the skull. Drs. Sickles and Myers extracted this piece, and no serious result was anticipated. Corbin was arrested for an assault and battery, and placed under bail. In a few days Easton grew worse, and a new warrant was issued for Corbin, but he had fled. His bail on the assault and battery case had been fixed at only $25. Easton lived two weeks after being wounded, and then died. It was supposed that, at the time of the altercation, the four men were under the influence of liquor. Information pertaining to the killing of Hamilton and Easton has been obtained largely from *The Excelsior*.

The Killing of Hiram Townsend.—This affair took place

during the heat of the political campaign of 1880, at a pole raising at the village of Coatsville, on October 23, on which occasion Henry Clay Dean was orator of the day. Hiram Townsend, William C. Niblack and others entered into a quarrel about politics, which led to a fracas in which several persons became engaged. The difficulty was commenced on the sidewalk, but the belligerents soon got into the street, where William C. Niblack, with a knife, stabbed and killed Hiram Townsend. Niblack was arrested, and, at the following October term of the circuit court was indicted for the murder of Townsend, and was held under $7,000 bond for his appearance at the next term of court. He was tried in July, 1881, before the following named jury: C. O. Everly, J. G. Oldham, William Moorehead, Samuel Shacklett, Elbon Fugate, John Haney, J. B. Villetoe, James Heaton, H. V. Craig, G. W. Hall, William Lunsford and John Morgan, and their verdict was "not guilty." He was acquitted on the ground of self-defense. The prosecuting attorneys in the case were C. Elliott Vrooman, circuit attorney, and U. S. Hall, of Kirksville, and defended by J. M. Knott, Higbee & Raley, and Shelton & Dysart. The killing being the result of a political quarrel, the case was attended with considerable excitement.

The Killing of Daniel Forsyth.—On the night of October 22, 1884, Daniel Forsyth, a section hand on the Keokuk & Western Railway, and Robert Powers and others, engaged in a drunken spree at the town of Coatsville, in Schuyler County. An altercation ensued between Forsyth and Powers, and the latter stabbed the former in the right side of the face, and killed him. Powers was immediately arrested, and taken before Squire John H. Hill, where he waived examination, and was committed to jail, to await the action of the grand jury. At the November term, 1884, of the Schuyler circuit court, he was indicted, tried and found guilty of manslaughter in the fourth degree, and was sentenced to serve two years in the penitentiary. He was prosecuted by Samuel A. Dysart, prosecuting attorney, and was defended by Higbee & Raley, and C. C. Fogle.

The Killing of John Barnes.—This event took place on the 16th of October, 1885, in the barn of George Lehr, about three and a half miles northeast of the town of Lancaster. John

Barnes was a close neighbor to Lehr, and it appears from the evidence that these men and their families got into a quarrel about some wood which Barnes cut on the land of Lehr, and was about to haul to market. It seems also that Barnes was told that he might burn the wood, but that he should not take it to town; that, on the day aforesaid, Barnes went to and into Lehr's barn, where he and his son George were at work, and the quarrel about the wood was immediately renewed. Then a fight ensued, in which Barnes was stabbed with a knife, or at least evidence to that effect was given at the preliminary trial. Barnes then went home, and there died from the effects of his wound on the same day. Afterward, on the 19th of the same month, the Lehrs were both arrested and given a preliminary examination before A. C. Bailey, a justice of the peace, and both were held under bail in the sum of $5,000 each for their appearance at the next term of the circuit court. At the November term, 1885, of said court, George Lehr, and George Lehr, Jr., were both indicted for murder in the second degree. The indictment charged them jointly with the murder of Barnes. The case was continued from term to term until June, 1887, when it was again called. A plea of not guilty having been made, a jury consisting of A. E. Owens, William T. Simmons, W. D. Ross, Samuel P. Ross, A. N. Alexander, W. P. Dawkins, Charles Richie, H. Gatlin, John M. Morgan, Sylvester Barker, A. L. Dawkins and A. M. Todd, were then empaneled and sworn to try the prisoners.

After hearing the evidence on the part of the State, the court instructed the jury to find the defendants not guilty. The jury then retired, and returned the following verdict:

We, the jury, under the instructions of the court, find the defendants not guilty.

SYLVESTER BARKER, *Foreman.*

The defendants were prosecuted by Edwin F. Payton, the prosecuting attorney, assisted by Smoot & Pettingill, of Memphis, and defended by C. C. Fogle, Higbee & Raley, and Shelton & Dysart, all of Lancaster.

Bench and Bar.—The following is a list of the judges who have presided over the Schuyler circuit court, beginning with its organization, and coming down to the present time; showing also the date of each one's term of service, to wit: Addison

Reese, 1846–59; Thomas S. Richardson, 1859–62; James Ellison, 1862–64; David Wagner, 1864–65; E. V. Wilson, 1865–72; John W. Henry, 1872–77; Andrew Ellison, the present judge, was elected in 1876, assumed the duties of the office in 1877, and has presided over the court ever since. As to the prosecuting attorneys, A. R. Abernathy served from 1846 to 1849; then James J. Lindley, J. Proctor Knott, John C. Anderson and John Foster occupied the office in the order named until 1866, and since that date the office has been filled as follows: William C. Hillis, 1866–72; Fletcher White, 1872–73; C. Elliott Vrooman, 1873–75; John B. Gamble, 1875–77; Joseph M. Knott, 1877–79; C. Elliott Vrooman, 1879–81; Frank C. Sickles, 1881–83; Samuel A. Dysart, 1883–85; and since the latter date by Edwin F. Payton, whose term expires in 1888.

Judge Addison Reese was a Kentuckian by birth, and in politics a Democrat. He possessed very fair legal abilities, and his long term of office as circuit judge qualified him well for the duties thereof. His decisions gave satisfaction not only to the bar, but the community generally. His errors in judgment were generally given on the side of mercy.

Judge Thomas S. Richardson settled in the town of Sand Hill, in Scotland County, Mo., in 1841, and there commenced the practice of law. He removed to Memphis in the same county in 1844, soon after the county seat was moved to that place. Like all young men in this part of the State, at that time, he did not have an opportunity to gain a thorough education, yet his industry and energy made amends for this deficiency, and by hard study and perseverance he made rapid strides in his profession. The Democratic party, of which he was a member, soon selected him as a leader in the vicinity of his home, and by his pleasing and gentlemanly manner he became very popular, even with those who were his political opponents. He was chosen, when quite a young man, to represent Scotland County in the Legislature of the State, where he soon gained an influence very rare to a man so young in a legislative body. He was also chosen a member of the convention to revise the constitution of the State, and was one of the committee of three appointed by the Senate to revise the statutes in 1856. He also served a term of four years in the

State Senate. At a special election in 1859 he was elected circuit judge by about 1,000 majority, over James Ellison, who was also a Democrat. Although Judge Richardson was a zealous politician, he disappointed the expectations of even his friends, who entertained fears lest his long political career might be prejudicial to him in his new position upon the bench, but he showed himself to be fully competent to perform the duties of his office, and gave general satisfaction to all parties. Being a Kentuckian and a pro-slavery Democrat, he took a strong interest in the success of the Southern cause at the commencement of the Rebellion. He was a Secessionist, but not a rebel. He was strongly opposed to the war, and, after hostilities had commenced, he used every effort in his power to induce Col. Martin Green to take his troops from this part of the State. He was even threatened with arrest by some of the rebel officers in Green's camp, while he was there for that purpose. He was in favor of peaceable secession.

When Memphis was occupied by home guards, under the command of Col. Moore, he was arrested, but not deprived of his liberty. After the Twenty-first Missouri Regiment was organized and returned to Memphis in the month of November, Richardson was again put under arrest, and confined in the court-house, although no definite charge was made against him. On the night of November 18, 1861, while he was engaged in reading a newspaper to the prisoners confined with him, in the center room of the court-house, on the west side of the building, he was assassinated by a shot from a carbine or musket, killing him instantly. It has always been supposed that he was killed by some criminal, or a friend and accomplice of some criminal, against whom he, in his judicial capacity, had previously rendered sentence of punishment. And it may be that the murderer had joined the army in order to get an opportunity to accomplish the hellish deed. Col. Moore immediately offered a reward for the capture of the murderer, but he was never apprehended.

James Proctor Knott, having once been a prosecuting attorney in the Schuyler circuit court, and having since gained both a State and national reputation, is entitled to a brief sketch in this connection. He was a Kentuckian by birth and education. He commenced the practice of law at Memphis, Mo., and soon afterward entered the political arena, and was elected to the State Legislature in 1858. In the impeachment of Judge Jackson, Knott, as chairman of the judiciary committee, was very active in bringing that officer to trial. When Jackson was brought to trial before the Senate, Knott was solicited to conduct the prosecution in behalf of the State. The legal ability displayed on that trial caused him to be appointed attorney general of the State, to fill a vacancy in that office. In the Democratic convention which met at Jefferson City in 1860, Knott received the nomination for attorney general, with C. F. Jackson for Governor, and was elected on the general ticket. In March, 1861, he represented Cole County in the convention which met at St. Louis, and though a strong Southern sympathizer, he warned them of the danger of secession, and opposed the movement to that end. Afterward, about the middle of the war period, he moved back to Kentucky, from which State he has since served several terms in Congress, and has recently retired, at the end of his term, from the office of Governor thereof.

Joseph Wilson and S. C. Thompson were the only resident attorneys of Schuyler County who signed the first roll of attorneys at the organization of the circuit court, all the others being non-residents. Wilson was a good man, and a fair but not very able lawyer. He remained in the bar about ten years, and then left the county. Thompson remained only a short time. John W. Minor, an attorney, settled in the county in 1844, and, though the record does not show that he was present at the first term of the circuit court, he became a practitioner immediately after the court was organized. He met with good success, and became an orator of State reputation. He was a good lawyer, and honorable in the practice of his profession. He was intimately connected with the business of the county, and was appointed by the county court as commissioner of the swamp lands, and served as such. He left the county during the Civil War, and afterward died at Nebraska City, in Nebraska. Isaac N. Ebey was also a shrewd and able lawyer and a good public speaker, but, being, as he was, clerk of both the county and circuit courts from their organization until 1851, he could not practice his profession

SCHUYLER COUNTY, MISSOURI 91

****

until after that date. Soon thereafter he went to Oregon, where he was killed by the Indians. He was very popular among the people, and carried with him their regrets when he left. Francis P. Hall settled in Lancaster in 1847, and soon became, and for a number of years continued to be, the leading attorney of the bar. He was a close legal reasoner, paid strict attention to business, was perfectly reliable, and with all very prominent, but not a brilliant advocate before a jury. Being a strong Southern sympathizer, he was arrested in Lancaster during the late war, and compelled to take the oath of allegiance to the United States. He then moved to Monticello, in Lewis County, where he died in 1865.

John McGoldrick settled in Schuyler County about the year 1847, and afterward became a practitioner at the bar. He was a good theoretical lawyer, sound and honest, a good pleader, and a moderate advocate. He is still a member of the bar, but retired from active practice about the year 1877, since which time he has given his attention mostly to farming. He lives in town and owns a farm a short distance east thereof, and does, of his own choice, a great deal of manual labor. He represented the county in the Legislature from 1862 to 1866. He is a fine classical scholar, and is highly esteemed as a citizen. Judge Richard Caywood settled in the county in 1842, and his history as a lawyer is co-existent with that of the county. He was the third surveyor of the county, and is now judge of the probate court. He has been cognizant of the county business and intimately connected therewith ever since its organization; and there is probably no man living who is more familiar with the history of the county since its organization, than Judge Caywood.

Andrew J. Baker began the practice of law in Lancaster during the Civil War, and soon after the close of that struggle he served one term as clerk of the county court. In 1872 he was elected on the Liberal Republican ticket to the office of attorney-general of the State of Missouri, and, after having served his term out, he moved to the State of Iowa, where he is now serving his second term as attorney-general of that State. His success speaks sufficiently of his ability. He is an able lawyer and brilliant orator. Among other prominent members of the

Schuyler County bar, it is proper to mention the name of Felix T. Hughes, who was an able and successful lawyer. He now resides at Keokuk, Iowa, and is the president of the Keokuk & Western Railway. Also J. M. Knott, a son of Samuel C. Knott, of Memphis, and nephew of the noted J. P. Knott. He served a term as prosecuting attorney, and was noted in criminal cases. Prominent also was James Raley, who came to Lancaster at the close of the war. He was a fair lawyer, and by his industry and speculation in lands, especially with tax titles, he acquired a large amount of property, and recently moved to Texas. Another man who was admitted to the Schuyler County bar must have a special, but not a favorable, mention His name was John S. Farris. He was deputy clerk, but was never recognized as a lawyer. In 1850 the county court, having confidence in the man, gave him an order to draw certain public funds belonging to the county from the State treasury, and sent him to Jefferson City for that purpose. He went there and drew the funds, and remitted the school funds to the county, and kept the balance, amounting to about $2,000, and made his way to California, where he was afterward seen by Mr. Edwin French, of Lancaster. Farris was never brought to justice.

The Lancaster bar at the present writing is composed of the following named gentlemen, none of whom have grown old in the practice, to wit: N. M. Shelton and Samuel A. Dysart of the firm of Shelton & Dysart, Edward Higbee, C. C. Fogle, J. B. Gamble, Ed. F. Payton, E. L. French, T. C. Tadlock and L. Sanderson. It is proper also to classify John McGoldrick and Judge Caywood, of whom mention has been made, as members of the bar, though not now in full practice.

MILITARY AFFAIRS.

The Iowa War.—The first war in which the people of Schuyler and Putnam Counties were interested was one in which no battles were fought and no lives were lost. It was the one known as the "Iowa War," the history of which is as follows: The act of Congress of March 6, 1820, authorizing the people of the Territory of Missouri to form a State government, provided

that the boundaries of the proposed new State should be as follows: "Beginning in the middle of the Mississippi River on the
parallel of thirty-six degrees (36°) of north latitude; thence
west along that parallel of latitude to the St. Francois River;
thence up and following the course of that river in the middle of
the main channel thereof, to the parallel of latitude of thirty-six
degrees (36°) and thirty minutes (30'); thence west along the
same to a point where the said parallel is intersected by a meridian line passing through the middle of the mouth of the Kansas River, where the same empties into the Missouri River;
thence, from the point aforesaid, north along the said meridian
line to the intersection of the parallel of latitude which passes
through the rapids of the river Des Moines, making the said line
to correspond with the Indian boundary line; thence east from
the point of intersection last aforesaid, along the said parallel of
latitude, to the middle of the channel of the main fork of the said
river Des Moines; thence, down and along the middle of the main
channel of the said river Des Moines, to the mouth of the same,
where it empties into the Mississippi River; thence due east to the
middle of the main channel of the Mississippi River; thence, down
and following the course of the Mississippi River, in the middle
of the main channel thereof, to the place of beginning."

The act of April 20, 1836, establishing the Territory of Wisconsin, and of April 12, 1838, establishing the Territory of Iowa,
prescribed that the southern boundary of each* should be the
" northern boundary of the State of Missouri." By an act of the
Missouri Legislature, approved December 21, 1836, it was made
the duty of the Governor to appoint commissioners to " ascertain,
survey and establish the northern boundary line of the State;"
and it was further made his duty to open a correspondence with
the President of the United States, and with the Governor of
Wisconsin Territory, and request the appointment of commissioners, to act in conjunction with the Missouri commissioners,
and to request the service of a United States civil engineer, "for
the purposes aforesaid;" if the service of the latter could not be
secured, then the "commissioners were to employ a skillful engineer." The chief duty prescribed to the commissioners was—

*The Territory of Wisconsin originally comprised what is now the State of Iowa.

Sec. 2. To ascertain by astronomical observations the true latitude and longitude of the eastern point of termination of the north boundary of this State in the rapids of the river Des Moines, and thence, passing west with the same parallel of latitude, to the point where the same strikes the Missouri River, and to ascertain by the same means the true latitude and longitude of the point last aforesaid.

No appointment of commissioners and engineer was made by either the Governor of Wisconsin or the President, and in the months of July, August, September and October, 1837, the survey was made by the Missouri commissioners exclusively. The report was laid before the Legislature at its session in 1838–39, and the line as run and marked out was declared the northern boundary of the State by an act of the General Assembly approved February 11, 1839.

Subsequent to the Missouri survey, as it was called, but before the report was filed, on June 18, 1838, Congress directed a survey of the same boundary to be made under the direction of a United States commissioner, in conjunction with a commissioner from the State of Missouri, and one from the Territory of Iowa. In case, however, the State and Territory refused to make an appointment, then the Federal commissioner was to act alone. The President appointed Maj. Andrew Miller Lea, of Maryland, commissioner on the part of the United States. In his report to James Whitcombe, commissioner of the general land office, under date of January 19, 1839, Maj. Lea says:

* * * I promptly repaired to St. Louis, where I had previously informed the Governors of Missouri and Iowa I would receive their communications in regard to the appointment of the commissioners of the State and Territory, respectively. On my arrival at St. Louis, 1st September last, I received a letter from the acting Governor of Iowa, asking me, on the part of the Territory, to defer before going further, also a letter from the Governor of Missouri, suggesting the propriety of deferring and suspending operations till I could hear from the Secretary of State of the United States, to whom His Excellency had written on the subject. His Excellency stated that he had no right to appoint a commissioner on the part of the State of Missouri, and desired the proposed survey to be postponed till after the meeting of the State Legislature. In reply I informed His Excellency that I would confine my operations to the ascertainment of facts necessary to be known before the line could be properly established, and with this arrangement he expressed himself satisfied. On September the 8th, I received notice from His Excellency, Robert Lucas, that he had appointed Dr. James Davis the commissioner on the part of the Territory of Iowa.*

* Davis County, Iowa, was named for this Dr. James Davis, and not for Jefferson Davis. Lee County, Iowa, was named for Maj. Albert Lea, and not for Gen. Robert E. Lee. The error in the spelling of Lee County is as singular as it is certain. It should be spelled Lea. It has been often asserted that the two counties were named for the Confederate leaders mentioned.

The accounts of both surveys are very interesting, but must be omitted here for lack of space. The Missouri commissioners decided at last that the rapids of the river Des Moines, referred to in the organic act, were in the said river in latitude 40° 44' 6'', longitude 91° 46' 40'', nearly opposite where now stands the town of Bentonsport, Iowa, and the distance from the said Des Moines River west to the Missouri River to be 203 miles, 32 chains and 40 links. The line so run was adopted as the northern boundary of the State by an act of the General Assembly approved February 11, 1839, and extended that boundary about nine miles north of the present limit.* United States Commissioner Lea, however, reported, January 19, 1839, that there were four lines, any one of which might be taken as that intended by the act of March 6, 1820, as the northern boundary, viz.: 1. The old Indian boundary (surveyed by Col. John C. Sullivan, and often called Sullivan's line) extended west of the Missouri River; 2. The parallel of latitude passing through the old northwest corner of the Indian boundary; 3. The parallel of latitude passing through the Des Moines rapids in the Mississippi River; 4. The parallel of latitude passing through the rapids at the Great Bend (Keosauqua) in the Des Moines River.

The organic act provided expressly that the northern boundary line of the State should "correspond with the Indian boundary line," and it is difficult to understand Maj. Lea's reasons for asserting that any one of four lines might be taken, instead of the old Sullivan line. His survey and report, therefore, settled nothing, only that they did not confirm the report of the Missouri commissioners, and endorse the position and action of the Legislature. The Iowa authorities, however, accepting the conclusions of their commissioner, Dr. Davis, declared that the southern boundary of their territory—or the northern boundary of Missouri—was the old Sullivan's line, or, as it was now called, "the Indian boundary line," to which the parallel mentioned as "passing the rapids of the river Des Moines" was required to "correspond." There was, therefore, a strip of territory about nine miles in width, between the Des Moines and the Missouri

---

* At the eastern end of the line, at the Des Moines River, the difference between the northern boundary as claimed by Missouri and that finally established, was eight miles, sixty-three chains and twenty links; at the western end it was exactly eleven miles.

Rivers, which was claimed by both the Territory of Iowa and the State of Missouri.

August 23, Gov. Lilburn W. Boggs issued a proclamation setting forth the condition of affairs, particularly citing the act which had been passed by the Iowa Territorial Legislature, at Burlington, entitled "an act to prevent the exercise of a foreign jurisdiction within the Territory," under which act the sheriff of Clark County was afterward arrested and imprisoned. The Governor also called upon the proper officers to execute the laws of this State within its boundaries, as they had been defined by our Legislature, and if obstructed to call to their aid the militia of the district if necessary. The officers of the militia were directed to hold themselves and their commands in readiness to assist the sheriffs and other civil officers of this State in discharging their duties. Gov. Robert Lucas, of Iowa, in a counter proclamation, denied the title of Missouri to the disputed tract, claiming the same as within the boundaries of the Territory, authorizing the arrest and trial, before the judicial tribunals of Iowa, of all persons who should, within such portion of the territory, attempt to exercise any official function not granted or secured by the laws of the Territory of Iowa," and calling upon all the citizens of Iowa to be " vigilant in the detection and arrest" of all such alleged offenders.

The relations between the people of this State and those of Iowa now became strained and unfriendly, and in time grew to be positively hostile. At this time (fall of 1839) the only settlements on the disputed territory were within what is now Van Buren County, Iowa, then claimed by the Missourians to be a portion of Clark County, Mo. In August, 1839, the sheriff of Clark County, Uriah S. Gregory, commonly called " Sandy " Gregory, went on the debatable land and demanded taxes of some of the people, as due from them to the State of Missouri. South of Farmington, at a house-raising, he called upon half a dozen men there present, but they greeted the demand with great contempt, not only refusing to pay, but advising Sandy to " get back to his own State as quick as possible," and never again attempt to exercise authority in Iowa by virtue of a commission issued in Missouri. The sheriff returned to Waterloo, then the county seat of Clark County, and reported that he was resisted and obstructed in the attempt to collect the revenues, and asked for instructions, whereupon Gov. Boggs, having been advised of the facts, issued a strong proclamation, urging all officials to do their whole duty.

Another incident occurred at this time which intensified the feeling. A Missourian cut three bee-trees on the disputed tract, and the owner, an Iowan, sought to have him arrested and tried before a magistrate holding an Iowa commission. The arrest was not effected, but a judgment for about $1.50 was rendered against the Missourian, and the constable, with a strong posse, was on the watch to collect it.

On the 20th of November, Sheriff Gregory went again upon the debatable ground to collect taxes, and was at once arrested by Sheriff Henry Heffelman, of Van Buren County, who, with a strong posse, was in watch for him. The charge was "usurpation of authority." The prisoner was taken to Farmington, where a large crowd had assembled and where there was much excitement, and from thence to Burlington, the then capital of the Territory, and Muscatine, and here he was confined in jail a brief time, being released on his own recognizance.

The news of the arrest and incarceration of Sheriff Gregory occasioned great excitement in Missouri. The Clark County court convened in special session at the tavern of John S. Lapsley, in Waterloo, on November 23, Judges John Taylor and Jesse McDaniel present. The action taken may be best understood by the following abstract of the record:

It being proven in open court, by the oath of John Whaley, that U. S. Gregory, sheriff of Clark County, was forcibly seized on the 20th inst. by the sheriff and citizens of Van Buren County, Iowa Territory, and brought to trial in said Van Buren County on the 21st inst., when he was condemned of having violated the laws of said Territory, by collecting and attempting to collect, taxes on the disputed ground between this county and said county of Van Buren, which by the laws of this State, is in the organized limits of this county, and that said Gregory was detained in custody.

Wherefore, it is, on mature consideration, ordered by this court that Gen. O. H. Allen, of the Second Brigade, Fourteenth Division of Missouri Militia, be and he is hereby required to muster the forces at his command to aid in sustaining the civil authorities of this county in exercising exclusive and unmolested jurisdiction within the boundaries of this county, and especially on the disputed ground above named contained within the same. It is further ordered that

David Willock, major-general commanding the Fourteenth Division of Missouri Militia, be and he is hereby likewise required to muster the forces at his command, or as many as he shall think necessary, also to aid the authorities of this county in maintaining their jurisdiction over said disputed ground, and demanding reparation from the Territory of Iowa for the misconduct of its officers and citizens as above mentioned if sanctioned by its government.

Meanwhile public meetings, were held in Clark, Lewis and Marion Counties to consider the situation, and resolutions were adopted to enforce the laws of the State against the Iowans at all hazards. These meetings were usually gotten up and managed by aspirants for political preferment, anxious to precipitate a difficulty, and be on the side of the war party, knowing full well that the troubles would be settled without serious consequences to themselves. A local satirist (John I. Campbell) hit off the situation very neatly with a bit of doggerel verse in the Palmyra *Whig* of October 26. Portions of this poem (?), which was entitled "The Honey War," are here given:

THE HONEY WAR.

TUNE—"*Yankee Doodle.*"

Ye freemen of the happy land
  Which flows with milk and honey,
Arise! To arms! Your ponies mount!
  Regard not blood or money.
Old Governor Lucas, tiger-like,
  Is prowling 'round our borders,
But Governor Boggs is wide awake—
  Just listen to his orders.

Three bee-trees stand about the line
  Between our State and Lucas.
Be ready all these trees to fall,
  And bring things to a focus.
We'll show old Lucas how to brag,
  And seize our precious honey!
He also claims, I understand,
  Of us three-bits of money!

Conventions, boys, now let us hold,
  Our honey trade demands it;
Likewise the three-bits, all in gold,
  We all must understand it!
*   *   *   *   *   *   *

Why shed our brother's blood in haste,
  Because "big men" require it.
Be not in haste our blood to waste,
  No prudent men desire it.
*   *   *   *   *   *   *

SCHUYLER COUNTY, MISSOURI 99

****

> Now, if the Governors want to fight,
>   Just let them meet in person,
> And when noble Boggs old Lucas flogs,
>   'Twill teach the scamp a lesson.
> Then let the victor cut the trees,
>   And have three-bits in money,
> And wear a crown from town to town,
>   Anointed with pure honey.
>
> And then no widows will be made,
>   No orphans unprotected.
> Old Lucas will be nicely flogged,
>   And from our line ejected.
> Our honey trade will then be laid
>   Upon a solid basis,
> And Governor Boggs, where'er he jogs,
>   Will meet with smiling faces.

In the meantime Maj.-Gen. David Willock, pursuant to the orders of Gov. Boggs, called for 2,200 men from his division (the Fourteenth) of militia. The General himself, with twelve men, rode from his home in Palmyra to the border, and found the Iowans under arms. With rare good sense, he did nothing to precipitate matters, but remained up in Clark, watching and waiting. Brig.-Gen. Allen was, however, a touch-and-go sort of man, hasty and impetuous. Ordered into service, he hastily set his squadrons in the field, and by the 7th of December had Col. Chauncey Durkee's Lewis County regiment *en route* for the seat of war, without tents, almost destitute of blankets, and only imperfectly supplied with arms and ammunition. At La Grange some men of this regiment broke into the store of Mr. Charles S. Skinner, and helped themselves to his stock of groceries, blankets and other supplies to the amount of some hundreds of dollars. Mr. Skinner had recently come to the country, and his goods were new and fresh. The appropriation of his stock was approved by Gen. Allen, and he was afterward wholly or partially reimbursed.

The Lewis County regiment, with Col. Dedham's Clark County battalion, went into camp on Fox River, near Waterloo. The snow was deep, and the weather very inclement. A reinforcement from what is now Knox County, then a part of Lewis, was received, and perhaps 600 men were in camp.

On the other side of the line preparations for war were making. The territorial militia of Iowa was mustered, 300 men were under arms at Farmington, and an encounter seemed imminent. Gov. Lucas proposed to command his own forces. Among his captains was James W. Grimes, afterward United States senator. Mounted pickets were stationed to herald the advance of the Missourians, and emissaries sent over to observe their movements, and if possible to learn their plans. At a public meeting in Farmington resolutions were adopted, "that we act on the defensive; that we will neither aggress nor be aggressed upon, and we will defend our soil and our rights against any invasion at any cost of blood and treasure!"

The plan of the Missourians was to assemble an army of militia in Clark County; then to send up the sheriff again into the disputed territory, at the head of his army, as his posse, and let him renew his duties as tax gatherer. If interfered with in any way, there was to be a fight, and the blood of the slain would be upon the Iowans, and not upon the Missourians, who would be within the peace of the law. On the 2d of December the Clark County court, in special session, ordered that Col. John Dedman, of the Seventy-fifth Regiment of Missouri militia, "detail so many men as he shall deem necessary to accompany the sheriff of Clark County to the northwestern boundary of said county in order to enforce the civil laws of the State of Missouri therein." But on the 4th of December the Clark County court took steps to prevent actual conflict by the appointment of a committee to confer with the Iowa Territorial Legislature, and ascertain whether or not a peaceable and equitable adjustment of the controversy might be affected. This committee was composed of Robert P. Mitchell, Abraham Wayland, William McDaniel,* Rev. Andrew Broaddus and Mays Johnson. The object of the conference, the court declared, was

To procure, if possible, an amicable adjustment of the difficulties now existing between the Territory of Iowa and the State of Missouri in relation to the subject of jurisdiction over a certain tract of country lying on the southern limits of said territory and the northern limits of Missouri, commonly known as "the disputed territory," and that all hostile operations may cease on both sides, and that the mutual friendly relations heretofore existing may be re-established.

---

* Mr. McDaniel was a prominent Democratic politician, and known by his sobriquet, "Billy Mac the Buster." In 1846 he was elected to Congress from the State at large to fill the vacancy occasioned by the resignation of Sterling Price, who resigned to enter the Mexican War.

To the Legislature of Iowa the court asserted its pacific desires and laudable disposition by the declaration that:

This court entertains toward your honorable body, and the citizens of Iowa generally, the most friendly feelings, and would express their sincere hope that all obstacles may be removed that tend to intercept the exercise of those feelings.

The delegation then set out for Burlington, where the Iowa Legislature was in session, followed by the best wishes for the success of their mission on the part of all right thinking men.

Meantime the citizens of Marion County had moved to bring about a sensible termination of the troubles. A large public meeting held at Palmyra, on the 9th of December, adopted resolutions deprecating the existing excitement and prospective strife, and calling for a suspension of further action on the part of the Missouri authorities until the question in dispute could be settled by either Congress or the Supreme Court of the United States. Thomas L. Anderson, William Carson, Francis H. Edmondson and S. M. Grant were appointed a committee to repair to Waterloo, and present to the authorities of Clark County the proceedings of the meeting, and to urge upon them the propriety of a suspension of hostilities or measures looking thereto.

The same day the Clark County court met in regular session, and its first order directed Gen. Allen to call together the Seventy-fifth Regiment of militia in order that the delegation sent to Iowa might make known their proceedings. [Further proceedings of the county court in this connection are to be found on pp. 114–15. book "A," Clark County court records.] It was soon learned that the Iowa Legislature had met, and welcomed in the kindliest manner and most generous spirit the overtures of the Missourians. Resolutions of a very pacificatory character had been adopted, a committee sent to bear them to the authorities of Clark County, and Gov. Lucas was ordered to transmit a copy of the same to Gov. Boggs.

On the 12th of December "peace" was established and declared. The Clark County court convened at Waterloo in special session; all three of the judges, John Taylor, Jesse McDaniel and David Hay were present. There were in attendance the Marion County delegation, Col. Thomas L. Anderson at the head; the Clark County delegation, and certain prominent citizens, and Col. William Patterson, Dr. J. D. Payne and L. B. Hughes, the commissioners from Iowa. The latter presented the following preamble and resolutions of the Territorial Legislature, which were, on motion of Col. Anderson, ordered to be spread upon the records:

WHEREAS, An unfortunate crisis has arrived in the difficulties hitherto existing between the State of Missouri and the Territory of Iowa, in relation to the boundary line between the two governments; and,

WHEREAS, The Territory of Iowa would, under any circumstances, deprecate any military collision between the forces of the said State and the said Territory, fully believing that the most friendly feelings exist between the great mass of the citizens of the respective parties; and,

WHEREAS, The organic laws of said Territory render it impossible for the constituted authorities of said Territory to accede to the proposition hitherto made by the citizens of Missouri, although they fully reciprocate the kind feelings evinced by the late delegation from the county court of Clark County, therefore,

Resolved, By the Council and House of Representatives of the Territory of Iowa, that the officers now on duty on the part of the State of Missouri be respectfully requested to suspend all further military operations on the part of the said State, until these resolutions can be submitted to His Excellency, Gov. Boggs.

Resolved, That His Excellency, Governor Boggs, be requested to authorize a suspension of hostilities on the part of the State of Missouri until the first day of July next, with a view of having the unfortunate difficulties now existing between the State of Missouri and the Territory of Iowa adjusted by the action of Congress.

Resolved, That His Excellency, the Governor of Iowa, be requested to suspend all further military operations until the decision of His Excellency, Gov Boggs, may be obtained to the propositions herein contained.

Resolved, That the Governor be requested to forward a copy of these resolutions to the Governor of Missouri, one to the county-court of Clark County, Mo., and copies to the officers in command on the disputed ground, to be by them presented to the officers of the Missouri forces.

STEPHEN HEMPSTEAD,
President of the Council.
ED. JOHNSTON, *Speaker of the House of Representatives.*

The resolutions were presented by Col. William Patterson, who, in behalf of his delegation, and, as he said, of the people of Iowa, made a very acceptable address to the court and the audience. He was followed by Col. Thomas L. Anderson, on behalf of the Marion County delegation, and William McDaniel spoke for Clark County. Col. Anderson's speech, it is said, was in sentiment very eloquent, and in depicting the horrors of war very terrifying. His auditors were moved by his earnest words, and

were by turns frightened and in tears. He showed very clearly
that war was entirely unjustifiable on the part of either the State
or Territory; that it would settle no question involved, decide
no principle at stake, produce nothing but ill consequences; that,
if the forces then in the field should fight until all were slain, the
boundary line would still have to be established by the authority
of the general Government, since neither contending party had
jurisdiction over the matter. Drawing a picture of the horrors
of internecine strife, as contrasted with the blessings of peace
and the delights of brotherly love and neighborly friendship, he
pleaded earnestly for concession, conciliation and peace. Allud-
ing to the condition of the men of Gen. Allen's command, then
shivering about their camp fires on Fox River, the thermometer
below zero, and themselves half fed, insufficiently clad, and not
at all properly provided for; "Send them home to their families," said he, "send them to those who at this inclement season
need them, and who are watching anxiously for them, and praying for their safe and speedy return. And, in the name of the
God of Mercy and Justice, gentlemen, let this monumental piece
of absurdity, this phenomenal but cruel blundering, have an end!"

The speakers, the commissioners and the county justices all
protested that they did not want war or bloodshed, and the attain-
ment of complete peace was easily and speedily accomplished.
By a unanimous vote the county court published the following
statement and accompanying order:

A committee from the County of Marion produced to this court a preamble
and resolutions from the citizens of said county, relative to the difficulties existing between the State of Missouri and the Territory of Iowa; also, there was
presented a copy of certain proceedings on the part of the Legislature of said
Territory, in relation thereto, by a special delegation of said Legislature, request-
ing on the part of the State a cessation of hostilities, for certain reasons stated
in said resolutions, and deeming said request reasonable, we therefore order that
Maj.-Gen. D. Willock and Brig.-Gen. O. H. Allen be and they are hereby
informed that we do not desire longer the aid of the militia of the State in the
enforcement of our laws. It is further ordered that the clerk of this court
forthwith forward a copy of the foregoing proceedings to His Excellency, the
Governor of the Territory of Iowa, one to Maj.-Gen. D. Willock, and one to
Brig.-Gen. O. H. Allen.

There was a general and hearty fraternization of all the
parties, and mutual congratulations that the troubles had been
settled. Gen. Allen and a few of the military officers, who were

drawing respectable pay so long as they were in active service, received the order for the withdrawal of the militia with much dissatisfaction, but their men were more than satisfied. On their return to Monticello, Gen. Allen, Col. Durkee, Addison Reese, and a few other warriors and bellicose gentlemen assembled at Pemberton's hotel, organized what they called a "public meeting," and passed sanguinary resolutions threatening fire and sword, and denouncing everybody that had been instrumental in bringing about peace and preventing strife and bloodshed. Gen. Allen was especially "disgruntled," and not until he and his associates were duly sober did they consent to be comforted and to be reconciled to the fact that the war was over.

Gen. Allen disbanded the Clark County regiment, the Seventy-fifth, at Waterloo; Col. Durkee marched the Lewis County regiment, the Fifty-eighth, back to Monticello, where it was discharged.

Meanwhile the Fifty-sixth Regiment of Missouri militia, composed entirely of men from Marion County, and commanded by Col. John Lear, had been called on for 200 men. That number refusing to volunteer, a draft was ordered, and the 200 secured after a great deal of protesting, remonstrance, and some hiring of substitutes. The men assembled at Palmyra on December 12, and took up the line of march for Waterloo. The first night the detachment went into camp over the Fabius, several miles from Palmyra. There was great distress. A deep snow fell, and the weather was bitter cold; the men suffered severely, being without tents, and for the most part without blankets. Only the large fires built and kept up saved them from freezing. The next morning the detachment was divided into four companies of fifty men each (a less number to the company would have prevented the captains from drawing pay), and the march was resumed through the cold and snow. The second night camp was pitched in Lewis County, not far from Monticello.

This night, too, news reached the camp that peace had been declared, and that the Marion County men were to return to their homes the following morning. A great cheer, half derisive, half joyful, went up. In a little while the men resolved to end their campaign with certain contemptuous proceedings toward the two

Governors, who, as they believed, were the cause of what had happened, and the ridiculous termination of the threatened "war." Accordingly a haunch of venison was cut in two, one piece labeled "Gov. Lucas of Iowa," the other "Gov. Boggs of Missouri," and both hung up and fired into with rifles. Then they were taken down and buried with mock funeral solemnity, and with burlesque honors of war.

Before starting on the return trip for home, the following resolutions were adopted at an impromptu meeting of the militiamen:

Resolved, That as this is the third winter in succession that the troops have been ordered from Marion, and had to furnish their own tents and blankets—therefore, we who have them now will keep them for the war next winter, as our notice has hitherto been so short.

Resolved, That the Governor be requested to furnish us with guns by next fall.

Resolved, That we think it high time we had our pay for the Mormon campaign last year.

The men then marched for home. Some of them turned their coats and wore them inside out when they reached home, in honor, they said, of their distinguished services in and safe return from the "honey war."

The Thirty-second Regiment, also from Marion County, was called on for 200 men, in companies of fifty each. These were organized into a battalion, led by the commander of the regiment, Col. Jordan J. Montgomery. The battalion set out from Palmyra, independent of Col. Lear's regiment, and a day later. The first night it camped across North River, near Oldham's spring, afterward known as Todd's spring. It was very cold and disagreeable, but the men built big fires, and, as they had taken five days' rations with them in wagons, they had plenty to eat. The command marched next day early, and that night went into camp two miles from La Grange.

Here the men, half desperate at their situation, gave themselves over to certain wild and unmilitary conduct. A half a mile of a settler's rail fence was burned as speedily and unceremoniously as if a battalion of Jim Lane's jayhawkers had done it. Several packs of cards were produced, and a great deal of playing was indulged in—some for money. It is said that the next

grand jury of the county indicted about 100 of the militiamen
for gambling.

In this camp the peace commissioners were met, also, and the
next morning Col. Montgomery faced his command about and
returned to Palmyra. Along the route, on the return trip, the
men indulged in a great deal of rough and wild sport. Like
their comrades of the Fifty-sixth Regiment many of them wore
turned coats when they reached Palmyra.

A company from Shelby County, under Capt. Scott Matson,
had encamped north of Newark, *en route* for Waterloo, when it
received the intelligence that peace had been declared.

In March, 1840, Congress legislated on the subject. In a
strong memorial of the Legislature, and by oral arguments from
the senators and others, Missouri presented a very plausible case.
The point relied on, mainly, was that in the organic act the word
" line " in the phrase, " making the said line correspond with the
Indian boundary line," meant the " meridian line " running north
through the mouth of the Kansas River, and forming the western
boundary of the State, and not the line running east and forming
the northern boundary. But the claim was not tenable. The
decision was in favor of Iowa, and " the Indian boundary line,"
run by Col. Sullivan, was declared to be the true northern boundary of the State. Notwithstanding this legislation on the part
of Congress, the question remained unsettled, and both governments continued to exercise authority over the disputed territory.
In the organization of Schuyler County, in 1845, the nine-mile
strip was included, and covered by Independence and Wells
Townships (see organization). And at the first term of the
Schuyler circuit court, it being in April, 1846, Samuel Riggs,
sheriff of Davis County, Iowa, was indicted " for taking upon
himself the office of sheriff," or in other words for assuming jurisdiction on the disputed territory; whereupon he appeared in
person and gave bond for his appearance at the next term of
court. Prior to this, however, in 1845, soon after Schuyler
County was organized, Jonathan Riggs, the first sheriff thereof,
was indicted in the district court of the Territory of Iowa for the
county of Davis upon a charge of " usurping and exercising the
office of sheriff " on the disputed territory. Jonathan Riggs lived

on this territory, and was a brother of Samuel Riggs mentioned. The cases against these men were continued, by the contending powers, from term to term, and finally dismissed. Schuyler County continued to claim jurisdiction over the nine-mile strip until 1848 or 1849, when it appears from the records that it was abandoned. In 1850 the State line was again run by commissioners from both States, and some corrections made, and the following letter relative to the subject written by Judge H. B. Hendershot, of Ottumwa, Iowa, dated December 1, 1887, will best explain how the State line was finally established to the full recognition of the contending powers:

Dear Sir:—I am in receipt of yours of 29th ult., in reference to the boundary, survey, etc., between Missouri and Iowa. The work to which you refer, was done by the commissioners, Mr. William G. Minor, on the part of Missouir, and myself on the part of Iowa, commencing in the field about the 1st of May, 1850, and we closed in October, 1850. After the field work was done, the commissioners made report to the December term, 1850, of the Supreme Court of the United States, and on the 3d day of January, 1851, the matter came up before said court, and the report of the commissioners showing the establishment of the true boundary line between the two States, Missouri and Iowa, was in every respect confirmed, and on that day, January 3, 1851, the decree of the court fixed the line established by the commissioners as the "true and permanent boundary line between the States of Missouri and Iowa."

Yours truly,

H. B. HENDERSHOT.

The cost of the Iowa War to Missouri was about $20,000. Of this sum, $19,000 was for the payment of troops and the attendant expenses. [Acts XI, Gen. Ass., p. 21.] Gens. Willock and Allen and their "escorts" received about $600, and $351.56 were paid to Franklin Levering, of Clark, to reimburse him for damages and costs sustained in the suits brought against him for false imprisonment by the three Iowans whom he had arrested at St. Francisville, in December, 1839. [Ibid, p. 223.] There were some other items paid for not worth mentioning.

The Great Rebellion.—Following the difficulty of the so-called Iowa War, the people of Schuyler County had nothing of a warlike nature to disturb their tranquillity until the War of the Rebellion began to approach their territory. Then, when the alarm of war was sounded, it was found that a majority of the citizens were in full sympathy with the Southern or secession cause. For the political status of the people of the county at that time the reader is referred to the votes cast at the presidential election of 1860. Though the majority were hostile to the general Government, it seems that at first all parties were anxious to avert the calamities of war, and the people on the Iowa side of the State line were also anxious to avoid trouble along the border, and to avert this a company of Home Guards was organized in Schuyler County to act conjointly with a command to be organized on the Iowa side, to preserve peace and enforce neutrality along the line. William Hombs was elected captain of this company. This experiment of enforced neutrality soon proved to be a failure, in consequence of which Capt. Hombs resigned his position, and the company disbanded. On the 13th of May, 1861, Judge Thomas S. Richardson appeared in Lancaster, and opened the May term of the Schuyler circuit court, and had just begun business when a messenger arrived with the news that the Federal forces had moved out from St. Louis, and had captured Camp Jackson, and were on their way to Jefferson City, the capital of the State. Then the excitement and commotion prevailed to such an extent that court was immediately adjourned, and the multitude resolved itself into a public meeting to consider the safety of the community. Those in favor of the Southern cause, being in the majority, now took the initiative, and eloquent speeches were made by certain lawyers and others present. Men realized that the "dogs of war" had been let loose, and that the terrors thereof were not far distant from their homes. The Union men being in the minority, and exceedingly loth to engage in a warfare with their fellows and neighbors, for the time kept silent. Thrilling appeals were made by the excited speakers for all to sell their lives dearly as possible, rather than to be ruled by the Lincoln Government. Then the men of Lancaster and vicinity, who favored secession, constituted themselves into "State Allegiance and Home Protective Guards," and encouraged the work of enlistment for the State Guards, under the call of Gov. Jackson, for a volunteer force to serve six months, to save the State from invasion by the United States army. Then men gathered in groups on the public square and discussed the situation, each feeling his ability to conquer the foe of several times his number. Soon the enlistment of men for the State Guards began in earnest, and seven companies, commanded respectively by Capts. William Dunn, James Buford, Samuel Shacklett, John McCully and——Slacum, Carmon and William J. Gates, were raised and organized in the county, and became a part of a regiment of the State Guards, of which Cyrus Franklin was colonel, and W. C. Blanton, lieutenant-colonel. These companies did a great deal of hard service in Northeastern Missouri and elsewhere, and at the end of the six months nearly three-fourths of them entered the regular Confederate army, and served therein to the close of the war. Of the balance, some returned to their homes and afterward took the oath of allegiance to the United States, some fled to other States, and a few subsequently enlisted in the Federal army. The men composing the foregoing companies together with all those that went outside of the county and joined other commands, and all subsequent recruits, are carefully estimated to have reached nearly 700 in the aggregate, which from first to last served in the rebel army.

In October, 1861, it was rumored that Col. David Moore, in command of a Federal force (the Twenty-first Missouri), was at Memphis, in Scotland County, and was threatening to move westward into Schuyler County. Then a number of the leading Southern sympathizers of Lancaster assembled in the store of William S. Thatcher, at the southeast corner of the public square, and appointed four Union men, viz.: Edwin French, William Garges Joseph Rhoads and William Casper (the latter declined), to go to Memphis, and entreat Col. Moore not to enter Schuyler County, as all was peace therein, and would remain so unless his or some other Federal force would invade it. Accordingly, the next day Messrs. French, Garges and Rhoads, being also anxious to keep the war from their homes, went to Memphis, and there met Judge Richardson, who informed them that Col. Moore and his command had not yet arrived. They then returned to Lancaster, and reported. Meanwhile recruits were being enlisted for the Confederate cause, and some of the men, so anxious for peace at home, and that no Federal force should invade the county, were and had been doing all in their power to induce their fellows to enlist in the army of the enemy of the United States.

Soon after this Col. Moore, with his regiment, took possession of Memphis, and, on the 24th of November following, he moved with a portion of his command, and took possession of Lancaster. Capt. John McCully, with his company of State Guards, anticipating the approach of the Federal forces, took position, the day before, about one-half mile south of the town, with the intention of resisting Moore's advance; but it seems the latter met with but little resistance until after he had taken possession of the town, and sent a foraging party to the west side thereof to bring in some hay for his horses. This was late in the afternoon, and Capt. McCully had advanced with his company into the hollow southwest of the town, and south of the house where Hon. Francis Hall then lived. Here an engagement took place between Mc-Cully's men and the guard of Col. Moore's foraging party, and William Garrison, one of the latter party who was on a haystack near by, was killed; and Capt. McCully and his two sons, Marion and George, and his son-in-law, Harrison Epperson, were also killed. The State Guards then fell back, and Col. Moore retained quiet possession of the town, which he held for about two weeks, and then took his troops back to Memphis. This allowed time again for the enemy to recruit and gather strength, until the latter part of January or early in February, 1862, when Capt, Mitch. Marshall, a recruiting officer of Keokuk, Iowa, and who had been recruiting in Putnam County, Mo., came to Lancaster with a small company of recruits, numbering about twenty men, and took quarters in the old brick (Christian) church which stood on the east side of the street, immediately and directly south of the railroad bridge, on Washington Street. Here, then, the captain at once began the business of recruiting soldiers for the Federal army.

This was exceedingly distasteful to the recruiting officers of the Southern army who had previously, and up to this time, held almost undisputed sway in the county, except the time that Col. Moore had been in possession of the field. And not being willing to give the territory over to Federal recruiting officers, a company of the State Guards marched into Lancaster on the night of February 11, 1862, and being aware of the small number of men in Capt. Marshall's company, resolved to drive him out or capture his force; and in order to do this, and as a precautionary measure, they erected a barricade across Washington Street just west of the southwest corner of the public square. This barricade was constructed of old counters, tables, work-benches, sleds, wagons, beds, planks and anything that would stop a bullet, and, when completed, the firing on the brick church began, and skirmishers were thrown out on the wings to cross fire on the Federal fortification. Capt. Marshall had but a small supply of ammunition, and therefore did not waste much of it firing at a concealed foe in the darkness. The firing by the State Guards continued for some time, and until it was found that the Federals would not come out of their stronghold, and then the siege was raised and the Guards retired in good order, and when morning came Marshall and his men were in full possession of the town and the abandoned fortifications. The latter, with the exception of some property returned to the owners thereof, was burned by Marshall's men. In this engagement one Federal recruit, Elias Yates, who was standing guard at the church, was shot through the leg, but no other damage was done except the indentures made upon the walls of the old church.

As soon as Capt. Marshall, the recruiting officer, had recruited a number of men, and got the business of recruiting fairly established, he left it in the hands of Capt. Perry D. McClanihan and others, and took his departure for another field of labor. On one occasion, in the month of March, 1862, Capt. McClanihan and a squad of twelve men visited the southern part of the county, and on their way back they were waylaid near the tobacco factory, three miles south of Lancaster, and three of their number, named Snyder, Funk and Davis, were killed. The latter was not a soldier, but was coming in to enlist as one. Poor fellow, he lost his life before his name reached the muster-roll! The following named soldiers of the squad, Zach Taylor, Moses Civets and Frank Gatlin, were severely wounded, and Charles Keesoker, slightly. Recruiting for the Federal army continued at Lancaster on this occasion until two full companies of eighty men each were composed and organized, and commanded respectively by Capts. Perry D. McClanihan and Thad. S. Wescott. Being thus organized, Col. John McNeil came to Lancaster about the middle of April, 1862, and assuming command, marched them to Canton, Mo., where they were assigned positions as Companies B and C in the Second Cavalry Missouri State Militia, and mustered into the United States service.

Among those belonging to these two companies who enlisted at Lancaster, Mo., are the following, whose names have been kindly furnished by Joseph F. Mellender, who was one of their number, and now resides at Lancaster: Thomas Brewer, John Blurton, Robert Blurton, John Blurton, Jr., Thompson Burgan, Isaac Burgan, David Brower, Moses Civets, George Combs, John M. Coons, Gotlieb Diereling, William Edwards, Charles H. French, Thomas Frazer, Alonzo T. Foster, Joel Graves, Abraham Gardine, Isaac Gardine, John Malone, J. D. Farris, A. D. Farris, George Combs, George Pruner, Samuel and Job Grag, John Van Buskirk, James P. Grindle, Charles Rodgers, Richard Galispie, Joseph Gilbert, Frank Gatlin, William Gregory, James Hubbard, William Homosin, Elisha Hayden, John A. Hays, Henry Heincy, Jacob Hornback, James Israel, Milton Israel, Sylvester M. Johnson, Henry Johnson, Charles Keeseker, Alexander Kemp, David Lazileer, Thomas Leedom, George Leedom, Jesse Maize, Thomas McGihon, Joseph F. Mellender, Burrel Pruett, Jacob Rhoads, Joseph Rhoads, Joseph Robinson, Elbert Robinson, Samuel Rhoads, Thomas Stanton, Eli F. Stanton, William Thompson, Warren Terry, Michael Shelton, Samuel Tipton, Thomas Stephens, Van Stephens, Henry Yeams, George Evans, Thomas Rodgers, Robert Canady, Isam Brewer, James Coffman. A few of the foregoing came from Iowa, and the following came from Putnam County, Mo.: Zachariah Brofford, John Pickering, Ellis Pickering, Matthew Ash, Isaac Featherly, Zach. Admire, George Admire, Bass. Cullom, Josiah Pickenpaw, John Yates, Elias Yates and Samuel Millirons. Joseph F. Mellender and several others of the foregoing named soldiers re-enlisted in the Thirteenth Regiment Missouri Volunteer Cavalry, and served therein until the regiment was mustered out after the close of the war.

Second Cavalry Missouri State Militia.—This regiment was recruited from Schuyler and other counties in Northeastern Missouri in the spring of 1862, and was mustered into the

United States service at Canton, in Lewis County. John McNeil was appointed colonel, and James H. Crane, lieutenant-colonel of the regiment, and after an active summer campaign against the rebel forces in Northeastern Missouri, it was consolidated with the Eleventh Cavalry Missouri State Militia, in obedience to Special Order No. 151, from the adjutant-general's office at St. Louis, dated September 2, 1862. The regiment retained its original number, and the new field officers were John McNeil, colonel; John P. Benjamin, lieutenant-colonel, and John B. Rogers and J. B. Dodson, majors. On the 6th of January, 1863, the regiment marched from Palmyra, Mo., to Southeastern Missouri, and took post at Bloomfield. On the 21st of April following, the advance of a rebel force under Marmaduke, surprised an outpost at Chalk Bluffs, consisting of Company H, Second Cavalry, and captured all but Lieut. Wilson and six privates, and all of the company's horses, arms, camp and garrison equipage. After this disaster the regiment fell back to Cape Girardeau, Mo., where it helped to repulse the attack of Marmaduke's whole force on the 26th of April. The regiment remained in Southeastern Missouri, with headquarters at Cape Girardeau, until it was mustered out at the close of the war. Meanwhile it was constantly engaged, serving by detachments in scouting through Southeastern Missouri and Northeastern Arkansas, where it carried on a successful warfare against guerrilla bands, many of whom it killed and captured. The several companies, while on detached duty, participated in many sharp engagements, in which they were generally victorious. On the whole the Second Cavalry Missouri State Militia was a noble regiment, and did a great deal of good service for the Union.

In the month of June, 1862, a Federal force, consisting of about 400 men and two pieces of artillery, under command of Col. Halbert, entered Lancaster one morning, about two hours before daylight, and began the work of confiscating certain property. They backed their wagons up to the closed storehouses of William S. Thatcher, and at the drug store of Wright and the store of Elijah Thatcher, and broke open the doors, and quietly and undisturbed, loaded the contents of each store into their wagons, and departed in the afternoon of that day for Kirksville, where the goods were afterward sold at auction for the benefit of the Government. The owners of these stores were Southern sympathizers, who were charged with aiding and assisting the Rebellion, and especially the rebel bushwhackers; and their property was confiscated in retaliation therefor, and to reimburse the Government for the damages they had done. It is not denied that these men were Southern sympathizers, but as to what proof the Federals had of the charges alleged against them, it is now impossible to say.

Skirmish at Downing.—This place is located on the Keokuk & Western Railway, in Schuyler County, and near the eastern line thereof. It was then called Cherry Grove, and the fight was known as "the skirmish at Cherry Grove." About the first of July, 1862, the engagement took place between the Second Battalion of the Eleventh Missouri State Militia (cavalry), under command of Maj. (afterward colonel) Rogers, and a portion of Col. Joe Porter's Confederate troops. In this engagement the latter were defeated with a loss of four men killed. The Federals lost one man, Capt. York, of Company B, of Eleventh Missouri State Militia, who was reported at the time as severely, if not mortally, wounded, but died a few days thereafter, at Memphis, in Scotland County. They also captured a few prisoners, horses, arms, etc. Following this engagement, and also the battle of Kirksville (an account of which is given elsewhere in this work), Maj. Rogers, with his battalion, entered the town of Lancaster on the 9th of August, and held possession of the place about two weeks.

Enrolled Missouri Militia of Schuyler County.—In 1862, Hon. John McGoldrick, of Lancaster, was appointed by the proper Federal authority as enrolling officer, and under his administration three full companies of the Enrolled Missouri Militia were raised and organized in Schuyler County, during the months of August and September of that year. These companies were first commanded, respectively, by Capts. Robert J. Maize, Nathan Williams and J. W. Eggleston. They were mustered into the Twenty-ninth Regiment Enrolled Missouri Militia, and the following is the roster of the field officers of the regiment, and of the officers of the aforesaid companies:

SCHUYLER COUNTY, MISSOURI 115

****

Col. William H. Parmort, commissioned March 13, 1864, to rank from March 13, 1864; commission not signed.

Lt.-Col. John Gildred, commissioned May 4, 1864, to rank from May 4, 1864; vacated March 12, 1865.

Maj. James Means, commissioned October 1, 1862, to rank from September 27, 1862; vacated March 12, 1865.

Adjt. William Kays, commissioned March 14, 1863, to rank from September 27, 1862; vacated March 12, 1865.

Quartermaster Thomas Little, commissioned October 6, 1862, to rank from September 27, 1862; vacated by Special Order, No. 126, 1864.

Quartermaster William Simpson, commissioned October 20, 1864, to rank from October 17, 1864; vacated March 12, 1865.

COMPANY E.

Capt. Robert J. Maize, commissioned September, 1862, to rank from August, 1862; vacated December, 1862.

Capt. Henry Grimshaw, commissioned March 14, 1863, to rank from December 20, 1862; vacated March 12, 1865.

First Lieut. John Gildred, commissioned March 14, 1863, to rank from December 20, 1862; promoted to lieutenant-colonel May 4, 1864.

Second Lieut. Geo. W. Alexander, commissioned August 7, 1863, to rank from October 17, 1862; vacated March 12, 1865.

COMPANY F.

Capt. Nathan Williams, commissioned September 24, 1862, to rank from August 30, 1862; vacated by Special Order, No. 126, 1864.

First Lieut. M. R. Bruce, commissioned September 24, 1862, to rank from August 30, 1862; vacated March 12, 1865.

Second Lieut. Joseph Gray, commissioned September 24, 1862, to rank from August 30, 1862; vacated March 12, 1865.

COMPANY G.

Capt. J. W. Eggleston, commissioned September 24, 1862, to rank from September 6, 1862; vacated by Special Order, July, 1864.

Capt. Jacob Miller, commissioned July 18, 1864, to rank from July 18, 1864; vacated March 12, 1865.

First Lieut. W. R. Jones, commissioned September 24, 1862, to rank from September 6, 1862; died March 30, 1864.

First Lieut. William H. Barnes, commissioned July 11, 1864, to rank from July 11, 1864; vacated March 12, 1865.

Second Lieut. John Dirigo, commissioned September 24, 1862, to rank from September 6, 1862; vacated March 12, 1865.

The other seven companies of this regiment were raised in adjoining counties in Northern Missouri. After the defeat of Col. Porter with his Confederate forces at the battle of Kirksville, and his retreat to the south side of the Missouri River, it was thought that the business of recruiting for the Confederate service in Northeastern Missouri was effectually ended, and that the Enrolled Militia, if organized, would be sufficiently able to keep the Southern element under subjection; hence the formation of this branch of the service. The Twenty-ninth Regiment of Enrolled Missouri Militia remained north of the Missouri River, and the companies remained mostly in the counties where they were raised. But they found all they could do to keep the enemy in subjection at home until the year 1864, and their services for that purpose were needed until the close of the war.

The three companies mentioned that joined the Twenty-ninth Enrolled Missouri Militia, and the two companies that joined the Second Cavalry, Missouri State Militia, together with all those that went to Iowa and to adjoining counties in Missouri, and there joined other commands, and including, also, those who subsequently enlisted in the Thirty-ninth and Forty-second Regiments of Missouri Volunteers, are carefully estimated at about 600 in the aggregate, who served in the Federal army from first to last during the Civil War.

Skirmish at Lancaster.—On Sunday, September 6, 1862, a portion of Capt. Maize's Company of the Enrolled Militia was stationed in Lancaster, with a few sentinels posted on the outskirts of the town. The guns of the company and a very few men were in the court-room at the court-house, but most of the men of the company were sitting on the south side of the public square (probably in the shade), and some were scattered elsewhere; all feeling that no enemy was near. John McGoldrick, the enrolling officer, had just put on his Sunday clothes and a silk hat, and was walking "up to town," and on reaching the southwest corner of the public square he espied the enemy coming from the north, then waved his hat to the militia, seated as aforesaid, and ran to the court-house, but was fired upon before reaching it. He ran into the court-room, and aroused the few inmates and urged them to action. He was followed closely by Capt. John Baker, who immediately took charge of the "firing squad." At this juncture the militiamen on the south side, unarmed, fled southward into the hollow for protection. A force of the enemy consisting of foot soldiers and mounted men, the former commanded by Capt. William Searcy, and the latter by Capt. Leeper, had passed the sentinel, who failed to perform his duty, at the northwest corner of the town, and had nearly reached the public square before being discovered. On nearing the square they shot and wounded Henry Hilton, a young lad not a member of any military force, but probably mistaken by them for a militiaman. They also shot and killed "Gideon," a free negro, and a militiaman by the name of William White.

On coming into the square they were fired upon from the windows of the court-room, and thus checked in their advance. Capt. Searcy was shot in the breast, the bullet being discharged from a squirrel rifle. The firing continued for some time, during which Edwin French, one of the men in the court-room, carried water from his residence for his comrades who did the firing. He was thus exposed to great danger. Finally the enemy, finding that they could not oust the firing squad in the court-house, turned and left the town. There were only nineteen men, all told, including Mr. French, that were in the court-room, and who did all the fighting on the Federal side. When the attacking party retreated, they carried Capt. Searcy with them about two miles, and there left him for dead. He was brought back to town the same day, and was cared for until he was sufficiently recovered to be taken to Macon City, Mo., where he was tried by a Federal court martial, and, in obedience to the sentence thereof, shot and killed. The evidence against him was, that he had no commission from any authority whatever. He and his men were therefore regarded, by the Federals, as guerrillas.

Skirmish near Unionton.—The fullest and most complete history of this engagement is believed to be embodied in the official report of Lieut.-Col. John Baker, of Lancaster, which is as follows:

LANCASTER, Mo., October 21, 1862.

Dear Sir:—I have the honor to report to you the skirmish that took place twelve miles northeast of Lancaster, on the 18th inst., between a portion of the Enrolled Missouri Militia, under my command, and a detachment of the Second Missouri Cavalry, and about 150 guerrillas, under command of the notorious Capt. William Dunn. On the morning of the 17th inst. I sent out Capt. David G. Maize, in the direction of Unionton, in Scotland County, with a small force of the Enrolled Missouri Militia from this post, to look for the rebels. At daylight next morning Capt. Maize discovered that he was in the neighborhood of a large force of them, and sent back for reinforcements to me at Lancaster. I sent what men I could spare, under command of Second-Lieut. Thomas Law, of the Second Missouri Cavalry, and First-Lieut. M. R. Bruce, of the Enrolled Missouri Militia, of this place, making a force, all told, of fifty-seven men and officers.

They came up with the rebels, posted in a thicket one and a half miles south of the village of Unionton, in Scotland County. Capt. Maize, assisted by Lieuts. Law and Bruce, opened fire on them. Capt. Bell, of the Enrolled Missouri Militia of Adair County, came up about the same time with a considerable force under his command and aided us in the fight, which lasted one and a half hours, and resulted in the total rout of the rebel forces. Seven of the rebels were reported killed, and a number of them wounded. Ten were taken prisoners, and among them the noted guerrilla, Tom Palmer. The number of horses captured by my men was twelve, arms, saddles and blankets unknown, as they were gathered up by various companies engaged, and carried off. Capt. Bell, of Kirksville, took charge of the prisoners and most of the horses, and took them with him.

The rebels wore white bands on their hats, and this saved them from utter destruction, as our men mistook them at first for our own men. We had none of our men killed or wounded in this skirmish. On the morning of the 18th, let me add, Capt. N. Williams and Lieut. Grimshaw, with seventeen men, were marching into the village of Unionton. When near the village they were fired on by some twenty men, who, they thought, were the Enrolled Missouri Militia, as they all had on white hat bands, but before they found out their mistake the guerrillas fled out of the village. One man of the Enrolled Missouri Militia was wounded; also three horses. The skirmish first mentioned in this report took place late in the evening, and the rebels made good their retreat under cover of night.

I have the honor to be, sir, your obedient servant,

JOHN BAKER,

Lieutenant-Colonel Commanding Post at Lancaster, Mo.

BRIG.-GEN. MERRILL, Macon City, Mo.

In the foregoing, Col. Baker says " seven of the rebels were reported killed," but from reliable information it is thought that none were killed. The white hat band referred to was a mark of distinction adopted and worn by the Enrolled Missouri Militia. Capt. William Dunn and his friends, who still live in Schuyler County, deny the charge made in the foregoing report, that he and his men were guerrillas, but claim that they were soldiers, first in the State Guards, and subsequently in the Confederate army, and that Capt. Dunn was a regularly commissioned officer. The latter claims that there were only about seventy-five men of his command engaged in the foregoing skirmish, instead of 150, as stated in Col. Baker's report.

Incidents of the War.—In 1861 Benjamin Brown, a farmer and Southern sympathizer, living about two miles northeast of Green Top, saw a party of Union soldiers approaching, and, being frightened, started to run, when they shot and killed him. The same year a Mr. Follett, living about nine miles southeast of Lancaster, was killed by some one belonging to Federal scouts. In the summer of 1862 a skirmish took place in the northeast part of the county between a party of Union men, who were threshing grain, and a party of rebels, and John Israel, a Union man, and John Leeper, a rebel, were killed. The following winter John Leeper, Sr., who lived about three miles northwest of Lancaster, was killed by a Union soldier. In 1863 David Conklin, a rebel soldier well acquainted with the country, and who acted in the capacity of a pilot for Confederate parties, was arrested in the southeast corner of Schuyler County, by a squad of Union troops, and by them shot and killed. The same year Peter Clark, a Southern sympathizer living about five miles east of Lancaster, was shot and killed. In 1864 Luther D. Sales, a rebel soldier, while at his home ten miles east of Lancaster, was shot and killed by a party of Federal scouts from Scotland County; and the same year James Ford, a Southern sympathizer living about two miles west of Glenwood, was shot and killed by a man belonging to a party of Federal scouts. Also during the war Graham Biles, who lived about five miles southwest of Lancaster, was killed by some personal enemy, as it is believed; and Isaac Varner was killed at a place about seven miles east of Lancaster by some Federal scout.

If these individuals had been killed by order of Federal officers, it would have been a severe reflection upon them. But it is fully believed that nearly all, if not quite all, with the exception of Conklin, were killed voluntarily by their individual enemies, who made use of and perhaps sought the opportunity thus to gratify their revengeful spirits. There were soldiers, bad men, in both armies, who seemed to think that their positions gave them license to kill; and it made no difference with them whether they killed a man in a skirmish or battle, or whether they deliberately murdered him when he was alone and defenseless.

*Early in 1863 Federal scouts under command of Col. Cantron lingered in the vicinity of Lancaster, and one evening six men went to the house of a tried Union man, and desired to see George Fletcher, who in the early days of the conflict had joined the rebels, but had returned to Lancaster homeless and half

---

*The Excelsior.

starved. They chased him with brick bats, but did not kill him. After disposing of him they returned and did likewise with Stephen Caywood, also firing on him, but he, too, escaped. They then turned the excursion into a raid on the office of Richard Caywood, and demolished his furniture, and distributed his books and papers about the public square and streets.

In 1864 the Federal element was in the ascendancy, and the Home Guards sent a deputation of twelve men to the house of an Englishman who was in the army, and where Bill Dunn was, to take him. These men rode up to the front of the house, and sent six men to guard the rear, and were about to demand a surrender, when the front door was thrown open and a volley of musketry from the party within came forth. Then Dunn and his party rushed out and fled to the woods. It being nightfall, the Home Guards filed into the house and demanded supper, and remained there till morning; and then two of them ventured out, and when a short distance from the house the contents of a gun were lodged in the back of Seth Hathaway. Sorely wounded, he managed to get back to the house, and there fainted on the threshold. He was laid on the bed, when lo! the eleven mounted their steeds and fled, leaving the wounded man. Dunn and his men then re-entered the house, and but for the entreaties of the Englishwoman, Hathaway would have been killed, but he was permitted to remain and live.

Soldiers' Bounties.—At a special term of the Schuyler County court, held on the 30th of August, 1864, a petition, signed by 446 citizens and taxpayers of the county, was presented to the court, praying that a bounty be offered to each recruit that would enlist in the United States army. And the court, after due examination of the matter, made an order to appropriate "$8,000 out of the county fund, to be expended in the payment of bounties to volunteers in the United States service for twelve months, under the last call of the President; or that a bounty of $100 be paid to married men, or single men who have helpless parents or brothers and sisters dependent upon them for support; and a bounty of $60 to all other acceptable volunteers who are residents of Schuyler County, Mo., said bounties to be paid in warrants drawn on the county fund, directed to the treasurer of the county, and to be given to the recruit or his legal agent, one-half at the time of his being mustered into the service, and the facts certified back by the colonels of their respective regiments, and the other half at the end of said service, on their producing of an honorable discharge."

Afterward, on the 15th of December following, a certificate of the commanding officer of the Forty-second Regiment Missouri Volunteers, containing the names of all persons who had responded to the aforesaid call, and had been mustered into Company G, of said regiment, was filed with the court, and thereupon a county order was issued to the following named persons for the sum of $50 each: Michael P. Boatman, George N. Bradley, James Bradley, Charles B. Wheeler, Charles W. Burnett, Phil. J. Emmet, Milton Israel, G. W. Jones, Elias Owens, Elias W. Owens, James P. Potter, Howel Sebring, Isaac J. Thompson, Thomas Vining, Davis Wyatt and James W. Wright. And a county order was at the same time issued to the following names, volunteers, for the sum of $30 each: Ed. R. Alexander, Mich. R. Bruce, David Brower, John W. Bailey, Elisha Bowen, John Blurton, William F. Curier, William L. Crump, James E. Crump, Albert H. Gray, Joseph Gray, James W. Gatlin, James P. Gatlin, William Hodges, Richard Hall, M. F. Jones, Colven Johnson, Taylor Johnson, Henry Jacoby, Samuel J. Jewett, William H. Lile, Cicero E. Mann, David Manier, Albert Manier, O. S. Middleton, John Manier, John N. Middleton, John Needom, George W. Ow, William H. Owen, William J. Phillips, L. J. Raridon, David B. Ray, Samuel P. Roberts, F. M. Rhoads, Timothy D. Simmons, Elias Speer, Francis Simeral, Nicholas Sloop, Joseph Wickham and Thomas H. Woods.

Afterward, on the 13th of February, 1865, a certificate of the commanding officer of the Thirty-ninth Regiment, Missouri Volunteers, containing the names of all persons who had enlisted under the aforesaid call, in Company K, of said regiment, to whom bounties from Schuyler County were due, was filed with the county court, whereupon it was ordered that orders for the sum of $50 each be issued to each of the volunteers, as follows: Isaac Andrews, Sol. Bass, Thomas Chamberlain, Thomas Coe, Charles P. Everly, F. M. Hughes, William C. Meader, Robert Taylor, Henry

Watkins, Sam M. White and Henry Winkler. And at the same time orders for $30 each were issued to the following named volunteers, to wit: John Burns, Camel Edwards, Wilber D. French, Fred Gardner, William F. Hartman, Wilson H. Hixon, John J. Israel, William C. Kelley, G. W. Koons, James M. Knight, George Murrell, Samuel Murrell, Robert Mayes, David G. Mayes, John Reed and Andrew J. White.

Recapitulation.—Company G, Forty-second Missouri Volunteers, sixteen men at $50 each, $800; Company G, Forty-second Missouri Volunteers, forty-one men at $30 each, $1,230; Company K, Thirty-ninth Missouri Volunteers, eleven men at $50 each, $550; Company K, Thirty-ninth Missouri Volunteers, sixteen men at $30 each, $480; total amount of first orders issued, $3,060.

Afterward, in accordance with the original order of the county court in offering bounties to volunteers, the same amount as shown in the foregoing statements was paid upon orders, to each volunteer or his "legal agent" at the close of his term of service, or upon presentation of his "honorable discharge;" consequently, to ascertain the total amount paid out by the county as bounties to soldiers, the total amount as shown above must be doubled, which makes the sum of $6,120. The offer and payment of these bounties was made to save the county from a draft, which otherwise would have been made by the Federal authorities.

CITIES, TOWNS, ETC.

Tippecanoe.—This town was established a number of years before Schuyler County was organized, and was the first town in the territory of which the county is now composed. It was located about two and a half miles southeast of Lancaster. In 1840 John M. Fish and Edwin French opened a store at Tippecanoe with a small stock of goods, but sufficient to supply the few settlers in the surrounding country. Their business increased with the increasing settlements until they had an extensive patronage. In 1846 they dissolved partnership, but both continued in business at Tippecanoe. In 1850 French quit business, and went to California, and in 1852 he returned and opened a store in Lancaster. Fish, after dissolving partnership with French, formed a partnership with Sargent and Gibson, and the new firm had great financial ability, and did an extensive business until 1852, when Fish retired and moved to Iowa. The same year that Fish & French began business John Jones erected a wool carding mill near Tippecanoe, to which was added a run of buhrs for grinding corn. Soon after the above firm began business at Tippecanoe other industries were established, such as blacksmithing and wagon-making by Samuel Tipton and William Schofield; milling by Lesley & Waldrip; cabinet work by Charles M. London, who at one time employed twelve men and boys in his shop.

The most renowned and extensive manufactory in Tippecanoe was the "Wheat Fanning Mill Establishment" of Dixon & Ralls, who employed probably twenty-five men and boys in the manufacture of their fanning mills and "cupboard safes." They also employed several two-horse teams to haul their goods to market. There were also two corner groceries at Tippecanoe, and two attorneys, Stephen C. Thompson and Richard Caywood. The town prospered for a number of years, and was at one time a rival of Lancaster for the seat of justice; from 1846 to 1854 it did a heavy business, and then it began to go down, and has since become so completely overshadowed that it has no existence now except in name and memory.

Lancaster.—The origin of the town of Lancaster, the county seat of Schuyler County, has been given on another page under the head of "County Seat." The first house in Lancaster was a log cabin, built in the southeast part thereof by Judge James C. Cochrane; and it was in this house where the county court in July, 1845, held its first session in the established county seat. The first store house was built by Manuel Richardson and Samuel Ow, in the spring of 1846, for a man by the name of Kent. The roof, counter and shelves were all made of clapboards. The same season James Bryant built the first hotel, a story and a half log building, which is still standing near the northeast corner of the square. He shortly after put up a store room on the corner; it is also one of the few old landmarks left. Thomas McCormack built a store house, and brought on a stock of goods the next year. William Buford and Shelton M.

Grimes shortly afterward brought on a stock of goods. James
C. Cochrane opened the first grocery in the town, in a one-story
log house on the southeast corner of the public square; and at
the October term, 1846, of the county court, he obtained " license
to keep a tavern at his house in Lancaster," and he had to pay
$10 into the State fund, and $5 into the county fund, for such
license. The early merchants already named were followed in
that business by Edward Trabue, William S. Thatcher, S. M.
Grimes, Thomas Jeffries, Alverson, Lindsey & Dennis, Buford &
Grimes, Garges & Lindsey, Foster & Grier, Rector & Melvin,
W. P. Owens & Co., Jeffries & Bradley, and Edwin French.
The latter commenced in 1852, after returning from California.
The above comprises the leading merchants of the town from its
incipiency to the war period. They were not, however, all doing
business at one time; some of them dropped out from time to
time, while others continued until compelled to close on account
of the war.

Among the early settlers and business and professional men
of Lancaster, may be mentioned the following: Don C. Roberts,
one of the first physicians, settled in 1845, and was only eighteen
years of age, but had his diploma, and soon became famous as a
physician and surgeon, and also as a brilliant orator. He represented the county twice in the Legislature, and when the war
came on he joined Price's army as a surgeon, and at the close of
hostilities he went to Utah, and died in Provost City on Christmas
day, 1884. Yelverton Payton established a tanyard in what has
since been known as Gray's meadow, and for a time did an extensive business, but no traces of the establishment now remain.
Asa Leedom settled in Lancaster in 1848, and opened a tailor shop.
Dr. Jason Brown settled near Lancaster in 1852, and moved into the
town in 1856; and George W. Melvin, the present efficient and
accommodating postmaster, became a citizen of Lancaster in 1853.
The same year Moses Baker came from Kentucky and settled in
the town, and in 1856 Wesley Farrel came from Maryland and
established a tan-yard in the south part of the town, near where
the railroad is now located, but did not continue it long. The
first 4th of July celebration was held in the year 1845, half a
mile north of the town of Lancaster, in the old barbecue style,

and Isaac N. Ebey delivered the oration.   Dr. George W. Johnson read the declaration of independence, and William Blansett beat the drum, and everybody enjoyed themselves hugely.   This celebration was followed for a number of years by celebrating the 4th in the good old style of contributions by the citizens and a barbecue dinner gotten up on the ground.   The latter-day style of picnics was then unknown.

From 1857 to 1861 there was more business done in Lancaster than in any of the neighboring towns, Memphis, Kirksville or Bloomfield, but in 1861 and 1862 it was almost entirely depopulated of its male inhabitants, as nearly all of them went into the Rebel army, or moved to other parts.   At the close of the war it began to recover, and in 1866 the business of the town was conducted by the following parties: General stores by J. F. Fenton, J. N. Shelton, Gildard & Figge, Edwin French & Co., William B. Hays, Baker & Melvin (post-office store); drug stores—Lambert & Baker and T. B. Jones; boots and shoes—J. N. Shelton, A. Royer; family grocery—W. H. Starrett; saddles and harness—Sizemore & Hooyer; stoves and tinware—C. Frederick; meat market—John Dirigo; wagon and plow factory—M. Shaffer; cabinet shop—M. Baker; blacksmith shop—Steete & Thompson.

On the 2d of October, 1873, the citizens of Lancaster met at the court-house, and adopted articles of incorporation for a hotel company.   Directors were elected for the first year, consisting of Edwin French, C. Figge Jr., A. Royer, William Casper and W. B. Hays.   The capital stock was limited to $5,000, and it was decided to use $3,000 to build a hotel.   The proposed location was one block west of the public square, on the way to the depot but it was subsequently changed to the southeast corner of the square, when the present two-story brick block, with double store room on the first floor and the hotel on the second, was erected soon thereafter.   The large stone and brick flouring-mill of William Schaefer & Co. was erected in 1874, and in December of the same year the "First National Bank of Lancaster" was organized, and began business in January, 1875, with a capital of $50,000, C. H. Howell of Centerville, Iowa, being president, Edwin French of Lancaster, vice-president, and C. Figge, cashier.   The directors were C. H. Howell, C. Figge, R. S.

Justice, Ed. Higbee, Edwin French, C. H. French and William A. Coffey. This bank was succeeded in January, 1877, by the Schuyler County Bank, with Edwin French, president; H. S. Justice, vice-president, and C. Figge, cashier. The present officers were elected January 7, 1885, as follows: L. Schmidt, president; C. H. French, vice-president, and C. Figge, cashier. The present board of directors are C. Burkland, R. Caywood, C. H. French, S. A. Dysart, C. Figge and L. Schmidt.

To show how the town of Lancaster recovered during the first ten years after the close of the Civil War, the following business directory for January 1, 1876, is here given: Dry goods and general merchandise—W. A. Richardson, E. French & Co., Brunk & Son, W. B. Hays, A. Royer; groceries—W. P. Murphy, Evans & Dysart, Summerlin & Co., G. W. Melvin; hardware—G. W. Melvin, Evans & Dysart; drugs—Niblack & Locey, B. B. Potter & Co., J. W. Brown, F. W. Mueller; boots and shoes—Jack Town, C. C. Hooyer, John Grist, H. A. Farris; millinery—Mrs. M. Barns; hotels—Lancaster Hotel, by Brunk & Son; livery—W. H. Starrett, Stretch Bros.; furniture—F. D. Nater; photo gallery—Mrs. H. A. Farris; saddles and harness—Garrett Hooyer; lumber yard—Lee & Wirth; cabinet shop—R. K. Grant; flouring-mills—William Schaefer & Co.; wagon and blacksmith shops—Scholz & Heller, Jos. Baumer, I. L. Anderson, Graves & Steele; stoves and tinware—C. Frederick; restaurants—Mr. Lane, T. H. Dillon; jewelry—D. Hamilton. In addition to the foregoing, there was the First National Bank; two churches—Methodist and Christian; one school-house; a lodge each of Masons and Odd Fellows, nine lawyers and five doctors, and a good supply of mechanics.

To show how the business of the town has increased since 1876, and of what it consists at the present writing, the following is inserted: General stores—Murphy & Miller, W. C. Graves, A. P. Primm, F. P. Hays & Co.; drugs and books—Elias Crim, Dr. John Reid; hardware and agricultural implements—George W. Melvin, Daniel Bunnell, P. C. Hays; stoves and tinware—Carl C. Frederick; harness and saddles—Garrett Hooyer; restaurants—John M. Taylor, A. J. Ballew; wagon and blacksmith shops—William Roberts, Joseph Baumer; millinery and dress-making—Miss Hays & Miss Dillon, Mrs. Mary W. Barnes; hotels—Lancaster Hotel, by C. B. Royer; boarding houses—H. T. Arnold, Mrs. Sallie Nutter, Mrs. Ann E. Sizemore, Mrs. Bettie Royer; carpenter shop—James Essex; saloon—Louis Schmit; billiard hall—H. T. Arnold; meat market—Shoemake & Hern; photo gallery—W. F. Bunch; barber shop—W. S. Mulady; lumber yard—McNulty & Roberts, Charles Wirth; livery stables—Stretch Bros., W. H. Starrett; blacksmith shop—Frank Sholty; furniture—R. G. Huston; boot and shoe shops—Jack Town, John W. Grist; flouring-mills—William Schaffer; saw and corn-mill—Turner & Evans; insurance agents—T. C. Tadlock, W. M. Hunter, E. L. Mitchell, J. L. Baker; real estate agents—Fogle & Hunter, Shelton & Dysart.

In addition to the foregoing, the two firms of Murphy & Miller and F. P. Hays & Co. each have grain warehouses, and deal extensively in grain. There are also two banks, the Schuyler County Bank, of which mention has heretofore been made, and the Hays Banks, which was established in 1886 with a paid up capital of $10,000, and of which William B. Hays is president, and Frank P. Hays, cashier. There is also a cheese factory, established by a joint stock company; and one of the leading enterprises is the celebrated stud of imported stallions and thoroughbred horses, kept by Becraft & Co. This company has over $7,000 invested in their horses. They also have an imported Holstein bull. The town also contains two printing presses and two newspapers, *The Excelsior* and the Lancaster *Republican*, two churches—Christian and Methodist—one large and commodious school-house, the Lancaster Medical Infirmary, and the railroad depot, etc.

Physicians.—Among the first physicians of Lancaster was Daniel Roberts, the father of Dr. Don C. Roberts, of whom mention has been made. Daniel Roberts was an able practitioner and continued to practice in Lancaster and vicinity until his death, which occurred in 1865. Dr. Warner resided near Tippecanoe, and practiced from about 1845 to 1851, and then went to Oregon. Dr. George W. Johnson was also one of the very early physicians of Lancaster, and Drs. Fort and Mains settled in the town about the year 1848, and practiced only a few years. Dr.

Cochran, a very prominent physician, practiced in Lancaster from 1850 to about 1858. Dr. Cantley Stewart settled in Lancaster about 1858, and practiced until 1862, and later went to Texas, where he died two years ago. Dr. William Moore practiced at Lancaster from about 1855 to 1859. Dr. R. J. Christie came from Maryland and settled in Lancaster, in 1857, where he practiced until 1861, and then became a surgeon in the Confederate Army, and at the close of the war he located in Monticello, in Lewis County, Mo., and afterward went to Pueblo, Col., then returned to Monticello, and afterward located in Quincy, Ill., where he now resides. He is a noted physician and surgeon. The present physicians and surgeons of Lancaster are William F. Mitchell, B. B. Potter, H. S. Justice, W. F. Justice and Jason W. Brown. For information pertaining to the attorneys of Lancaster see Bench and Bar, and also Biographical Department of this work.

Incorporation.—Lancaster was incorporated by a special act of the Legislature, in 1857, and some amendments to the charter have since been made, so that at the present writing the government of the town consists of a mayor, council and other officers. The present officers are as follows: Edward Higbee, mayor; John H. Evans, marshal; Charles W. Bunch, secretary; Charles Wirth, treasurer.

The members of the council are W. P. Murphy, Elias Crim, Dr. W. F. Mitchell, Charles Wirth and Charles W. Bunch. The town is in good financial condition, being entirely out of debt; and though it is larger than at any former period of its existence, it is still a small town, having a population of about 800. The completion of the railroads has caused so many other towns or villages to spring up in the county that neither of them can ever expect to become very large. Each will command the trade of its own locality, and thus prevent a concentration of business at any one point.

Societies.—*Lodge of Love, No. 59, A. F. & A. M.*, at Lancaster, Mo., was chartered about the year 1857, and on the 24th of June, 1858, the corner-stone of the hall of the lodge was laid with appropriate ceremonies. The building containing the lodge room or hall was erected one block north of the northeast corner of the public square where it is still standing in a good state of preservation. It is a two-story frame building, set upon a stone foundation, with the Masonic hall on the second floor; the first story being now occupied by *The Excelsior* printing press. Among the charter members of this lodge were Dr. W. A. Cochran, I. B. Alverson, William Buford, Dr. Daniel Roberts and his son, Dr. Don C. Roberts, Samuel Merrel and others. The members of the lodge labored in harmony until after the Civil War closed, and then, on account of a disturbing element which had gained admission to it, the charter was surrendered to the Grand Lodge, in order to get an opportunity to reorganize without such disturbing element; and afterward a new charter, No. 259, was granted, under which the lodge now exists. The present officers are Edward Higbee, W. M.; De N. Jewett, S. W.; H. S. Justice, J. W.; Richard Caywood, Sec.; W. B. Hays, Treas.; E. Eggers and E. F. Payton, Deacons; F. P. Hays and T. P. Line, Stewards; Henry Eichmire, Tyler. The lodge owns the Masonic building, mentioned, is in good financial condition, and the members thereof labor in peace and harmony.

Schuyler Lodge, No. 117, I. O. O. F., was instituted in 1859, and during the Civil War the charter was sent to the Grand Lodge for safe keeping, and the work of the lodge suspended until the close of that conflict, after which the charter was returned, and the work resumed. This lodge has forty-five members at the present writing, and it owns a large and well-furnished hall in the second story of the brick block east of the southeast corner of the court-yard; the first store being occupied by Murphy & Miller, merchants. This hall was erected in 1886, and cost the lodge about $2,000. The society is out of debt, in good financial condition, and since its organization it has expended over $2,500 for charitable purposes. The present officers of the lodge are as follows: John C. Mills, N. G.; William L. Casper, V. G.; C. C. Fogle, Sec.; P. C. Hays, Treas.

Lancaster Lodge, No. 236, A. O. U. W., was organized under a charter dated December 2, 1881. The charter members were De N. Jewett, W. P. Leedom, W. P. Murphy, O. D. Caywood, H. A. Miller, W. C. Jeffries, John W. Grist, Henry Eichmire, Edward Mott, Thomas H. Dillon, Dr. W. F. Mitchell, Elias

Crim, J. M. Knott, Frank A. Irvin, P. C. Hays, N. T. Roberts, Nat. M. Shelton, Ben. R. Melvin, W. S. McGoldrick, T. P. Leedom, John J. Slighton, Henry A. Leyhe and John Sisler. The present officers are De N. Jewett, M. W.; George W. Ferrey, For.; Charles Burkland, Over.; John W. Grist, F.; Elias Crim, Receiver; William P. Leedom, Rec.; William Mulady, Guide; P. C. Hays, P. M. W.; William P. Leedom, Lodge Deputy, and W. F. Mitchell, representative to Grand Lodge, with P. C. Hays, alternate. This lodge has a present membership of thirty-one, and it meets in the city hall over Crim's drug store. Its financial condition is good.

T. H. Richardson Post, No. 92, G. A. R.—This post was organized under a charter dated June 30, 1883. The charter members were T. H. Dillon, A. Zugg, W. H. Starrett, A. L. Merrick, J. M. Taylor, W. P. Leedom, A. P. Primm, W. B. Wayland, G. W. McClellen, E. R. Kirkpatrick, J. L. Anderson, S. J. Jewett, A. J. Booth, Edward Ball, T. N. West and Leonard Schaffer. The present officers are A. L. Merrick, P. C.; Z. A. Macomber, S. V.; James B. Hackett, J. V.; John C. Caywood, Surg.; E. R. Kirkpatrick, O. D.; W. P. Leedom, Q. M.; S. J. Jewett, O. G.; E. R. Kirkpatrick, Adjt.; J. F. Mellender, Chap. The post has twenty-eight members, and is in good financial standing. It meets in the city hall.

The Press.—The first newspaper published in Schuyler County was the Lancaster *Herald*, established at Lancaster, in 1856 by Huon Jackson, of La Grange, Mo., who continued its publication about a year, and then sold it to Wilber Wells, who published it about two years longer. It was succeeded in 1859 by the Lancaster *Democrat*, which was established by Mains & Elder, and published by them until the year 1861, when it was discontinued on account of the war. From that date there was no paper published in the county until 1866, when Capt. H. D'B. Cutler established the *Weekly Lancaster Excelsior*, a Republican paper, at Lancaster. Some time thereafter he associated with himself Capt. F. M. Wilcox, and by them the paper was published until 1871, when they sold it to Samuel Dysart and Henry A. Miller, who changed its politics, and made it Democratic. The latter afterward purchased the interest of Mr. Dysart, and continued to publish the paper until September, 1883, when he sold it to W. M. Hunter, who has since and still continues its publication. It is now printed on a steam power press, and is named *The Excelsior*, the word weekly having been dropped from the head of the paper. It is a forty-eight-column-paper, the pages being 15x22 inches in size, and is ably edited, and has a large circulation. The Lancaster *Republican* was established in Lancaster by Grant M. Potter, and the first number was issued on the 30th of December, 1887. It is a twenty-eight-column paper, and starts out with Republican principles.

Additions to Lancaster.—French's addition to Lancaster was laid out by Edwin French in August, 1855. It contains twelve lots in all, and lies south of and adjoining the southwest part of the original plat of the town. Dr. Potter's medical infirmary stands on this addition.

Buford & Wilson's addition was laid out in July, 1856. It contains four blocks containing twenty lots in all, and lies north of and adjoining the northwest part of the original town. It is not improved, being almost void of buildings. The foregoing additions were surveyed by Richard Caywood.

Ow's addition was laid out by Samuel Ow in March, 1857. It contains six blocks—three of nine lots each, and three of sixteen lots each—and lies east of and adjoining the original plat between Jackson and Monroe Streets.

Rector's addition was laid out in May, 1857, by Bennett Rector. It contains three blocks or thirteen lots in all, and adjoins the original town on the west, and lies on the north side of Washington Street.

Watson's addition was laid out in May, 1857. It contains four blocks of ten lots each, and lies directly south of Rector's addition, and joins the original town plat on the west. The railroad right of way runs through the north half of it.

Thatcher's addition was laid out in July, 1865, by William S. Thatcher. It has two blocks, and contains thirty-three lots in all, and lies south of the old town plat and east of French's addition.

Downing's addition was laid out in April, 1873, by James Raly and Edwin French as trustees of the Lancaster Real Estate

Company. It contains more land than the original town and all the other additions together, that is, by including its several out-lots of several acres each. It lies northwest of the old town, and contains the railroad depot, flouring-mill and a number of fine residences.

Glenwood, situated on the north branch of the St. Louis, Kansas City & Nebraska Railroad, about five miles south of the State line, and two miles west of Lancaster, was laid out in November, 1868, by Stiles E. and Alexander Forsha. The original plat of the town contains a public square and forty-four other blocks.

Forsha's addition to Glenwood comprising a tract of land both north and east of the original plat, and containing a large number of lots of several acres each, was laid out in January, 1870.

Freemon's addition, containing twenty-four blocks, mostly of eight lots each, and lying immediately south of the original plat of Glenwood, was laid out by Leon Freemon in May, 1871.

Potter, Hughes & Forsha's addition to Glenwood, lying west and northwest of the original plat, and reaching to the junction of the aforesaid railroad with the Keokuk & Western Railway, was laid out in September, 1874, by the Glenwood Real Estate Association.

The first dwelling house in Glenwood was built by John B. Glaze in October, 1868. S. E. Forsha erected a storehouse in October and November of the same year, also a number of dwelling houses, and a school-house the following winter. The town was incorporated in the spring of 1869, but after a few years the corporation was abolished. Also, in 1869, a two-story brick block, with four storerooms, was erected, and the following year Buford & Neely built and started a large woolen factory, and the foundry and machine shop of Dunbar Bros. was erected about the same time. From this time forward, and for a number of years, the town grew rapidly, and in 1873 the business men and merchants were John Scovern, Stanley & Forsha, J. N. Shelton, Forsha & Irvin, William Moore, Chattan & Forsha, H. D'B. Cutler, George Eldridge, W. C. Trew, C. W. Walton, P. F. Swarts, A. H. Lane and Joseph Kitering.

Glenwood has suffered many heavy losses by fire. The flour-ing-mill was burned down in 1870, and has since been rebuilt.

The foundry has been burned down and rebuilt twice; also a wagon factory, which has been rebuilt. On the 5th of April, 1877, a fire originated in the lumber sheds, near the railroad depot, and from the sheds a train of box cars took fire, and two of them were consumed and three damaged. From the cars the fire went to S. E. Forsha's stable, and a long warehouse containing about seventy tons of hay and a quantity of corn, salt, lime, cement, dried fruits, agricultural implements, etc., nearly all of which were consumed; next the fire reached the large store building of S. E. Forsha, which contained several thousand dollars' worth of goods. The goods, however, were all removed except two heavy safes, which remained in the fire. The total loss was estimated as follows: The lumber shed and contents, owned by S. E. Forsha, $1,100; box cars, $1,200; stables, $200; warehouse and contents, $2,500; agricultural implements on commission, $300; storeroom, $1,500; contents of storeroom and goods lost and damaged, $950. The latter belonged to Logan & Co. Some boys had been playing cards in the lumber shed where the fire originated.

The following is a summary of the business of Glenwood, at the present writing:

Dry goods and groceries—Blackwood & Hombs, E. E. Hale & Bro., C. A. Hays and V. C. Rose; groceries—A. J. Greenwell, William Coburn and G. W. Ballew; drugs, books and stationery—Spencer & Gray and Jones Bros.; boots and shoes—William Coburn; restaurant—G. W. Ballew; notions—J. Coons; millinery and notions—Mrs. F. Beard and Miss Nellie Buford; hardware, stoves, harness and lumber—W. Chattin & Bro.; hardware, stoves and queensware—C. Smith; hardware, stoves, queensware and saddlery—A. Campbell; dressmaking—Misses Maize & Magee, and Mrs. L. C. Hanson; livery—L. H. Case and Shattuck & Davis; billiard hall and lunch counter—T. S. Lewis; jewelry—C. W. Walton; sewing machine repairer—Jesse Jones; furniture—J. Kitering; barber—E. Johnson.

In addition to the foregoing, there is the extensive woolen factory of A. J. Williams, the foundry and machine shop of Dunbar Bros., the roller process flouring-mills of Stanley & Bickle, the wagon and blacksmith shop of Ben. F. Woodson, the handle factory of John Storm, the handle factory and cooper shop of John McMinn, the marble shop of W. P. Mullins, and the large, commodious and well-kept St. Nicholas Hotel, I. W. Stanley, proprietor. H. D'B. Cutler is a notary public and insurance agent, with office in Logan's bank; and G. D. Gray runs a land, loan and insurance office upstairs, near the bank. The physicians and surgeons of Glenwood are J. H. Rambo and J. T. Jones; and the dental surgeons are L. V. White, H. C. Rowe and A. B. Johnson. There is also a good railroad depot, and at the junction, nearly a mile from Glenwood proper, there is a railroad depot and eating house combined, and also a small railroad repair shop. Glenwood contains about 700 inhabitants.

Logan's Bank.—This bank was established in January, 1875, by C. H. Howell, of Centerville, Iowa. He sold it in January, 1877, to Capt. H. D'B. Cutler, and in May, 1882, the latter sold it to William Logan, the present owner. The capital stock is $10,000, and the accumulated surplus on the 1st of January, 1888, was $46,814.49, and the amount of the deposits at the same time was $129,672.20.

The Press.—The Glenwood *Criterion* was established in 1870, by Messrs. Cutler & Wilcox, and in 1872 Cutler became sole proprietor, and continued the publication of the paper, with the exception of one year (1876), until July, 1884, when he sold it to G. D. Gray, who published it about a year, and then sold it to Grant M. Potter. The latter ran it six months, and then sold it to G. C. Miller and others, who conveyed it, in May, 1887, to W. D. Powell, the present editor and publisher. During the year of the campaign of 1876 it was published by H. Martin Williams, in the interest of the Democratic party, and, with this exception, it has always been published in the interest of the Republican party. It is a five-column folio, is ably edited, and has a large circulation.

Societies.—*Glenwood Lodge No. 427, A. F. & A. M.*, was organized under a charter dated October 17, 1873. Among its charter members were W. C. C. Steele, W. M.; Stephen Caywood, S. W.; W. F. Staples, J. W.; Aseph Dunbar and William Buford. The present officers are William Logan, W. M.; O. B. Spencer, S. W.; H. A. Jones, J. W.; A. H. F. Smith, Treas.; H. D'B. Cutler,

SCHUYLER COUNTY, MISSOURI 135

****

Sec.; G. R. Hombs, S. D.; V. C. Rose, J. D.; and M. Kennedy, Tyler.

Glenwood Lodge, No. 233, I. O. O. F., was instituted at Glenwood under charter dated May 17, 1870. The charter members were G. D. Gray, Hufty Dye, Henry Chattin, Leroy Hays and Charles Daniel. The present officers are C. W. Walton, N. G.; J. H. Rambo, V. G.; J. P. Stewart, Rec. Sec.; G. D. Gray, Per. Sec., and W. Chattin, Treas. This lodge and Glenwood Lodge, No. 427, A. F. & A. M., own one of the finest halls outside of the large cities. It was erected jointly by the two lodges in 1885 at a cost of about $1,600. It consists of the second story of a brick block containing two large store rooms on the first floor. The hall contains ample reception and preparation rooms and other conveniences, and is used by all the secret societies of the town.

Glenwood Encampment, No. 34, was instituted under a charter dated May 23, 1873, and the charter members were John Baker, G. D. Gray, F. T. Hughs, A. J. Baker, Wesley Ferrell and A. K. Cowgill.

Libby Lodge, No. 71, Daughters of Rebekah.—The charter members of this lodge were G. D. Gray, O. Thompson, James W. Howard, Robert N. Bartlett, Henry Chattin, William Chattin, Emma Gray, Cornelia Thompson, Hattie L. Howard, M. P. Bartlett and Mary Chattin. This lodge is auxiliary to Glenwood Lodge, No. 233, I. O. O. F.

Glenwood Lodge, No. 301, A. O. U. W., was organized under charter dated January 11, 1884. The charter members were F. M. Rose, William Chattin, John H. Rambo, M. A. Brann, M. M. Mann, A. D. Johnson, G. D. Gray, W. E. Beemer, A. H. Sears and Myron U. Mann. The officers for 1888 are A. B. Johnson, M. W.; J. H. Rambo, Foreman; William Chattin, Overseer; G. D. Gray, R.; H. Chattin, Financier; J. H. Rambo, Receiver; H. W. O'Briant, Guide; H. W. Smith, O. S. W.; John W. Bryan, I. S. W.; W. Chattin, Rep. Grand Lodge; J. H. Rambo, Alternate; A. J. Tisdale, Trustee for three years.

David A. Roberts Post, No 25, G. A. R., was established under charter dated August 24, 1882. The charter members were H. D'B. Cutler, G. D. Gray, O. Thompson, Henry Mulch, G. N.

Bradley, H. Clay Woodson, Alvis H. Boze, J. Ross Brown, G. Matherson, Jesse Jones, George Daniels and W. Hole. The officers for 1888 are T. B. Dodson, P. C.; William Hole, S. V.; W. Crump, J. V.; G. D. Gray, Q. M.; G. N. Bradley, Surg.; A. H. Boze, Chap.; A. J. Tisdale, O. D.; F. M. Hughs, O. G.; A. J. Tisdale, Del. State Encampment; G. D. Gray, Alternate; C. D. B. Austin, Adjt.

The Woman's Relief Corps, No. 33, since organized, and auxiliary to the foregoing post, had the following charter members: Mrs. Agnes Austin, Mrs. Catharine Johnson, Mrs. Carrie Tisdale, Mrs. Mary Boze, Mrs. Mary M. Coburn, Mrs. Evaline Stanley, Mrs. Carrie Cutler, Mrs. Hattie Howard, Mrs. Harriet E. Jones, Mrs. Harriet Owens and Misses Frankie McDowell, Kittie Allen, Annie Hale, Emma Woodson and Mrs. Carrie Hays and Mrs. Catharine Dodson.

All of the foregoing societies are in good financial condition, and all are laboring harmoniously to promote the objects for which they were organized.

Downing.—This town is situated on the Keokuk & Western Railroad, three-fourths of a mile west of the east line of Schuyler County. It was laid out for the Missouri Town Company by H. H. Downing, president thereof, in September, 1872. The original plat of the town contains thirty-five blocks, mostly of twelve lots each. Lockett's addition to Downing, containing two blocks of twelve lots each, was laid out in August, 1887, by H. W. Lockett. The first merchants of Downing were Collins & Clapper, LeGrand & Gamble, D. L. Ringler, W. F. Petty and Stephen Gnash. In January, 1874, a fire got too close to a keg of powder in Dr. Petty's drug store, and it exploded, and burst the building wide open, and set it on fire. It was consumed, and the loss was about $1,000. The town has had substantial prosperity, and the business thereof at the present writing is shown by the following list of merchants and business men, and the several business enterprises: General stores—William A. Barbee, John M. Smith, W. H. Bailey & Son and N. A. Lane; drug stores—McCanlass & Gamble and Dr. W. B. Smith; hardware—Camp Cowell and E. Fraker; groceries—Robert Boss and J. C. Carroll; furniture—John S. Isaacs; restaurant—J. B.

Mudd; saloon—Freshwater & Lockett; wagon maker—A. M. Todd; blacksmith—James E. Pulliam; handle factories—Morgan & Co., and Stacey, Pool & Co.; confectionery and meat market—George Whitlock; harness and saddles—Robert T. Gamble; millinery—Mrs. Ann Clapper.

In addition to the foregoing, N. A. Lane and Bailey & Son have each a grain house and a tobacco warehouse, and both do an extensive business in buying grain and tobacco. There are two saw and corn-mills combined, and owned and run respectively by S. Barker and Shackelford & Co. The latter firm has also a hoop factory. There are also two hotels kept respectively by J. P. Smith and D. D. Freshwater. The physicians of the town are W. B. Smith, W. H. E. Bondurant, James Bridges and W. G. Payton. Of the secret societies, there is a lodge each of Masons, Odd Fellows and Triple Alliance. Downing is a thriving town, and the shipments therefrom of grain, tobacco and live stock, have become extensive, and are rapidly increasing. The two houses that deal in tobacco have ample facilities for the transaction of the business, and the farmers in the surrounding country have recently engaged extensively in the cultivation of that article. It is claimed that more tobacco is shipped from Downing than from any single station in a large territory surrounding it. The town contains two church buildings, one owned by the Christian denomination, and the other by the Methodist Episcopal Church and the Methodist Episcopal Church South. There are also two school-houses, both on the same lot, for the use of the public schools.

Queen City.—This town is situated on the St. Louis, Kansas City & Northern Railway, in Prairie Township, in Schuyler County, about eight miles south of Glenwood, and four miles north of Green Top. It was laid out in May, 1867, by Dr. George W. Wilson, and, according to the plat thereof, it contains a public square and fifteen other blocks, containing 178 lots in all.

In December, 1868, the railroad addition to Queen City was laid out by Lewis W. Coe and William B. Hays, and in May, 1876, another addition, containing eight blocks, was laid out by Dr. Wilson. The first house in the town was built by Dr. Wilson, and the first hotel by Henry Bartlett.   The merchants of the town in 1873 were George Bamberger, W. B. Hays, Jacoby & Co., Herman Herboth and C. W. Hight; but the following in regard to the business at the present writing will show how the town has since improved: There are five general stores, kept respectively by Miller Bros., Herman Herboth, Dufer Bros., S. Perin and J. H. Morris; two drug stores, by O. W. Avery and C. W. Wright; two hardware stores, by P. Schwartz and John Sloop; two grocery stores, by John Sloop and Capt. Patterson; two hotels, by S. Perin and Miller & Shipley; two wagon and blacksmith shops, by George Lauer & Son and John Diehl; an extensive harness and saddle store, with shoe shop attached, by J. H. Ryan; a stove and tinware store, by F. J. Biggs; a music and millinery store, by F. M. Powers; a millinery store, by Mrs. Jennie Dotson; a jewelry store, by Mr. Shupert; a lumber yard, by John Sloop; a gunsmith shop, by John Blurton; a barber shop, by O. M. Crapson; a photograph gallery, by Joseph Kent; two livery stables, by Shipman & Lyle, and Crapson & Bass; and last, but perhaps not the least frequented place, a saloon, by J. H. Ryan.

In addition to the foregoing, there is the flouring-mill of John Humes, and the grain houses of J. H. Morris and John Sloop, both of whom deal extensively in grain; and John Bowen deals in grain and hay.   There are also two church buildings, owned respectively by the Methodist Episcopal Church and the Methodist Episcopal Church South, and one public school building.   The physicians of Queen City are A. W. Parrish, J. O. Coffey and O. W. Avery.   The town is situated in the midst of a good agricultural country, and so far away from any strong competing point that its prosperity for the future is assured. The annual shipments of grain, live stock, railroad ties, and hoops, are quite extensive.   The ties and hoops are obtained principally from the timber country along the Chariton River.

The Queen City *Transcript*, a six-column folio newspaper, was established early in November, 1887, by D. G. Swan.   It is neutral in politics.

Queen City Lodge, No. 380, A. F. & A. M., was organized under charter dated October 13, 1871, and the charter members were Jacob Miller, Jacob D. Miller, J. D. Galloway, H. M.

Jacoby, G. A. Wilson, F. E. Jacoby, James Carter and R. D. Gardener. The present officers are Thomas W. Henton, W. M.; D. J. Tipton, S. W.; James P. Logan, J. W.; J. G. Miller, Sec.; H. H. Brenizer, Treas.; James Carter, S. D.; John Black, J. D., and J. H. Walker, Tyler.

Green Top.—This village is situated on the St. Louis, Kansas City & Northern Railway, at the south line of the county. It was surveyed and laid out in April, 1857, by Stephen Caywood, for George W. Gatlin, the proprietor. According to the plat then made, it contained a public square and eighteen other blocks, containing 168 lots in all. An addition thereto, containing ten blocks, was laid out in February, 1870, by William A. Sickles and others. It has considerable trade in railroad ties and hoop poles from the Chariton timber, and is conveniently accessible to coal on the west. It has never improved to any considerable extent. In 1873 it contained the following named merchants and business men: Evoe Mullanix, David Wells, S. W. Wright and A. L. Bledsoe. It was incorporated in February, 1867, under the name and style of the "Town of Green Top," and the directors appointed were G. W. Gatlin, W. S. Gatlin, G. P. Blaze, Jacob Witmer and George Lowre. At the present writing Green Top has two general stores, kept, respectively, by W. B. Reynolds and Tice & Parker; two drug stores, kept, respectively, by W. A. McKeehan and William Van Note; a grocery and the post-office, by N. Spear; a furniture and undertaker's establishment, by Jacob Whitmer, and a hardware and grocery store, by Gatlin Winfree.

Coatsville.—This town is situated on the St. Louis, Kansas City & Northern Railway, at the State line between Missouri and Iowa. It contains, according to the plat thereof, forty-three blocks of different sizes. It was laid out in February, 1869, by Alexander H. Wells, John B. Holbert and James T. Guinn. The following is a business directory of the town in 1874: Dry goods—Hatton & Welch and John F. James; general stores—James F. Fenton and James & Lacker; drugs—Samuel Rhodes, Niblack & Morrow and William B. Gilbert; hotel—John Dowlin; doctors—A. J. Eidson, M. M. Cook and Sarah B. Coffman; also one school-house, in which a good school was being taught by F. R.

Fleagle. Four years later (1878) the town contained two dry goods stores, two drug stores, one grocery, a blacksmith and wagon shop, the school-house and a Missionary Baptist Church, and had a population of about 100. It is said to be a great place in which to get married, and that James Coffman, during his term as a magistrate, married more people than any other magistrate in Missouri, in the same length of time. At the present writing there are two general stores at Coatsville, kept, respectively, by Thomas H. Mitchell and Simmons & Holbert; two drug stores, kept, respectively, by A. J. Eidson and J. L. Tadlock, and a grocery kept by W. F. James. There is also one church and the public school-house.

EDUCATION.

The Log School-house.—Years ago some pioneer settler published in *The Excelsior* the following retrospective view of a backwoods' school-house, fifty years ago: "When enough had settled in a neighborhood, say from three to four miles around, some sage old veteran would suggest to his neighbors the necessity for a school. Then by common consent they met at a convenient place to wood and water, with chopping ax and frow in hand a school-house to build, and while some of them do cut and haul, others hew and maul puncheons for the floor; and at night they have it ready for the school. Then who is to teach comes up. There is one of them who has learned to read and write, and cipher to the rule of three, and he proposes to teach six months if they will raise twenty-five scholars, he to teach for $1.50 per scholar per quarter of thirteen weeks, and board round; if not he must have $1.75 and board himself; in either case the tuition to be paid at the end of each quarter. School commences, and the little fellows have blue primers and wooden back Continental spellers, and the older ones have slates and Dillsworth's or Smiley's arithmetics, and in the bosom of their hunting shirts the English reader; and the school must be taught from an hour after sunrise until an hour before sunset. They are arranged on long benches, and at such places Corwin and many others were educated, and the teacher was paid in coon skins, bear meat, venison, etc."

The foregoing is a fair description of the first efforts of the pioneer settlers on the frontier for the education of their children, as civilization moved westward from the Atlantic coast, where our forefathers landed and built the first rude and rustic log school-houses. Such school-houses continued for many years in all the newly settled portions of the United States, but the teachers who always contracted with the pioneers to teach "reading, writing, and arithmetic to the rule of three," did not continue long in the business of teaching after the public school systems were established and became operative. Fortunately for the pioneers of Schuyler County, there were no teachers among them hedged in by the "Rule of Three," but on the contrary there were many persons among them who were well educated. The first school-house in Schuyler County stood a few miles south of the site of Downing, and close to the county line; and in this rude cabin Miss Hathaway, now the wife of Edwin French, taught the first school in the county in the spring and summer of 1841; and the second school was taught in the summer of the same year by Jesse K. Baird, at the old town of Tippecanoe. In 1842 James Johnson began teaching a school at a point about one mile northeast of the site of Lancaster, and about the middle of the first term he died with hemorrhage of the lungs, and Miss Hathaway was then employed, and she taught the school to its close.

Log school-houses then sprang up in various parts of the territory of the county where there were enough settlers to sustain a school; and after the organization of the county, the first action of the county court preparatory to the establishment of public schools took place at the May special term in 1847, when enumerators were appointed to ascertain the number of white children, of the proper school age, in each of the several townships, as follows: James Hepburn for Liberty, George F. Palmer for Fabius, John Willis for Independence, Benjamin Ray for Wells, George W. Rorhr for Chariton, and John Fayette for Salt River. These, it must be remembered, were the original townships, when Wells and Independence embraced the nine-mile disputed strip of territory. The court then began from time to time to number the congressional townships preparatory to the sale of the public school lands.

Public School Lands.—These lands consisted of the sixteenth section in each congressional township, and were donated by the general Government to the State, when it was admitted into the Union, for the purpose of creating a permanent fund to be loaned to borrowers, and the annual interest thereon to be appropriated for the support of common schools. The State then passed laws regulating the sale of these lands, and by an act of the Legislature, approved March 19, 1835, it was provided that whenever school lands in any congressional township were sold to the amount of $800, the county court should establish school districts therein not exceeding four, and thenceforth the districts so established became a body politic and corporate. The act also provided that school trustees should employ teachers, and keep up schools six months in each year, in which all white children between six and eighteen years of age should be free to enter; and when the income from the aforesaid school fund was not sufficient to keep up the schools six months, the trustees were to apportion the delinquency in proportion to the number of pupils attending the schools, and collect it from their parents or guardians. The same act also provided that all fines and forfeitures collected for the use of the State or county should become a permanent fund for the use and benefit of the schools of the counties where collected.

According to the foregoing law, no public schools could be established until school lands in a single congressional township were sold to the amount of $800, consequently none were established in Schuyler County until several years after it was organized. And the interest on the amount for which any one of the school sections was sold was never sufficient to support a single school for six months, consequently rate bills had to be made out and collected for many years after the county was organized. The aforesaid act of the Legislature laid the foundation for two very important school funds, viz.: "The Permanent Township Public School Fund" and "The Permanent County Public School Fund; the former being derived from the sale of the school lands, and the latter from the accumulation of fines, forfeitures, etc.

The sale of the school lands in Schuyler County began the

same year that it was organized, and continued from time to time until all were sold, excepting a very small tract in Township 65 north, Range 16 west, which still remains unsold, and at the same time the loaning of the proceeds commenced, the first loan being made to James C. Cochran. The principal of this loan was $50, and the fund belonged to Township 65 north, Range 15 west. The loan was made for twelve months, and the interest was charged at 10 per cent. The second loan was made to David Floyd, the amount being $113.50, for one year, at the same rate of interest. The amount received from the sale of the school lands in each congressional township in Schuyler County, together with the aggregate amount, is as follows:

Township 64 north, Range 13 west.....................$	131 40
Township 65 north, Range 13 west.....................	506 79
Township 66 north, Range 13 west.....................	345 97
Township 67 north, Range 13 west.....................	13 32
Township 64 north, Range 14 west.....................	638 00
Township 65 north, Range 14 west.....................	948 80
Township 66 north, Range 14 west.....................	477 45
Township 67 north, Range 14 west.....................	551 14
Township 64 north, Range 15 west.....................	531 22
Township 65 north, Range 15 west.....................	825 00
Township 66 north, Range 15 west.....................	1,009 80
Township 67 north, Range 15 west.....................	771 30
Township 65 north, Range 16 west.....................	519 56
Township 66 north, Range 16 west.....................	85 00
Township 67 north, Range 16 west.....................	698 39

Aggregate amount...............................$8,053 24

According to the report of the county court clerk to the State school superintendent for the year ending July 1, 1887, the county then held secured notes for $6,986.88, that being the total amount of the fund derived from the sale of the school lands now owned by the county; consequently the sum of $1,066.36 of the aggregate amount has been lost.

Permanent County Public School Fund.—This fund, as already stated, consisted at first of the accumulated fines and forfeitures, but was afterward largely augmented from the net proceeds of the sale of the swamp and overflowed lands, of which mention has been made in a former chapter. In April, 1876, Schuyler County received the sum of $6,137.84 as a swamp land idemnity from the general Government of the United

States. This fund is constantly increasing, and under the present law it will continue to increase as long as men continue to commit crimes and forfeit recognizances. The increase from fines, forfeitures, swamp land sales, etc., in Schuyler County, for each of the last eleven years, has been as follows: 1877, $77; 1878, $200; 1879, $596.10; 1880, $208.40; 1881, $1,653.58; 1882, $991.37; 1883, $374.30; 1884, $2,266.79; 1885, $1,082.78; 1886, $643.56; 1887, $580.37. The amount of this fund belonging to Schuyler County on the 1st of July, 1887, as shown by official report of that date, was $37,387.07, to which add the $6,986.88 belonging to the permanent township school fund, and the total, $44,373.95, is the sum of the two permanent school funds of the county at that date. These funds are constantly loaned to individual citizens of the county, and the annual interest collected thereon is appropriated to help support the common schools.

The State School Fund.—This is also a permanent fund, which is controlled by the State officers, and the interest is annually collected thereon, and distributed to the counties to assist in the support of the common schools. It was created by an act of the Legislature, approved December 12, 1855, which provided that "all moneys heretofore deposited, or which shall hereafter be deposited with the State, according to act of Congress, entitled 'An Act to regulate the deposit of the surplus revenue,' passed June 23, 1836. Also the proceeds of all lands, now or heretofore belonging to the State, known as the Saline Lands, and all lands vesting in the State, by escheat or forfeiture of taxes." This act of the Legislature provided that all white children, between the ages of five and twenty years, should be entitled to the privileges of the common schools.

Prior to the late war the common schools of the county were supported mostly with the proceeds of these two funds and by the payment of "rate bills" by the parents and guardians of the pupils; but no adequate system for the maintenance of free schools existed in the State until after the close of the war, when the present system was inaugurated, and provision was made for the establishment of separate free schools for the benefit of the colored children.

Sources of School Revenue.—The sources from which the

school revenue is derived under the present school system are various. The State school fund from which each county gets its annual distributive share is fully defined in Section 7095 of the present laws, which reads as follows: " There is hereby created a public school fund, the annual income of which shall be applied as hereinafter directed. The proceeds of all lands that have been or may be hereafter granted by the United States to this State, and not otherwise appropriated by this or the United States; also, all moneys, stocks, bonds, lands, or other property now belonging to any fund for the purpose of education, except wherein the vested rights of townships, counties, cities or towns would be infringed; also the net proceeds of the State tobacco warehouse, and of all sales of lands and other property and effects that may accrue to the State by escheat or for sale of estrays, or for unclaimed dividends or distributive shares of the estate of deceased persons, or from fines, penalties or forfeitures; also any proceeds from the sale of public lands which may have been or hereafter may be paid over to this State if Congress will consent to such appropriation; also all other grants, gifts or devices that have been or hereafter may be made to this State, and not otherwise appropriated by the terms of the grant, gift or devise; which shall be invested under the direction of the State board of education, either in bonds of the United States or bonds of the State of Missouri, the income of which, together with 25 per cent of the State revenue, shall be applied annually to the support of the public schools and university, provided for in this chapter, to be divided and apportioned as hereinafter provided."

The present law also requires the school board of each school district to levy a direct tax upon the taxable property thereof, which, when added to the income from the foregoing funds, shall produce a fund sufficient to sustain a school for the time required by law (four months), or for a longer period if so ordered by the annual meeting of the district. The sources of revenue for the support of the public schools in Schuyler County, together with the amount derived from each, is comprehensively shown by the report of the county court clerk, showing the amount of the annual distribution for the year ending July 1, 1887, which is as follows:

Cash on hand with county treasurer, July 1, 1886....$2,654 70
Amount received from State fund for 1886.. .... 3,444 40
Interest received from County fund for 1886.......... 3,553 87
Interest received from township fund for 1886........ 544 54
Amount received from direct taxation............... 9,585 99
                                                    _____
     Total amount.................................$19,783 50
Total amount expended as shown by settlement with
     treasurer, July 1, 1887........................$17,363 54
                                                    _____
Cash on hand with treasurer, July 1, 1887...........$ 2,419 96

Having shown the sources of revenue, and the amount collected and expended in one year in Schuyler County for the public schools, the workings of the present school system will be seen by a compilation of statistics taken from the report of the State superintendent of public schools for the year ending June 30, 1886.*

Number of school children in Schuyler County, white—males, 2,035: females, 1,960; total, 3,995; colored—males, 2.

Number enrolled in the public schools, white—males, 1,014; females, 1,096; total, 2,110; colored—none.

Total number of days' attendance...... 205,113
Average days' attendance........................... 97
Number of days of school taught.................. 9,554
Average number attending each day............... 1,364
Number of teachers 88
Average salary per month.......... . ... $25
Number of rooms occupied......................... 68
Seating capacity of all rooms.................... 2,485
Number of white schools.......................... 62
Number of colored schools........... ....
Average cost per day per pupil................... $0 5½
Value of school property......................... $35,550
Assessed valuation of property in county $1,992,343
Average levy on each $100...... .... $0 43
Paid teachers......... ....$15,482 76
Paid for fuel.................................. .... $918 85
Paid for repairs and rent......................... $1,096 77
Paid for apparatus... .... $1,171 57
Paid for new buildings........................... $450 00
Sinking fund and interest. $1,249 18
Salary of district clerks......................... $298 50
Extended $11,145 78

By reference to the enumeration and enrollment, it must be observed that less than 53 per cent of the children enumerated, and entitled to school privileges, were in attendance at the schools; or, in other words, only a little over one-half of the

_____
*The report for 1887 not yet received.

children in the county, of school age, attended the public schools for the year covered by the foregoing report. And with a scholastic population of 3,995 white children, the seating capacity in the public school-houses was only sufficient for 2,485 pupils. It is understood, however, that the foregoing report does not embrace quite all of the pupils enrolled in the public schools, for the reason that the teachers of three or four districts failed to make a report. If these were included, the per cent of attendance would be slightly increased—perhaps to 55 per cent. It seems that the interest taken in education in Schuyler County is concentrated in the towns, the schools of which are much better sustained and are far in advance of those in the country. The people in the towns have recently taken advanced steps in the interest of education, and this gives an encouraging outlook for the whole county, and will, it is hoped, induce the people in the country to take a greater interest in the education of their children in their home schools, to the end that good schools may be taught in every district, and that nearly all children enumerated may be found in attendance at school.

The Lancaster Seminary.—By an act of the Legislature approved March 12, 1859, John M. Minor, Reuben Whitewell, E. M. Bradley, Richard Caywood, William Buford, R. J. Christie, I. B. Alverson, William S. Thatcher, and William V. Rippey were constituted a body corporate and politic by the name and style of the "Lancaster Academy." Thus it appears that the people of Lancaster and a few good citizens in the county were the first to take advanced steps in the interest of education. A good high school was then established, and continued in a flourishing condition until it was broken up by the beginning of hostilities in the late war. It remained disorganized until after the close of the war, when it was reorganized, and afterward became a public school under the new free school system. In 1869, a new frame school building, containing four rooms (now the Lancaster Medical Infirmary) was erected, and used for school purposes until 1886, when it was found that the school had outgrown the building, and that a larger and more commodious building was necessary for the accommodation of the rapidly increasing school. Accordingly, the present school building was erected, and completed in the summer of 1886, in time to be occupied at the beginning of the school year. It is a two-story brick building, 65x70 in size, set upon a stone foundation, and contains six school rooms, 25x30 feet in size, and a hall or room for entertainments, 25x68 feet in size, besides an entrance hall, stairs, four large wardrobes, and a number of small closets. It is substantially built, and has a seating capacity for 310 pupils; it cost, together with the wells and outbuildings, $7,500. This sum was raised by selling the bonds of the school district at par. Messrs. W. F. Bunch and D. D. Glenn were the contractors for the construction of the building. The assessed valuation of the taxable property of the school district of the town of Lancaster is $202,315; and the tax thereon for the support of the school is 85 cents on each $100.

To show the condition of the Lancaster graded public schools for the school year beginning July 1, 1886, and closing June 30 1887, the following statistics are taken from the official report of the school officers. There being no colored children of school age in the district, the words " white " and " colored " are omitted:

Total enumeration, males, 173; females, 181	354
Total enrollment, males, 158; females, 166	324
Average number of days in attendance by each pupil enrolled	100.27
Number of days school was taught during year	153
Average number of pupils attending each day during the year	212
Number of teachers employed in the district during the year	5
Average salaries of male teachers per month	$55
Average salaries of female teachers per month	$25
Salary of principal per month	$75
Salary of principal per year	$600
Average cost per day for tuition on enrollment	$4.57
Average cost per day on daily attendance	$6.98
Value of school property in the district, building, grounds, apparatus, library, etc	$10.000
Amount paid for teachers' wages in the district during the year	$1,407.55
Amount paid for district officers during the year	$10
Amount paid for janitor during the year	$78.85
Number of volumes in public school library	78

According to the foregoing figures, $91\frac{1}{2}$ per cent of the children enumerated were enrolled in the school. This is in striking contrast with the per cent of the number enumerated in the whole county, who were enrolled in the schools the previous year, as heretofore shown, and is proof conclusive that the educational interest manifested is centered in the towns. However, while the number of pupils enrolled is a high per cent on the number enumerated, the average number (212) in daily attendance shows that the pupils were not kept in school as regularly as they should have been. The figures being given, the readers are left to make further comparisons, and to draw their own conclusions. The Lancaster schools are now under the management of E. D. Luckey, principal, and the following able corps of assistants: Prof. R. I. Tipton, teacher of the first high school department; Miss Ludie Bartlett, second intermediate; Miss Emma Mullett, first intermediate; Miss Helen Higbee, second primary; Miss Emma M. Miller, first primary. The school, as a whole, is now in a flourishing condition, and is doing excellent work, and the report of the officers for the present year will show a marked improvement on the last.

The school board consists of the following officers: W. M. Hunter, president; S. A. Dysart, treasurer; H. A. Miller, Spencer Greer, Charles Burkland, and Edward Higbee, Secretary.

To show the condition of the Glenwood graded public schools for the school year beginning July 1, 1886, and ending June 30, 1887, the following statistics are taken from the official report of the school officers:

Total enumeration, males, 102; females, 106	208
Total enrollment, males, 77; females, 73	150
Average number of days in attendance by each pupil enrolled	$76\frac{87}{150}$
Number of days school was taught during the year	119
Average number of pupils attending each day during the year	$96\frac{57}{119}$
Number of teachers employed in the district during the year	3
Average salary of male teachers per month, $55; females, $45 and $35	$135
Salary of principal, per year	$330
Number of pupils that may be conveniently seated in the school rooms of the district	150
Average cost per day for tuition on enrollment	$6.80
Average cost per day on daily attendance	$8.39

Value of school property in the district, building,
    grounds, apparatus, library, etc................ ... $1,800
Assessed value of property in the district.............$107,254
Number of cents on each $100 levied for school purposes
    in the district................ 75
Amount paid for teachers' wages during the year..... $867
Amount paid for district officers during the year.......   ——
Amount paid for janitor during the year..............   ——

According to the figures given in the above we see that $72_{1\frac{1}{0}}$
per cent of the children enumerated were enrolled in the school.
This is far ahead of the average enrollment in the county, but
not as large as it ought to be.   There can hardly be a good reason why over one-fourth of the school children did not attend
school, and why, that out of 150 pupils enrolled, there should only
be 96 and a fraction over in daily attendance.   It can only be
accounted for by a lack of interest on the part of parents in edu-
cating their children.   The Glenwood public school-house, which
is now in use, was erected in 1873 at a cost of about $2,000.   It
is a two-story frame building with a one-story wing.   The main
building is 24x50 feet in size, and the wing 24x40 feet in size,
and the whole building contains three large school rooms.   A
first-class graded school is now being taught by the following
able corps of teachers: T. J. Thrailkeld, principal; Miss Allie
Updike, teacher of the intermediate department, and Miss Lula
Storm, teacher of the primary department.

RELIGION.

The Methodists.—With the poverty and rough garb of the
hardy pioneers and early settlers of this county, they brought a
love of social order, and an abiding faith in the doctrines of
Christianity.   So the voice of the Christian minister was heard
coeval with the first settlements, pointing out to them the way to
eternal life.   The first sermon preached in the county was delivered by Elder William White, of Boone County, a minister of the
Christian Church.   This was in the year 1837.   The second was by
the Rev. Abraham Still, a Methodist preacher, who shortly after
settled in the southern part of the county.   He was also a physician, and ministered to both soul and body.   In those days
there were no churches, and the meetings were held in the cabins

of the settlers in the winter and in bad weather; at other times the services were held in the groves, where they erected rude pulpits of slabs, and seats for the congregation of the same material. The entire population were church-going, and when a minister came into a neighborhood, it mattered little of what denomination, they all attended—Baptist, Methodist, Presbyterian, Christian, United Brethren, or Catholic—and all united together in giving praise and adoration to the same God; and I have no doubt that their love was as pure, their prayers as heartfelt, and listened to by Him who rules above with as much pleasure, at least, as they are now in the splendid temples and cushioned seats of the purse-proud Christians of the present day.

The first camp meeting was held in the county in the year 1840, and conducted by Rev. Abraham Still and Rev. Jesse Green, of the Methodist Church, on Battle Creek, in the southwest part of the county. They were both able men in the ministry, and quite a revival was had. Dr. Still was also the first circuit rider in this county, and the organization of the Methodist Church dates from about this time in this county. In 1844 the church divided, and under the terms of the division both branches held the right here to hold an organization, and the field has been occupied by both ever since that time until the present. (Extracts from Judge Caywood's history.)

The first Methodist Episcopal Church society in the county was organized at the house of Jefferson Fulcher about the year 1838. Mr. Fulcher's house stood on the northeast quarter of the northwest quarter of Section 5, Township 65, Range 15. Prominent among the original members of this class were Jefferson Fulcher and wife, Mansel Garrett and wife, Mrs. Threlkeld, John Fulcher, Richard Fulcher, W. L. Robinson and wife, George Naylor and Mrs. Mitchell. Other Methodist Episcopal Churches were soon organized, and when, in 1844, the question of slavery divided the church, a new church, the original members of which withdrew from the Methodist Episcopal Church, was organized under the name of the Methodist Episcopal Church South, and for a series of years, and until after the close of the Civil War, the latter was much stronger than the former in Schuyler County, but since that time the Methodist Episcopal Church has outgrown the

Methodist Episcopal Church South. These two Churches are
commonly designated as the Southern Methodist and the Northern Methodist, either of which is incorrect, especially as to the
latter, as there is not now, and never has been, a Northern
Methodist Church. When the officers and members of the
Methodist Episcopal Church in the slave-holding States withdrew
therefrom and organized the new church, they chose for it the
name "Methodist Episcopal Church South," the last word being
added to distinguish it from the original "Methodist Episcopal
Church," as organized under the reformation of the Wesleys in
England; but that did not change the name of the Methodist
Episcopal Church.

Prior to the year 1850, the Methodist Episcopal Church
South had an organization in Lancaster, and about the year
1854 this organization erected the frame church building in
Lancaster, which is now owned and used by the Methodist
Episcopal Church. The latter society or class was organized
about the year 1860, and has held its organization ever since,
but during the war period the Methodist Episcopal Church
South in Lancaster became disorganized, and has never been
reorganized, but a number of its former members have since
united with the Methodist Episcopal Church. The Methodist
Episcopal Church in Glenwood was organized in 1870, by Rev.
John Wayman, and among the original members were Edmond
Rogers and wife, J. W. Burns and wife, Wesley Case and wife,
Mrs. A. B. Case, Mrs. Henry Chattin, Mrs. Sarah Tannahill,
Alvis H. Boze and wife, Dr. Burgen and wife, Benjamin Woodson and wife, William Owens and others; and their church
edifice, which is a handsome frame building, was erected in 1870,
at a cost of $1,200, and was dedicated February 12, 1871, by
Rev. St. James Fry. Until April, 1887, this church belonged to
the Glenwood circuit, but at that time it became a charge, and
the circuit was abolished. This church has sixty-five members,
including probationers. The pastors of the Glenwood circuit
have been Revs. John Wayman, Oliver Williams, Robert Collins,
O. S. Middleton, H. B. Seely, A. H. Powell, J. C. Horn, N. M.
Enyeart, Ben. Stauber and James Allen. Rev. J. S. Wilson is
the present pastor of the Methodist Episcopal Church at Glen-

wood. In connection with this church a " Young People's Bible Reading Society " has recently been organized. Since the Glenwood circuit was abolished the Methodist Episcopal Church at Coatsville has been without a regular pastor, as it is not at present attached to any circuit. The Methodist Episcopal Churches at Queen City and Green Top have been attached to the Kirksville circuit. The church edifice at Queen City was dedicated on Sunday, October 22, 1871, by Revs. John Wayman and A. H. Hamlin.

The Downing circuit of the Methodist Episcopal Church embraces only one organization in Schuyler County, and that is located about four miles west of Downing, on the northwest quarter of the northeast quarter of Section 26, Township 66, Range 14. The other organizations belonging to this circuit are located in Scotland County. The Lancaster circuit of the Methodist Episcopal Church embraces three organizations or classes within Schuyler County, one located at Lancaster, another (Mount Tabor) about three miles south, and the other (Mount Zion) about five miles northeast from Lancaster, and all within Liberty Township. Rev. E. B. Lytle is pastor of the Lancaster circuit. The Methodist Episcopal Church at Lancaster formerly belonged to the Glenwood circuit, and the Lancaster circuit is of recent formation.

The Methodist Episcopal Church South has two organizations within Schuyler County, one located about three miles southwest of Glenwood, on the southeast quarter of Section 32, Township 66, Range 15, known as the Bethel Church, and the other located about five miles south and a little west from Lancaster, on the northeast quarter of Sections 11, Township 65, Range 15. These two churches have about seventy-five members. The Bethel Church society was organized about 1867, by Rev. John Perry, and among the original members were W. M. Patterson, William D. O'Briant, William Bailey and their wives, and Martha Caywood, Emily Willis, Jensie Stewart and Pertina Mitchell. The church edifice of this society, which is a frame building, was erected and dedicated in 1867. The material was mostly contributed by the members, and the carpenter work was done by Rev. John Perry. This church has a membership of about forty-five.

The following is a list of the names of pastors of the Methodist Episcopal Church South, in Schuyler County, since the late war: Revs. William Blackwell, John Perry, Fowler, William J. Jackson, Worley, William Sarter, Brewer, Doke, J. A. Snarr, Medley, J. W. Owen, Patton, Rooker, Williams and Capp. There is also a German Methodist Episcopal Church located two miles east of Sloop's mill, and a few miles south of Lancaster, the edifice of which was dedicated to the worship of God on September, 11, 1870.

The Baptists.—The first Baptist Church in Schuyler County was known as the Lynn Grove Church, and was organized about the year 1837. The first meeting house in which this society worshiped was a log cabin, which was erected on the south side of Bridge Creek, and about three-fourths of a mile south of the present Lynn Grove Church; and the next church building was also made of logs, and stood near where the present frame building now stands, which is between two and three miles south of Downing. Among the original members of this church were the families of William V. Rippey, Garden Petty, Mr. Lake and other pioneer citizens. Rev. A. T. Hite, who organized this church, was its first pastor, and served as such for a series of years, and until he left the county. An anecdote is told of him which occurred while he was preaching during the fifties; donations were not numerous then, and some parishioners forgot to pay their dues; Hite appealed to one of these delinquents one day, and the man gave him a calf if he would catch it. The proposition was accepted, and to work the preacher went, and, after a prolonged chase, in which his clothes were considerably soiled with mud, he succeeded in capturing the animal. Prior to the Civil War he moved to another county, and during the rage of that conflict he was shot and killed one night while sitting at his own fireside.

In the ministry at Lynn Grove he was succeeded by the following preachers in the order here named: William Seamstor, Luther Salee, George Line and — Shoemake. Rev. Luther Salee was another victim who was killed during the war at his home a few miles east of Lancaster. The Second Baptist Church in the county was organized soon after the organization of the Lynn Grove Church, at the house of David Floyd, in the southwest corner of the county, it being in Section 1, Township 64, Range 16. This denomination has an organization at Lancaster, but no church edifice. It has several organizations and churches throughout the county, but is perhaps not as strong in numbers as some other denominations.

The Christians.—The first Christian Church in the county was organized during the forties, by Elder Wills, of Boone County, Mo. George Nichols, John Sleighton and Josiah Hathaway were the first elders of the church. Rev. Isaac Foster succeeded as pastor, and continued preaching and organizing churches until about the year 1858. Prior to the year 1850 a church of this denomination was organized in Lancaster, and afterward a church building was constructed of brick, and it stood on the east side of the street, and immediately south of the present railroad bridge on Washington Street. This building, of which mention has been made in connection with the war history in this work, was taken down after the railroad was completed, and the new frame church which stands on the east side of the street, and a short distance south of the southwest corner of the public square, was erected in its stead. The Christian Church has grown in Schuyler County until it has as many and perhaps more different organizations than any other religious denomination. In 1884 these several organizations met together and organized a Christian co-operation, and the fourth annual meeting of the co-operation was held in Lancaster on the 9th, 10th and 11th of September, 1887. The officers present, and in their respective stations, were R. D. Gardener, President, E. L. French, Treasurer, and A. C. Bailey, Assistant Secretary. Devotional exercises were conducted by the president. H. R. Trickett, of Hancock County, Ill., addressed the meeting on Christian work.

On the second day of the session delegates from the several organizations in the county were enrolled, as follows: " Antioch, R. D. Gardener, J. L. Hollowell; Coffey, H. F. Minnium; Downing, J. K. P. Tadlock; Lancaster, A. C. Bailey, E. L. French, J. L. Baker, Moses Baker; Liberty, —— White, —— See; Pleasant Grove, F. M. Rose, Thomas McGoldrick, ——Shoemate; Tippecanoe, T. W. Yates and ——Marian. Bridge Creek, Darby, Fairview and Green Top were not represented."

Committee on permanent organization reported for president, R. D. Gardener; treasurer, E. L. French; secretary, A. C. Bailey; which report was adopted. The committee on future work then submitted a report in favor of employing an evangelist for all the time possible, and that for his support the several organizations of the church in the county were requested to contribute, as follows: Lancaster, $75; Antioch, $50; Coffey, $50; Downing, $40; Darby, $30; Liberty, $30; Pleasant Grove, $25; Fairview, $25; Bridge Creek, $25; Tippecanoe, $25, and Green Top, $25. It was then decided to hold the next annual meeting at Lancaster. The third day of the session, being Sunday, was devoted to devotional exercises. The present pastor of the Christian Church in Lancaster is H. R. Trickett, of Hancock County, Ill.

The Christian Church at Downing was organized in August, 1883, with W. B. Smith, Jerome Bridges and J. K. P. Tadlock, as ruling elders; and in 1885 the present frame church building was erected at a cost of about $1,300. The names of the pastors who have officiated for this church are J. A. Walters, F. M. Rose and G. T. Johnson. The membership is thirty-four in number, and embraces many of the best families in that vicinity.

Other Denominations.—There are a few other religious denominations that have organizations in the county, among which is a Lutheran Church, located about six miles south and east from Lancaster, and a Catholic Church organization in the northwestern part of the county. Pleasant Grove Union Church, which stands about two miles south of Coatsville, in Section 1, Township 66, Range 16, was erected in 1885, by all denominations represented in that vicinity, and by liberal contributions from nonprofessors. It is a frame building, with a seating capacity for 300 persons, and cost about $800. It was dedicated to the worship of God, the same year it was built, by Rev. Myrtle.

On the county court records may be found the following order made by that court at its January term, 1850: "Ordered that the clerk allow the following religious denominations to occupy the court-house for the purpose of worship, on the following days in each month, to wit: The Baptists on the fourth Sunday; the Methodist Episcopal Church South on the second Sunday; the

Presbyterians on the third Sunday, and the Reformers or Camp-
bellites on the first Sunday, and the week following each Sunday."
It is presumed that the latter clause meant that each denomination mentioned should have the use of the courtroom during the
balance of the week after the Sunday designated for each. By
the foregoing it will be seen that the Presbyterian Church had
an organization in the county in an early day. In about the
year 1870 the Congregational Church had an organization at
Glenwood, which built the brick church at that place, and used
it as a house of worship until 1878, and then sold it to an organization of the Presbyterian Church, which has since been dissolved, and the building is now standing idle and in a dilapidated
condition.

All of the existing churches in the villages of the county have
Sunday-schools connected with them, as also have several of the
country churches. The Methodists have continued to hold camp
meetings at different places in the county, from time to time, from
the pioneer days to within a recent date.

SCHUYLER COUNTY.

Dr. O. W. Avery, physician and surgeon, is a native of Prospect, Ohio, and was born in 1839. He is a son of Aaron F. and Elizabeth (Hoskins) Avery. The father was of English descent and born in Jersey City, in 1811. When a young man he went to Ohio where he was married, and about 1864 removed to Agency City, and in 1873 came to Queen City, Mo., where he engaged in the mercantile business and died in 1885. He was made captain of a company to enter the Mexican War, but while in camp at Columbus, peace was declared. The mother was born in Ohio in 1813, and died in Iowa in 1870. Both were members of the Christian Church. Our subject was reared at home and received a common-school education during his younger days. In 1858 he entered the American Eclectic Institute at Cincinnati, Ohio, from which he graduated in the medical course in 1861. He immediately began to practice at Essex, Ohio, and the next spring went to Montezuma, Ia., where he was married in 1862 to Miss Sarah, daughter of Samuel and Catherine Willey, formerly of Ohio, where Mrs. Avery was born. In 1862 he entered the United States Contract Surgery Service for a year, and then settled in Springfield, Ia., remaining until 1867, when he came to Schuyler County, and located at Queen City, where he soon established an extensive and lucrative practice and now ranks among the foremost of his fraternity. Since 1875 he has conducted a drug store in connection with his profession, and is one of the active business men, as well as a leading physician of the county. He is one of the oldest settlers of Queen City, and is the only resident of the city at the present time who resided there at the time of his location at the place. He is a Democrat and cast his first presidential vote for Douglas in 1860. He is a member of the Masonic fraternity, a Knight of Pythias, and belongs to the G. A. R.

William A. Barbee, merchant, was born October 20, 1845, in Marion County, Mo., and accompanied his parents to Scotland County, Mo., when a year old, and there grew to manhood. He began life for himself when twenty-five years old, and at the death of his father inherited $600, but the balance of his property is the result of his own labor and good management. He received a good education at the Kirksville State Normal

and the Troy (Iowa) High School.   He farmed until he engaged
in the mercantile business at Killwinning, Mo.   In February,
1876, he removed to Downing, and became a partner of Dr.
Lane in the mercantile business, but in February, 1882, sold his
interest to the Doctor, and then gave his attention to grain dealing, until April, 1884, when he built the block in which he is
now doing business, and where he owns a stock of goods valued
at about $7,000.   He has a comfortable residence in Downing.
June 27, 1880, he married Miss Francis A. Craig, daughter of
George and Elizabeth (Dorman) Craig.   To Mr. and Mrs. Barbee four children have been born: Frank E., Carrie, Claude
(deceased) and Charles E.   Mrs. Barbee is a member of the
Methodist Episcopal Church.   Mr. Barbee is a Democrat in politics, and is a Master Mason.   He is the eldest of eleven children of Elias and Amanda (Terrill) Barbee, natives of Fauquier
County, Va., and Garrard County, Ky., respectively.   The father
served as assessor of Scotland County, Mo., and was a son of
Joseph and Annie (Harris) Barbee, natives of Virginia, where
they lived and died.   Mrs. Amanda Barbee was a daughter of
Robert and Mary (Beazley) Terrill, natives of Kentucky, who
settled in Marion County, Mo., about 1827.

J. R. Blackwood, senior member of the firm of Blackwood
and Hombs, is a son of Joseph and Kittie (Jones) Blackwood,
who were married, and for many years resided in Kentucky.
At an early day they settled in Marion County, Mo., where the
father still lives; the mother died in 1852.   The father is a carpenter by trade, and both himself and wife were united with the
Presbyterian Church many years ago.   J. R. is the youngest of
six children, and was born January 12, 1852, in Marion County,
Mo., and was but an infant at the time of his mother's death.
His education was limited to the common schools of the country.
Soon after arriving at maturity he engaged in the stock raising
business with a cousin, but after two years embarked in the mercantile life in Hunnewell, Mo.   He remained there a year, when
he sold out and removed to Macon City, where he was employed
by the firm of Goldsbury & Stephens.   In 1882 he came to
Glenwood and opened a general store in partnership with W. H.
Sipple.   Later he sold his interest and engaged in the boot and
shoe business at Canton, but in a year returned to Glenwood and
became a member of the firm of Blackwood & Hombs, and is now
one of the enterprising and prosperous merchants of Glenwood.
In 1883 he was united in marriage to Miss Addie, daughter of
Dr. T. W. Reed of Macon City, Mo.   Mrs. Blackwood is a worthy
member of the Methodist Episcopal Church.   Politically Mr.
Blackwood is a Democrat,   In Masonry he is a member of
Greenwood Lodge, No. 427.

L. D. Bowen, merchant at Julesburg, was born in Schuyler
County, in 1856, and is a son of Levi and Maria (Zuck) Bowen.
The father was of English descent, and a native of New Jersey.
He was married in Ohio in 1837, and in 1850 removed to Lewis
County, Mo., but six years later came to Schuyler County, and
located near Queen City, where he has a fine farm, and enjoys
the esteem of the community. Our subject was reared at home,
and received a common-school education. He began life for himself as a farm hand, and in 1882 he and his brother Elisha established a grocery store at Queen City, where L. D. filled the
office of assistant postmaster. In December of the same year he
removed to Julesburg, where he conducts a general store, and
enjoys a flourishing trade. He is one of the active and prosperous business men of the town, and in 1883 was appointed postmaster. January 3, 1885, Mr. Bowen was married to Miss For-
rest Dove, daughter of James and Maria Bennett, early pioneers
of Schuyler County. Mrs. Bowen is a native of Iowa. In politics Mr. Bowen is a Republican, and cast his first presidential
vote for Grant. He is also a member of the K. of P. The first
store in Julesburg was established in 1881 by Julius Ortmann,
who conducted it until 1882. He was the first postmaster of the
place, and the post-office was named in his honor.

Henry H. Brenizer, a prominent farmer and stock raiser of
Prairie Township, was born in Delaware County, Ohio, in 1837,
and is a son of Jacob and Margaret (Griffith) Brenizer. The
father was of Dutch ancestry, and born in Pennsylvania about
1792. He afterward went to Maryland, where he was married
in 1821, and nine years later removed to Delaware County, Ohio,
(now Morrow County), where he spent the remainder of his life.
His death occurred in 1869. The mother was born in Maryland,
in 1803, and died in 1882, a member of the Baptist Church.
Our subject received a common-school education while living at
home, and in 1863 was married to Miss Frances, daughter of
Merrick and Emeline Barr, a native of Zanesville, Ohio, by whom
he has had six children, four living, viz.: Grant, Cicero, May
and Avis. Mr. Brenizer came to Schuyler County immediately
after his marriage, and purchased eighty acres of raw prairie
land two miles east of Queen City, which he has since increased to
360 acres, 120 acres being situated just south of the town. The
home farm is under a very high state of cultivation and improvement, the outbuildings being very fine. Mr. Brenizer is a self-made
man, and his property is the natural result of frugality and
industry. During the war he served a short time in the Missouri State Militia, and he is always interested in the general
welfare and prosperity of the county. He is a member of the

Masonic fraternity, a Republican, and cast his first presidential vote for Lincoln, in 1860.

James R. Buford was born in Missouri, in 1853, and is now a well-to-do young farmer of Chariton Township, and owns 160 acres of good land, well cultivated and improved. In 1880 he married Eliza Lasley, a native of Schuyler County, and to that union two children have been born: Carrie and Marvin. In politics he is a Democrat, as are his brothers and father. His parents have been residents of Schuyler County forty-three years. William, the father, was born in Bedford County, Va., in 1822, and when young worked in the woolen factory of his father. When eighteen years of age he came to Schuyler County, Mo., and built a woolen mill for John Jones, which he at first managed, and afterward purchased. It was located one mile east of Tippecanoe, and was the first woolen mill in the county. Mr. Buford also introduced the first reaper, mower, steam engine and sewing and knitting machines used in that region. He began life in Missouri with $6, which was all that remained of the money he received from a sale of a horse he rode from Virginia to St. Louis. He was an enterprising and industrious man, however, and at the time of the late war owned 4,500 acres of land, which the ravages of war swept from him. In 1849 he went to California, and from there to Nevada City, where he engaged in business, and built the first store of the town. He also successfully engaged in mining. In 1851 he returned home, and for several years sold goods in Lancaster and Glenwood. In 1843 he married Mary A. Jones, a daughter of John Jones, and born in Virginia, in 1828, and to them the following children were born: Henry, Mildred, Liza, James, Jane, Maryette, Don, William and Nellie. In 1861 Mr. Buford raised a regiment of 1,100 men, of whom he was elected colonel. While home visiting his family at one time he was taken prisoner, but was finally released upon giving a $22,000 bond to not engage further in the Rebellion. He also served some time as a recruiting officer. In 1867 he built the large woolen mill at Glenwood, and managed it for ten years. He is a member of the Masonic fraternity of the Royal Arch degree, and one of the oldest and most respected citizens of the county.

Charles W. Bunch, county clerk, is a native of Davis County, Iowa, and was born in 1851. His parents, Dr. David and Aditha (Walker) Bunch, are natives of Indiana. During his youth the father engaged in milling in Iowa, and removed to Davis County in 1850. During the war he began to study medicine, and attended the medical college at Keokuk, Iowa. In 1865 he came to Lancaster, Mo., and practiced until 1869, when he returned to Davis County, Iowa, where he has since resided, but on account of poor health has not been actively engaged at his profession. The mother was born in Indiana and is also living. Our subject is the fourth of twelve children and received his early education at the common schools. In the fall of 1865 he came to Schuyler County and worked on a farm, and afterward worked at the carpenter trade. He then clerked in a store at Lancaster for six or seven years, and in 1877 began business on his own responsibility, but in 1878 was elected county treasurer of Schuyler County, and re-elected in 1880. During 1883 and 1884 he farmed, and in 1885 went into the drug and grocery business. In the fall of 1886 he was elected clerk of the county court by a majority of ninety votes. September 30, 1887, he married Miss Dora N. Brown, daughter of Jason W. and Eliza (DeCorse) Brown, whose respective births occurred in 1826, in Berkshire County, Mass., and 1835, at Wilmington, Del. Mrs. Bunch was born in Shelby County, Ill., in 1854, and has borne our subject one son, Roy B. In politics Mr. Bunch is a Republican, and cast his first presidential vote for U. S. Grant. His wife is a worthy member of the Christian Church.

Charles Burkland, contractor and farmer, was born in Sweden June 14, 1851, and is a son of Andrew and Helen Burkland. The father was born in 1829 and died in 1873, and was a farmer by occupation. His wife was born in 1827 and is now a resident of her native country. She is the mother of six children, of whom our subject is the eldest. He was educated in Sweden and attended school from the age of seven to fifteen. When twenty years old he left the parental roof and emigrated to the United States, locating in Keokuk, Iowa. In January of the following year he began working on the Missouri, Iowa & Nebraska Railroad, laying track. In 1873 he became section foreman, and remained as such for ten years, locating in Lancaster in 1878. November 12, 1874, Mr. Burkland married Miss Christina Holstrand, who was born in Sweden in 1853, and came to America in 1873. By her he had three children, Fred William, Oscar, Leo Raymond and Charles Herbert. In 1879 Mr. Burkland bought 750 acres of land in Liberty Township, and since 1883 has spent his time in looking after his real estate and dealing in railroad ties, lumber and wood for the Keokuk and Western Railroad. He is a self-made man and his property is the result of his ability and industry. For the past two years he has been president of the Scandinavian Coal Company, and a director of the Schuyler Company Bank. In politics he is a Democrat, and cast his first presidential vote for Hancock in 1880, and two years later was elected a member of the town council of Lancaster. He is a member of the A. O. U. W. of the second degree, and himself and wife are members of the Methodist Episcopal Church, of which he has been steward and trustee for seven years.

George Bush, sheriff of Schuyler County, is a native of Bradford County, Penn., and was born in 1840. His father, Jonathan Bush, was of French and English descent, and born in Rhode Island in 1809, and was a carpenter and millwright by trade. When seventeen years old he went to Bradford County, Penn., and was married in 1839. In 1859 he immigrated to Schuyler County, Mo., and located in Independence Township. In 1861 he enlisted in the Confederate army, and served one year. In 1866 he moved to Howard County, Mo., where he died in 1884. His wife, Fannie (Beach) Bush, was of French descent, and was born in Bradford County, Penn., in 1821. She is now living in Howard County, Mo. Our subject was the oldest of six children, and accompanied his parents to Schuyler County in 1859. During his youth he was educated at the common schools in Pennsylvania, and when becoming of age began life as a farmer. He served in the Southern army two years during the late war, and after that engaged in farming in Howard County. In 1872 he returned to Schuyler County, and farmed about ten years. From 1877 to 1884 he clerked in a general store at Downing, and was then elected sheriff of Schuyler County. He was re-elected in 1886, and is now efficiently and faithfully discharging the duties of that office. In November, 1863, he wedded Mary (Pruner) Carroll, daughter of Christopher Carroll. This lady was born in Schuyler County, Mo., in 1842, and is the mother of nine children, seven of whom are living: Fannie (wife of Charles Peterson), Mary E. (now Mrs. Cox), Lina, Annie, Minnie, De Witt and Carroll. In politics Mr. Bush is a Democrat, and cast his first presidential vote for John C. Breckinridge in 1868.

Jesse Carter, farmer and stock raiser, was born October 24, 1829, in Lincoln County, Ky., and moved to Schuyler County, October 12, 1849, where he has since resided, devoting his attention to farming and stock raising, at which occupations he has been engaged since his boyhood. When twenty years of age he started out in life with but $5, and what he now owns is due to industry and perseverance, united with practical business ability. He now owns 430 acres of land, well stocked and improved, and is one of the prominent citizens of the county. In 1853 he was married to Malinda C. Brown, a native of North Carolina, and daughter of Benjamin and Charlotte Brown, natives of North Carolina. Mrs. Carter died July 7, 1855, and was the mother of one son—Benjamin. November 20, 1856, Mr. Carter was united to Miss Sarah Ann Munsell, a native of Miami County, Ohio, and daughter of Asa H. Munsell, a native of the same county. To this marriage eleven children have been born: William A., James T., Elizabeth J., Solomon L., Mary C., Peter E., Annie B. and Charles F. (twins), Jessie, John and Ward H. Mrs. Carter died March 3, 1874, and Mr. Carter was married, a third time, August 4, 1875, Miss Elzira W. Seamster becoming his wife. This lady is a daughter of Green B. and Sarah (Legrande) Seamster. To this union four children were born: Sarah M., Ella, Green and Emma. Mr. Carter is a member of the Christian Church, and is a Democrat in politics. He represented his county in the Legislature in 1872, and two years later was re-elected, and also in 1876. In 1860 he was elected county assessor, and served two years. He was the fourth of eight children, seven sons and one daughter, of Peter and Elizabeth (Nevin) Carter, natives of Virginia and Ireland, respectively. Mrs. Carter first came to the United States when twenty-four years old, and settled in Lincoln County, Ky., where she married Mr. Carter. Mr. Carter served as a soldier in one of the early Indian Wars.

Judge Hawley Cone was born in January, 1825, in Muskingum County, Ohio, and was reared upon a farm. When seventeen years old he went into the general merchandise and distilling business at Conesville, Coshocton Co., Ohio, and afterward at Adams Mills in Muskingum County, until about 1853, when he moved to Peoria, Ill. He then went into the grain business with Mr. Schnebly, and in 1855 went to Davis County, Iowa, where he began to farm. In 1848 he was married to Miss Jennie Davidson, daughter of Maj. Davidson, a native of Virginia, and who was among the early settlers upon the Muskingum River. Two children blessed this union: Howard J. and Junius B. (deceased). Mrs. Cone died about 1852, and in 1855 Judge Cone married Miss Lois N. Ross, daughter of Lyman Ross, an early settler in Muskingum County, Ohio, where Mrs. Cone was born. Four children have been born to this marriage: Emma E. (deceased), Converse C. (an M. D.), Mary R. and Jennie D. In politics the Judge is a Republican, and has served as county judge of Schuyler County very efficiently for two years, and has the honor of being elected on a Republican ticket in a very strong Democratic county. He is the second of seven children born to Jared and Eliza (Shoff) Cone, natives of Massachusetts and Pennsylvania, respectively. They moved to Cadiz, Ohio, in 1816, then to Licking County, and then to Muskingum County, settling upon a farm which has since been in the possession of members of the

Cone family. The mother of Judge Cone was the daughter of Philip Shoff, who was born in Carlisle, Penn., and settled in Guernsey County, Ohio, in 1804, where he lived and died. Judge Cone is a Wesleyan Methodist, and believes in the absolute necessity of being cleansed from all filthiness of the flesh and spirit, and perfecting holiness in the fear of God. With spirituous liquors and tobacco he pollutes not his mouth. He is a dear lover of children, and Sabbath-schools are his delight. Himself and wife are living alone upon a farm in moderate circumstances. He has had his full share of life's misfortunes and ills, and is patiently waiting his allotted time when the last change shall come.

William Cook, farmer and stock raiser, was born in Schuyler County in 1843, and has followed farming in his native county since his boyhood. He is the third of fourteen children born to Charles and Ann (Slightom) Cook, natives of England and Virginia, respectively. The father came to the United States in 1837, when twenty-four years of age, and settled upon a farm in Schuyler County, Mo., where he died in January, 1887, at the age of seventy-four. The mother was a daughter of John J. Slightom. William Cook was reared by his parents, and in July, 1862, enlisted in Company G, Twenty-seventh Missouri Infantry, being mustered out at Louisville, Ky., in June, 1865. He began life a poor man, but is now a well-to-do citizen of Schuyler County, and owns a finely improved farm of 223 acres, which is well-stocked and equipped for farming. In 1867 he was united in marriage to Miss Mary J. Lambert, daughter of James and Mary (Tingle) Lambert, natives of Kentucky. Mr. and Mrs. Cook have been blessed with eight children: Mary A. (deceased), Oscar (deceased), Edward, Viola, Ida May, Charles, Oliver (deceased) and Bertha. Mrs. Cook is a member of the Baptist Church, and a well esteemed and worthy lady. Mr. Cook is a Republican, and one of the enterprising and energetic farmer citizens of the county.

Judge Enoch Crim is a native of Clark County, Ky., and was born in 1827. His parents, John R. and Mildred (Sears) Crim, were both natives of the same county, and were born in 1806 and 1808, respectively. They were married, and lived in their native county until 1836, when they removed to Monroe County, Mo. After thirteen years' residence there they went to Lewis County, where they died in 1883 and 1879, respectively. Both were members of the Christian Church. The father was a farmer, and an ardent Democrat, and as such served as constable in Lewis County sixteen years. Enoch is the eldest of a family of nine children, and was reared upon the farm. His early edu-

****

cational advantages were very limited, his school life not exceeding a year, but by patient study and reading, by the light of a bark fire after his daily duties were discharged, he acquired a good practical business education.   At the age of twenty he was engaged to drive a team of oxen to Santa Fe.   He returned home in 1848, and was united in marriage to Nancy Peacher, a native of Howard County, Mo., born in 1832.   To them eight children were born: Ann C., Margaret E., John A., Enoch W., Frank P. and Warren E.   After marriage Mr. and Mrs. Crim located in Monroe County, and in 1854 removed to Lewis County, Mo., where they remained but two years.   They next located in Schuyler County, and settled upon the farm where they now reside, which contains 219 acres of fertile and well-cultivated land. Mr. Crim has now been a resident of Schuyler County, and lived in the same vicinity over thirty-one years.   He is a successful farmer, and one of the best citizens of the county.   He served as constable five years, and from 1874 to 1882 filled the office of probate judge, and for the last fourteen years has been a school director.   In politics he is a Democrat, and himself and wife are worthy church members, he belonging to the Missionary Baptist Church, and she to the Christian.

J. J. Daniels was born in Muscatine County, Iowa, in 1851, and is a son of Anthony and Nancy (Crosson) Daniels, natives of Virginia and Ohio, respectively.   During the Mexican War the father was mustered in, and organized two or three companies.   He also served in the late war as surgeon, and was a son of Joseph Daniels, a native of France, who was married in that country, and came to the United States when about twenty-four years of age.   The maternal grandfather of J. J. Daniels was a native of Ireland, who immigrated to the United States, and was married in Pennsylvania.   The subject of this sketch moved to Schuyler County in 1855, and lived at various places during the six years following 1861, and in 1866 moved upon the farm where he has since resided.   He has been a farmer since his youth, and his home place consists of sixty acres of nicely improved land, which he has accumulated through industry and good management.   In 1878 he was married to Miss Nancy R., daughter of David and Louisa Griggs, natives of Hancock County, Ill., and Bowling Green, Ky., respectively. Their parents, Leonard and Nancy (Thomas) Griggs, were born in Kentucky, and moved to Illinois, where the father died in 1875.   The mother was a daughter of John Scamster of Kentucky.   Mr. and Mrs. J. J. Daniels have been blessed with three children: Elbert W., Charles E., and one who died unnamed.   Mr. Daniels is a Democrat, and one of the honored citizens of the county.

Judge Harrison Davis, farmer and stock raiser, was born in what is now Alleghany County, Va., in 1809, and is a son of Richard and Mary (Wilson) Davis, natives of Virginia. The father was born in 1777, and married in 1803. He died in 1862, having spent his entire life in his native State engaged in farming. His father, Richard Davis, was a native of Northumberland County, Va., and his father was born in Wales, but was afterward an early pioneer of Virginia. The mother of our subject was five years her husband's junior, and died in 1835. Both belonged to the Methodist Episcopal Church. Harrison received a limited common-school education, and when nineteen years old learned the hatter's trade, but soon returned to farm life. He went to Missouri in 1832, returning to Virginia in a year, and in 1834 married Miss Margaret Ann, daughter of David and Margaret Rodefer, natives of Virginia. To this union only one of the five children is living, Frances, wife of Isaac N. Walker, of Trenton. In 1838 Mr. Davis came to Lewis County, Mo., where he lived until 1856. He then located three-fourths of a mile north of Queen City, in Schuyler County, where he now owns a fine and well-improved farm of 220 acres. He came here during the early history of the county, and has long been recognized as one of the prominent and highly honored citizens of Schuyler County. In 1859 he was first elected justice of the peace, in which capacity he has served in all over twenty years. In 1866 he was appointed judge of the county court, and held that office five years to the satisfaction of all. In 1866 he was appointed judge of the probate court, filling that position one year. He was reared a Democrat, and cast his first presidential vote for Gen. Harrison, who was a distant relative of his, but since the war has been a Republican. Himself and wife have for forty years been faithful and worthy members of the Christian Church, and are warmly admired and respected by their large circle of friends and neighbors.

Abraham Davis is the eldest child of Daniel and Sarah (Brake) Davis. The father was born in Princeton, N. J., and at the age of fourteen, enlisted in the Revolutionary War under Gen. Washington. While living in New Jersey he married and raised a family of five sons and three daughters. He then moved to Ross County, Ohio, where he lost his wife, and afterward married the mother of the subject of this sketch, by whom he had two sons and one daughter. In early life he learned the tanners' and shoemakers' trades, and also ran a coasting vessel seven years, but after moving to Ohio devoted his time exclusively to farming. In politics he was a Whig, and both himself and wife were members of the Methodist Episcopal Church.

His death occurred in 1851, and his widow survived him until 1883. She had been previously married to Sylvanus Morris, by whom she had four children. Abraham Davis was born in Ross County, Ohio, March 10, 1833. Being the eldest child, and the main support of the family, after the age of nine he naturally enjoyed very meagre educational advantages. In 1854 he married Cynthia A. Lucas, who was born in Highland County, Ohio, August 16, 1834. She is a member of the Methodist Episcopal Church. This union was blessed with eight children: Arthur born March 12, 1857; Emery, born in 1859; Minnie, July 13, 1861; Sarah Libbie, October 4, 1863; Luther E., September 9, 1865; Cashus C., October 17, 1867; and Chalmers Bertie, December 24, 1873. In 1856 the family moved to Schuyler County, Mo. At that time Mr. Davis had but little means, and for four years worked at the carpenter's trade. He then engaged in farming in connection with which he shipped stock, and is now the owner of a fine farm of 660 acres, and is one of the well-to-do farmers of the county. During the late war he served three years in the State Militia, and is a stanch Republican. He is a member of Lancaster Lodge of the I. O. O. F.

John R. Dawkins, of the firm of Munsell & Dawkins, lumber dealers and hardware merchants, was born in Carroll County, Ky., in 1839. When ten years old he was taken by his parents to Shelby County, Ind., and in 1856 moved to Schuyler County, where he has since resided. He was reared upon a farm, and when twenty-five years old learned the carpenter's trade, which he followed until 1879, and from that time to 1881 was engaged in the drug trade and the lumber business. February 24, 1887, he purchased a half interest in Munsell & Son's hardware and grocery store, and is now the junior member of the above firm, and one of the enterprising business men of Downing. He also owns town property, and as he was a poor man when starting in life for himself, ranks among the self-made men of the county. In July, 1868, he married Miss C. C. Lewis, a native of Kentucky, and to this union ten children have been born: Merrit L., James M., Lillie M. (deceased), Alva W., Bertie P., Della B., Sarah E., Edgar I. and two who died unnamed. In politics Mr. Dawkins is a Democrat. He was the third child of nine born to James and Mary H. (Lewis) Dawkins, natives of Kentucky. The father was a son of John Dawkins, of Virginia, and the mother a daughter of Richard Lewis, of Virginia, a soldier in the Revolutionary War.

James A. Dawkins, a prominent farmer and stock raiser of Independence Township, was born February 4, 1842, in Carroll County, Ky., and is the fifth of a family of nine children born to

James and Mary H. (Lewis) Dawkins, natives of Kentucky. The father was born in Henry County, and for the last three years has been deprived of the blessing of sight. James A. moved to Shelby County, Ind., in 1850, with his parents, and to Schuyler County, Mo., May 31, 1856, where he has since resided, engaged in farming and stock raising. He began life a poor young man, at the age of twenty-three, and now owns 382 acres of choice land, finely improved and cultivated. In 1864 he was married to Miss Hannah R. Coffey, daughter of William A. and Mary J. (Whiteside) Coffey, natives of Casey County, Ky. To Mr. and Mrs. Dawkins eight children have been born: Denton E., Emma C., Christopher E., Mary Clara, Jennie D., Bembridge H., Jesse M. and Eliud Arlando. Both Mr. and Mrs. Dawkins are members of the Missionary Baptist Church, of which the former has been a deacon for six years. In politics he is a Democrat, and in Masonry, a member of the Blue Lodge.

Albert L. Dawkins, a prominent farmer and stock raiser of Independence Township, was born in Carroll County, Ky., in 1848, and is the youngest child of James and Mary H. (Lewis) Dawkins. After living in Shelby County, Ind., he moved to Schuyler County, Mo., and has followed the occupations of farming and stock raising in that county ever since. He began life a poor man, but through industry, energy and good management is now the owner of 380 acres of well improved land, and is one of the well-to-do and enterprising farmers of the county. In 1870 he was united in marriage to Miss Samantha Coffey, daughter of William A. and Mary J. (Whiteside) Coffey, and to this union two children, James W. and Bertha L., have been born. Mrs Dawkins is a member of the Missionary Baptist Church. Mr. Dawkins is a Democrat in politics, and ranks among the honored and respected men of his township.

Jesse Dooley was born in Howard County, Mo., in 1825, and is a son of Henry and Sarah (Coffer) Dooley, natives of Kentucky, born in 1801 and 1799, respectively. They were married in 1819, and the same year removed to Howard County, Mo. Some years later they went to Boone County, Mo., and in 1840 moved to Davis County, Iowa, where the father died in 1856 and the mother in 1860. Mrs. Dooley was a niece of Daniel Boone, the celebrated bear hunter and Indian fighter. Both Mr. and Mrs. Dooley were members of the Missionary Baptist Church of which the former was a preacher about thirty years. While in Boone County he was captain of a militia company. In politics he was a Whig, and his occupation was that of farming. Jesse Dooley was the fifth of ten children, and being reared upon a farm when educational institutions were scarce, never learned to read or write, but by observation and experience has become a successful man and owns a good farm of 240 acres, which he has earned by hard labor since his arrival in this county in 1866. In 1847 he left the parental roof and married Mary E. Fenton, a native of Boone County, Mo., where she was born in 1831. To this union eight sons and six daughters have been born: Sarah J., Joel C., Francis M., Obadiah, Infant, William E., Lucy A., Jerusha E., Henry H., Leatha E., James L. and Lodemia E. (twins), John A. and Jesse A. Joel C., the eldest son, was county superintendent of public schools of Davis County, Iowa, for four years, and the third son holds the same position in Saunders County, Neb. Jesse Dooley, our subject, has been, respectively, a Whig, Republican and Greenbacker. Mrs. Dooley is a member of the Missionary Baptist Church.

James F. Dowis is a son of Isaac and Elizabeth (Rogers) Dowis, and is their youngest and only living son. He was born in Knox County, Ky., in 1836. The father was born in Newberry County, N. C., and the mother in Ashe County, N. C. When young both were taken to Knox County, Ky., where they were afterward married. In 1854 they removed to Nodaway County, Mo., where they spent the remainder of their lives, the mother dying at the age of seventy-two, and the father living to be over one hundred years of age, and never having been confined to his bed in his lifetime. He was a soldier of the War of 1812 in the Northern Expedition, and a Whig until the dissolution of that party, when he became a Democrat. His only occupation was that of farming; both himself and wife belong to the Christian Church. James F. spent his youth upon the farm, working for his father until twenty-five years of age. His educational advantages were very limited, he having attended school not more than a year in all. In 1863 he joined Company B of the Thirty-fifth Missouri Infantry, U. S. A., as sergeant, and after six months' service was discharged on account of disability. In 1865 he married Elizabeth Melvin, daughter of George W. Melvin. Mrs. Dowis was born in Lawrence County, Ind., in 1847, and to her union with Mr. Dowis nine children were born: Elizabeth F., Jesse L., Levi M., William F., Emma J., Rosaline, two infants (deceased) and James F. Both Mr. and Mrs. Dowis are members of the Presbyterian Church. In politics Mr. Dowis was formerly a Democrat, but a few years ago affiliated with the Greenback party. In 1874 he was chosen county judge, which office he held four years. He is a member of the A. O. U. W. Mr. Dowis is a self-made man, having begun life very poor, but after twenty-two years' residence in Schuyler County has become the owner of 400 acres of land, and is now one of the substantial farmers of the county. He is of German ancestry upon the paternal, and Irish-German upon the mother's side.

Camillus Dunbar, machinist, was born in Stark County, Ohio, in 1849, and when fifteen years of age moved to Howard County, Ind. He received a common-school education during his youth, and learned the moulder's trade at Kokomo, serving an apprenticeship of three years. In 1870 he came to Missouri, and after traveling around some time he and his brothers erected their foundry and machine works in Glenwood Township, where they are now in business, the firm name being Dunbar Bros. In connection with their manufactory they are also engaged in general repairing. He was reared a farmer, but as he did not like a farmer's life has devoted his time to mechanical occupations. In 1885 his marriage with Mary Rigg was solemnized. In politics he is a Republican, his first presidential vote having been cast for Gen. Grant. He is a son of Aaron and Jeanette (Doolittle) Dunbar, both natives of Connecticut. They afterward moved to Stark County, Ohio, where they passed the remainder of their days. Of six children (three sons and three daughters) our subject is the youngest son. Only two of the sons survive, both mechanics. The three daughters are living. At the death of his parents Mr. Dunbar was but five years old, and his early life after that time was spent with his guardian, Alexander Maxwell, of Portage County, Ohio.

Capt. William Dunn was born in Warren County, Ky., in 1831, and when two years old was taken by his parents to Henderson County, Ill. When nineteen years of age he went to California, and there experienced all the vicissitudes of a miner's life, and engaged in many conflicts with the Indians. In the winter of 1853 he accompanied Gen. Walker to Nicaragua upon his famous expedition, and there remained a little over a year. He then went to South America, and then to New Orleans, where he remained one winter. After that he went to Cairo, Ill., and conducted a woodyard. After some time he finally chose a location in Schuyler County, Mo., in September, 1858, of which place he has since been a resident. He began life with no capital, but is now the owner of a well-improved farm of fifty-two acres. In July, 1858, he was married, and to that union one child was born, which died unnamed. The mother died in May, 1859, and in 1866 Capt. Dunn married Miss Nancy Morris, by whom he had five children: John H., Addie, Ella, and two who died in infancy. Mrs. Dunn died in 1882. Capt. Dunn is a Democrat, and in 1861 enlisted in Green's Missouri Infantry, Confederate States of America, but after the disintegration of his regiment, enlisted in Col. Porter's Missouri Infantry, and also

served a while in Franklin's Missouri Infantry. He was elected
first lieutenant upon the organization of his company, but on
account of his efficient service, was promoted to the captaincy.
He was paroled in 1865 in Scotland County, Mo., where he was
captured. He was the fourth of eight children of John H. and
Charlotte P. (Dunn) Dunn, natives of Virginia and Kentucky,
respectively. The father was a son of William and Fannie
(Haley) Dunn, natives of Virginia, the father having been a soldier in the Revolutionary War.

Andrew J. Eidson, M. D., was born in Butler County, Ohio,
October 26, 1837, and is the eldest son of four sons and two
daughters born to William M. and Catherine (Daugherty) Eidson, natives of North Carolina and Ohio, and born in 1814 and
1817, respectively. They were married in Butler County, Ohio,
whither the father had gone when a young man. They afterward moved to Adams County, Ill., where their respective deaths
occurred in 1858 and 1886. After the death of Mrs. Eidson, the
father was united to Mrs. Eliza Nelson. During the Mexican
War he offered his services, but was not mustered in. Late in
life he became united with the Congregational Church. Our
immediate subject spent his youth upon his father's farm, and
although the educational advantages of those days were very
limited, he was very intelligent and studied assiduously, and
became qualified for teaching while a young man. He afterward attended Quincy College and attained the degree of A. B.
He then worked by the month and taught school until he had
accumulated enough money to forward him in his studies, and,
having decided upon a medical career, attended a course of lectures at McDowell's College, St. Louis, in 1859. In January,
1865, he graduated from Rush Medical College, Chicago, and in
February he enlisted in Company D, One Hundred and Forty-
eighth Illinois Volunteer Infantry, as a private, but was soon
taken to the hospital. After his partial recovery he was made a
ward master of the hospital, and then acting surgeon, which
position he filled until discharged on account of disability. He
then located in McDonough County, Ill., but in 1871 came to
Coatsville, where he has since enjoyed a large and lucrative practice. His wife owns a drug store, which was established in 1880,
and 505 acres of land near Coatsville, besides considerable town
property, and the Doctor owns 280 acres of land in Fulton
County, Ark. Andrew J. Eidson was twice married: his first
marriage occurred in February, 1863, Miss Lucinda M. Monroe,
of Cass County, Ill., becoming his wife. To this union two
daughters were born, viz.: Araminta, twenty years of age, the
wife of Charles C. Dean, son of the late Hon. Henry Clay Dean.

Mr. and Mrs. Dean reside upon what is know as the Hamilton farm, situated one mile from Coatsville. The second daughter, Miss Lillie Maud, is eighteen years of age, and is living in Salem, Fulton Co., Ark. She was reared by Alfred M. Wheeler, and is now the wife of Frank Waters, son of Dr. Waters, of Salem. In March, 1871, Dr. Eidson was united in marriage to Miss Bethany M. Wheeler, a native of Van Buren County, Iowa, and born in 1850. This union has been blessed with three children: Mark M., Edmund E. and Kate C. The Doctor and his wife are both members of the Missionary Baptist Church. Dr. Eidson is a member of the Masonic lodge, at Glenwood, No. 427, and belongs to the I. O. O. F. fraternity. Dr. Eidson is a writer of considerable note upon scientific and professional subjects, and a poet, the following being a product of his ready pen:

NO CHILDREN'S GRAVES IN CHINA.

No children's graves in China,
　The missionaries say;
In cruel haste and silence
　They put those buds away.
No tombstones mark their resting,
　To keep their mem'ry sweet;
Their graves, unknown, are trodden
　By many careless feet.

No children's graves in China,
　That land of heathen gloom;
They deem not that their spirits
　Will live beyond the tomb.
No little coffin holds them,
　Like to a downy nest;
No spotless shroud enfolds them,
　Low in their quiet rest.

No children's graves in China.
　No parents ever weep,
No toy or little relic
　The thoughtless mothers keep.
No mourners e'er assemble
　Around the early dead,
And flowers of careful planting
　Ne'er mark their lowly bed.

No children's graves in China,
　With sad and lovely ties,
To make the living humble,
　And point them to the skies.
No musings pure and holy,
　Of them when day is done;
Be faithful, missionary,
　Your work is just begun!

Harvey E. Epperson was born in Tennessee, in 1851, and is the fifth of seven children of Silas A. and Nancy (Beheeler) Epperson, natives of Virginia, and born in 1812 and 1814, respectively. The mother accompanied her parents to Kentucky, when very young, and was there reared and married in 1834 to Mr. Epperson, who was a near neighbor, having moved during his youth to Tennessee, where he lived just across the State line. After their marriage the young couple moved over the line into Kentucky, and there lived until 1851. They then moved to Marion County, Ill., and in 1854 came to Schuyler County, Mo., where the father died in 1886. The mother is now a resident of California. Both belonged to the Missionary Baptist Church. By occupation Mr. Epperson was a farmer, but learned the carpenter's trade, and built the first tobacco factory in the county. Harvey E. received a good common-school education during his youth, and spent his life upon his home farm until 1874. He then went to California and engaged in the lumber business, working at the carpenter's trade which he taught himself, having a natural mechanical ability. In 1877 he returned to his native State, and two years later married Jennie P., daughter of James T. Guinn [see sketch]. This union has been blessed with the following children: Carl D., Jennie G. and Mada. Mr. Epperson is now a successful farmer of 160 acres of land. In politics he is a Democrat. In Masonry he is a member of Glenwood Lodge, No. 427. Both Mr. and Mrs. Epperson are members of the Missionary Baptist Church.

John W. Evans is a son of Thomas and Esther (Wright) Evans, natives of Virginia, born in 1799 and 1807, respectively. After their marriage they resided in their native State until 1833, and then removed to Logan County, Ohio. Seven years later they went to Union County, where the mother died in 1849, and the father in 1853. Both were members of the Methodist Episcopal Church. During his early life the father was engaged as a teamster, but later turned his attention to farming. In politics he was a Democrat. John W. was the sixth of a family of seven sons and four daughters, and was born in Fauquier County, Va., in 1833. When six months old he was taken by his parents to Ohio, where he was reared and educated. In 1856 he married Fannie J. Cowan, who was born in New York, in 1826, and accompanied her parents to Ohio. To this marriage six children were born: Mary B., Bettie, Robert D., Charles L. and two infants. Of these, but Robert D. and Charles L. are living. Mr. Evans is of Irish and his wife of Scotch descent. In 1857 they came to Schuyler County, where they have since made their home, and now own a fine farm of 130 acres, a good evidence of their economy and thrift. During the war Mr. Evans served a short time in the Twenty-ninth Regiment of Enrolled Militia as sergeant. He has served four years as magistrate, and has ever borne the reputation of being an honest and upright citizen. Politically he was formerly a Democrat, having been raised in that faith. Of late years he has been more independent in his views, believing the best interests of his country can be served by voting for the best man, and not the party.

Christian Figge is a son of Christian and Catherine (Heinze) Figge, and was born in Hesse Darmstadt, Germany, in 1838. His parents were natives of Germany and born in 1810 and 1817, and died in 1880 and 1852, respectively. Both emigrated to America in 1851 and located six miles southeast of Lancaster. The father was a tailor in Germany but after coming to America engaged in farming and was the owner of 100 acres of land. Christian was the second of five children. He accompanied his parents to America and remained at home assisting in clearing the home place for one year. When fourteen years old he worked for $5.00 a month as clerk and chore boy, and attended school three months out of a year for three years in Lancaster. When eighteen years old he went to La Grange, Mo., and worked as clerk for $20 per month, board and washing. In 1861 he returned home and with the money earned by six years' labor purchased a small stock of goods and opened a store on the home place. In six weeks all his property was seized by the rebels and he barely escaped with his life. In November, 1861, he enlisted in Company A, Twenty-first Missouri Volunteer Infantry, and served for three years during the war receiving his discharge at Shreveport, Miss., in 1865. He was in the battles of Shiloh, Corinth, Red River and Shreveport among others and participated in numerous skirmishes. The last eight months of service, after being discharged as a soldier, were spent in the Commissary Department as chief clerk, Sixteenth Army Corps, at a salary of $100 per month and board. After peace was declared he resumed the mercantile business at Lancaster at which he was engaged until January, 1875, when he was elected cashier of the First National Bank of Lancaster, and when the Schuyler Company Bank succeeded the First National, in 1877, Mr. Figge was elected cashier and has since retained that position. He has also been one of the directors since the organization of the First National, and was one of the leading and prime movers of the organization. He owns a residence valued at $5,000, a stock of goods in Unionville, Mo., worth $12,000, a bank at Rush Centre, Kas., $15.000 capital, and has $4,000 of stock in the Schuyler County Bank. He also owns 160 acres of land at Rush Centre, Kas., valued at $4,000, ninety-eight acres near

Bloomfield, Ia., 110 acres near Moulton, Ia., which are highly improved, three houses and lots at same place, eighty acres of land in Schuyler County, and has a $4,500 mortgage on a valuable farm in Appanoose County, Ia., besides other means not herein mentioned, all of which make him one of the most wealthy men of his county. In 1866 he married Miss Mary F., daughter of A. K. and Jane Cowgill, who was born in Iowa in 1849. Mr. Cowgill was sheriff of Schuyler County at the close of the war, and since the death of her husband Mrs. Cowgill has lived with Mrs. Figge. To her union with our subject six children have been born: Clara, Belle, Cora May, Halena and Maglena (twins) and Christian, Jr. In politics Mr. Figge is a Republican but cast his first presidential vote for Douglas. Himself and wife are members of the Methodist Episcopal Church of which he has been steward and trustee for the past sixteen years.

C. C. Fogle, attorney at law, Lancaster, Mo., was born in Hardin County, Ky., July 28, 1847, and is a son of Samuel Newell and Matilda (Smith) Fogle. The father was born in Hardin County, Ky., in 1820 and was of German descent, and was married in 1839. In March, 1850, he moved to Scotland County, Mo., and bought a farm upon which he died in January, 1857. The mother was of Irish descent and was born in Hardin County, Ky., in 1819, and died July 11, 1877. Our subject is the fifth of nine children, all of whom are living, and when about three years old, went with his parents to Scotland County, Mo., and received his common school education in that county. In 1869 he entered the Normal School at Kirksville, Mo., and in 1872 graduated, but attended the same the following year. He holds a life State certificate. When twenty years of age he began to teach in the public schools; in 1873 was elected principal of a graded school at Glenwood, Schuyler Co., Mo.; in 1874 was chosen professor of mathematics in the Unionton Academy in Scotland County, Mo., which was a private institution, and the following year was made principal of that institution. In 1876 he came to Lancaster, and was made principal of the graded school there for two years. In 1878 he began the study of law in the law office of Messrs. Higbe & Shelton. In November of the same year he was admitted by Judge Andrew Ellison to the bar, and immediately began the practice of law with A. C. Bailey as a partner. This partnership continued but six months; he then practiced about two years alone. The first fee which he obtained of any importance grew out of the noted "Bill Young trial" in Clark County, Mo., where he was paid $100. He afterward became a law partner of Joseph M. Knott, which partnership continued for three years, when Mr. Knott moved to Texas; then our subject went in business with Edwin F. Payton, now prosecuting attorney, which partnership lasted about twelve months, since which time he has continued his practice of law by himself. He has been employed in all the important criminal cases in the county since his admission to the bar, realizing fees ranging from $100 to $750, and his success has been remarkable. In politics Mr. Fogle is a Democrat. But he says he "deserves no credit for being right in politics because his parentage on both sides as far back as he can trace them were Democrats." He cast his first presidential vote for Seymour and Blair in 1868. He has been spoken of in connection with several important offices but declines to accept any official position. However, he is active in politics and has been a delegate to county, senatorial, congressional and State conventions. In 1879 he was elected County School Commissioner of Schuyler County, and in 1881 was re-elected. In 1884 he was appointed attorney for the town of Lancaster, which position he still holds. In the same year he was elected a member of the school board, served three years, two of which he was president of the board, during which time there was erected a fine brick school-house in the town of Lancaster, owing largely to his exertions and influence in that direction. In 1881 he was elected town councilman of Lancaster and served two years. In November, 1879, he married Miss Minerva D. Childress, a lady of French and English descent and who had been educated at the Kirksville Normal School; she is a daughter of William Pryor and Melissa (Justice) Childress. Mrs. Fogle was born in Scotland County, Mo., December 25, 1855, and to her union with our subject three children have been born: Claude C., Earle E., and Hugh N. Mrs. Fogle is a member of the Methodist Episcopal Church and her husband of the Methodist Episcopal Church South. He is also a member of the I. O. O. F. and A. O. U. W. He is a leading lawyer, whose practice is large and lucrative and not confined to his own county. He is a logical and a forcible debator, an indefatigable worker and a close student. In political canvasses he is a strong man on the stump.

George W. Ford is a son of James H. and Catherine (Groseclose) Ford, and was born in Davis County, Iowa, in 1853. The father was born in Garrett County, Ky., in 1816, and the mother in Wythe County, Va., in 1823. When young both came to Schuyler County, where they married and settled upon a small farm, and spent the remainder of their lives in the county, with the exception of about eight years. They were among the very early settlers of the vicinity, and Mrs. Ford was one of the three young ladies who first came to the county. At the time that Texas was fighting for her independence Mr. Ford volunteered his services, but was never upon the scene of action.   In politics he was Democratic in his views, but was also a strong Abolitionist.   He was killed in 1862 by a party of bushwhackers.   George W. Ford was one of a family of eleven children, and when three months old was brought to Schuyler County by his parents, where he spent his youth upon the farm, and received a good English education.   After attending the district schools he attended the State Normal at Kirksville, and then, after teaching one term, devoted his attention to farming.   He now owns 700 acres of good land, well cultivated and improved, and devotes his time exclusively to agricultural pursuits.   He resides upon the old homestead, which was settled in 1838.   In 1879 he was united in marriage to Mary J. Mock, a daughter of Alfred Mock. Mrs. Ford was born in Putnam County, Mo., in 1854, and died in 1882.   She was the mother of two children—Harvey A. and James T.   In 1882 Mr. Ford married Martha D. Lucas, who was born in Schuyler County in 1860.   This union has been blessed by three children: Jessie L., George J. and a child yet unnamed. In politics Mr. Ford is a Democrat, and in Masonry a member of Glenwood Lodge, No. 427.

Edwin French, a retired merchant and old settler of Lancaster, Mo., was born in Worcester County, Mass., in 1817, and is a son of Isaac and Catherine (Davis) French.   The father was born in 1775 in Massachusetts, was a farmer and trusty and prominent business man, and settled many estates.   His father, John French, was a solicitor in the French and Indian War, in 1754–57, and died at the age of eighty-six in 1823.   Isaac died while in the prime of life, in the year 1826.   His wife, Catherine Davis, was born in Worcester County, Mass., in 1781, and was the mother of four children, our subject being the only one living.   Edwin was educated at the district schools of his native town, and attended a boarding-school two terms.   His father's death occurred when he was but nine years old, and when seventeen he began to teach in his native town.   He continued this occupation for three months.   In 1837 he went to the territory that has since been formed and organized into Scotland County, Mo., and engaged in the mercantile business there three and a half years, and in the fall of 1841 came to the territory since organized into Schuyler County, locating at Tippecanoe, three miles southeast of Lancaster, where he engaged in the same business. In 1853 he removed his stock of goods to Lancaster, and remained in business there until 1879.   He also engaged in farming, in connection with his other business, with good success.   In February, 1843, he married Miss Esther Hathaway, daughter of Josiah Hathaway.   This lady was born in Vermont in 1822, and is the mother of five living children: Charles H., Wilber D., Agnes, Julia and Edwin L., an attorney at law, at Lancaster. In 1879 Mr. French and wife went to Colorado, in 1881 to California, and in 1885 returned to Lancaster, Mo., where they now live a retired life. Previous to the war Mr. French was a Whig, but is now a Democrat, and cast his first presidential vote for William H. Harrison in 1840. He was elected representative of Schuyler County in 1846, being the first one from that county, and was re-elected in 1848. Ten years later he was elected treasurer of Schuyler County, and served so satisfactorily that he was re-elected in 1860. At the close of the war he was elected circuit clerk, and was afterward appointed by Judge Ellison, serving about fifteen months. He and his wife are members of the Christian Church. His son, Edwin L., was born in Lancaster, Mo., in 1856, and was educated there and at Christian University in Canton, Mo., which he attended three years, graduating with the degree of B. S. in 1876. He then taught one term of school in Schuyler County, and in January, 1877, began to study law with C. E. Vrooman. He was admitted to the bar in 1879, and was a partner of Mr. Vrooman for three years. He is a man of more than ordinary legal ability, and enjoys a fine practice. In May, 1883, he married Miss Belle Justice, daughter of Joseph H. Justice, of Keokuk, Iowa, and to Mr. and Mr. French two children have been born: Herbert Justice and Joseph Harvey. Himself and wife are members of the Christian Church.

James T. Fugate is a grandson of John Fugate, a native of Virginia, where he was united in marriage to Elizabeth Hamilton, who bore him five sons and five daughters, and died before he left his native State in search of a home in the west. He was a prominent man in those days and filled the offices of sheriff and magistrate, performing the duties of the latter more than thirty years. In 1845 he located near Queen City, Mo., and cultivated a farm. He soon after married Susan Hamilton, by whom he had one daughter. He died in his eighty-third year. Of his children two, Elizabeth and Elbert, are living in Schuyler County. The latter was born in Virginia in 1838, and was but seven years old when he accompanied his father to Missouri. Since that time he has been a resident of Schuyler County. In 1858 he wedded Nancy Hollcroft, who was born in Switzerland County, Ind., in 1838, but who accompanied her parents to this county when a young lady. To this union five sons and two daughters were born. Mrs. Fugate is a member of the Primitive Baptist Church. Mr. Fugate and his sons are strong Democrats, and the grandfather was also a member of that political party. Although farming is his principal occupation, Mr. Fugate held the office of constable for four years. Of his children two, James T. and Jeff D., are teachers, and the former is superintendent of schools in Schuyler County. He is a native of this county, and was born August 4, 1859. He was reared upon a farm and educated in the common schools of the neighborhood. At the age of eighteen he began to teach and has since taught eleven successive terms. In 1882 he married Laura Payton, daughter of Y. W. Payton, and a native of Schuyler County, Mo., and born in 1858, and by her one son, Clarence, has been born. Mr. James Fugate is one of the enterprising young men of the county, and has always been interested in its educational advancement. In April, 1887, he was chosen county superintendent, and is also discharging the duties of the office of magistrate. He has sixty-one schools under his charge, and besides looking after them satisfactorily, owns a farm of eighty acres of land well cultivated and improved.

James M. Fulcher, farmer and stock raiser, was born in Schuyler County, in 1844, and is the second of four children of John S. and Mary (Alverson) Fulcher. The father was of English-Irish descent, and born in Boone County, Mo., in 1819. His father, Jefferson Fulcher, was a native of Virginia and a soldier in the War of 1812, having fought in the battle of Tamer. He was an early pioneer of Madison County, Ky., and settled in Boone County, Mo., in an early day, while the present State was yet a territory. For some years he engaged in traffic with the Indians and made several trips each year to Santa Fe. In 1836, he settled in what is now Schuyler County, Mo., where he died in 1859. John S. was reared in Boone County, and came with his father to Schuyler County, Mo., in 1836. He was married in Howard County, in 1841, and located on the Grand Divide, where he farmed until his death in 1852. Having been reared in Missouri during the early history of that State, when Indians still inhabited the country, he associated with the neighboring tribes and learned their language, and also became very proficient in hunting and other sports. The mother of our subject was born in Madison County, Ky., and when eight years old was taken by her parents to Howard County, Mo. Both she and her husband were members of the Methodist Episcopal Church. Her death occurred in 1860. James M. lived with his mother prior to her decease, and received a common-school education. He was the main support of the family. In 1864 he was married to Miss Susannah, daughter of David A. and Rachel Roberts. Mrs. Fulcher was born in Schuyler County, in 1846, and has borne her husband nine children, seven living: Emma (wife of W. E. Stacy), John D., Etta, Cora, Eva, William and Reuben. He has resided five miles northwest of Queen City, near Julesburg, since his marriage, where he has a farm of 120 acres in one tract, and eighty acres in another. Mr. Fulcher was reared during the early days of Missouri, and endured the hardships of pioneer life during his youth, but has kept pace with the advancement of the State, and is now one of the enterprising farmer citizens of his county. He was elected justice of the peace, serving four years, and was then re-elected and served another term with equal satisfaction. Two appeals have been taken from his decisions as justice, and were both settled by appellants before the trial in the circuit court. In politics he is strictly Independent and votes for the man he thinks worthy without regard to party affiliation. His first presidential vote was cast for Grant in 1868. He has been a member of the Christian Church since thirty years of age, and has been an elder in the same for some years. His wife is also a member of the same church, as are also the four eldest children.

George A. Furry, farmer, is a son of Jacob and Maria (Hill) Furry, and was born October 27, 1847, in Perry County, Ohio. The father was of German and French descent, and a native of Pennsylvania. When young he went to Perry County, Ohio, where he was married. In 1851 he started for Iowa with his family by water, but died of cholera while on the Mississippi River, and was buried upon its banks. The mother continued her journey with her four children, and located in New London, Henry Co., Iowa. She was born near Zanesville, Ohio, and died in Iowa in 1864. George A. is the third child, and at the time of his father's death was four years old. He lived with his mother until seven years of age, and was then taken by Richard Griggs, a resident of Schuyler County, Mo., where George made his home until February, 1864, when he enlisted in Company M, Twelfth Missouri Volunteer Cavalry, and served two years. He was discharged at Fort Leavenworth, Kas., in April, 1866. He then returned to Schuyler County, and October 13, 1868, married Miss Mary P. Barnes, daughter of Jacob and Catherine Barnes. Mrs. Furry was born in Davis County, Iowa, September 29, 1851. Since his marriage our subject has made his residence in Schuyler County, with the exception of the three years which divide 1873 from 1876, which he spent in Pottawattomie County, Iowa, during which time he was foreman of the Bellview Nursery at Council Bluffs, Iowa. In the spring of 1887 he moved where he now resides. He is a well-to-do citizen, and a man of enterprise, and is the owner of two blocks in Lancaster, containing ten acres of land. He is a Republican, and cast his first presidential vote for U. S. Grant in 1868. He is a member of the A. O. U. W., and himself and wife belong to the Methodist Episcopal Church.

William S. Gatlin, senior member of the firm of Gatlin & Winfree, was born in Tazewell County, Ill., in 1832, and is a son of Hardy and Catherine (Gates) Gatlin. The father is of Irish and English ancestry, and was born in Tennessee in 1808. When a young man he went to Illinois with his parents, and was there married. In 1855 he removed to Adair County, Mo., and soon after to Green Top. He lived in Schuyler County some years, and then went to Kansas, and is now living in Cass County, Mo., farming and working at the blacksmith's trade. His father, Dempsey Gatlin, was a soldier in the War of 1812. The mother of our subject was born in Kentucky, was about three years her husband's junior, and died about 1849 in Illinois. William S. was reared at home, and received but a common-school education. In 1855 he married Miss Deborah Vannote, a native of Illinois, and this union was blessed with four children: Henry W. Hamilton (of Iowa), Charles A. (of Alexandria, Mo.), Emma Belle (wife of Peter B. Winfree, of De Witt, Mo.) and Ida May. Mrs. Gatlin died in 1872, and in 1874 Mr. Gatlin married Miss Elizabeth Hoover, a native of Virginia, but then living in Iowa. His second wife died in 1875, and in 1877 our subject wedded Mrs. Lovina Winfree, daughter of William Hall. In about 1857 Mr. Gatlin came to Schuyler County, where his home has since been, with the exception of the years between 1870 and 1875, which were spent in Iowa. He first located at Green Top upon coming to Missouri. Part of the time he had been engaged in farming and saw-milling, but was mostly in the mercantile business. He served about twenty years as postmaster of Green Top, and while in Iowa was assistant postmaster for a while. He has always been a public-spirited man, interested in educational and public enterprises, and his children are enjoying the advantages of a good education. He was formerly a Democrat, and cast his first presidential vote for Douglas in 1860, but since that time has been a Republican. During the war his sympathies were with the Union, but he was not allowed to serve, on account of his poor health. He is now engaged in the hardware and grocery business at Green Top, and enjoys a good and extensive patronage. He is a prominent member of the I. O. O. F., and his wife belongs to the Methodist Episcopal Church.

W. C. Graves was born in Schuyler County, in 1850, and is a son of Richard and Berrilla (Myrtle) Graves. The father is of English descent, and was born in Howard County, Mo., in 1826, and is a farmer by occupation. His father, David, was a native of Shelby County, Ky., and emigrated to Howard County, Mo., in 1820, and died in 1880. Richard H. was married in 1849, and soon after located three miles northwest of Lancaster in Schuyler County, Mo., where he bought and entered 160 acres of land upon which he has since resided, and which he has increased to 340 acres. He served in the Home Militia during the war. His wife is of English descent and was born in Howard County, Mo., in 1823. She is the mother of seven children: William C., James D., Hannah A. (wife of Thomas Burns), Reuben W., Samuel C., John B. and Lizzie. W. C. lived with his parents until twenty-one years of age, receiving a common-school education, and April 27, 1871, was united in marriage to Miss Annie G. Green, daughter of Hiram Green. She was born in Brown County, Ill., in 1849, and is the mother of six children: Clarence True, Florence E., Lena Belle, Edna Leonora, Hiram Leo and Addie Dimple. After his marriage our subject settled near the home place and began farming for himself. In 1875 he bought eighty acres in Liberty Township, and in 1885 came to Lancaster and purchased a half interest in a general store with John W. Milligan, who afterward sold his share to A. P. Primm. In January, 1887, he divided the stock of goods with Mr. Primm and has since conducted the business alone. He is a Republican, having cast his first presidential vote for U. S. Grant in 1872. Himself and wife belong to the Christian Church.

Gilbert D. Gray, loan broker, was born in Perry County, Ohio, in 1840, and is a son of Jonas H. and Achsah P. (Mills) Gray. The father was born in Muskingum County, Ohio, July 4, 1812, and the mother in Hartford, Conn., in 1814, but in infancy was taken by her parents to Perry County, Ohio, where she was married. Mrs. Gray was a daughter of Senator Mills, and after the death of Mr. Gray was married to Robert Greene, with whom she is now living in Iowa. Mr. Gray was a tailor by trade, and at the time of his death was the proprietor of a merchant tailor establishment. He was a Whig during the days of that party, and served as captain in the State Militia. Both Mr. and Mrs. Gray were members of the Methodist Church. Of a family of three sons and three daughters, only one son and two daughters are living. The grandfather of the subject of this sketch was of Irish descent; his great-grandfather, in company with a brother and a Scotchman, were prosecuted by the Catholics in their native land, and after the confiscation of their property escaped and went to sea in a yawl, and after being wrecked were picked up and brought to America about the year 1760. They settled in Virginia and their descendants are now scattered over the United States. Gilbert was reared in Perry County, and after the death of his father, when he was but ten years old, lived with his mother and two sisters, whom in later years he

cared for to the best of his ability. His education was necessarily somewhat limited, but while a boy he worked in a printing
office and became an expert type-setter. During the late war
Mr. Gray offered his services, which were rejected on account
of his small statue. He then organized a company of small
men and tendered them as sharpshooters, but the Government
rejected them. He soon went to St. Louis, Mo., and was finally
mustered into service as second lieutenant of Company D, of the
Tenth Missouri Infantry. He was promoted to the first lieuten-
ancy of the company in August, 1861, and in June, 1863,
became captain of Company B. At Vicksburg he was wounded,
and mustered out on account of disabilities in February, 1864.
He then returned home, but the following October organized
the eastern regiment of Davis County, Iowa, border troops, of which
he was elected lieutenant-colonel, and fulfilled the duties of that
office until the close of the war. In 1861 he was captured in
Callaway County, Mo., but effected an escape. In 1867 he came
to Lancaster and engaged in the drug business. In 1869 he
removed his store to Glenwood, and engaged in the drug business
until 1886, since which time he has been a loan broker. In 1863
he was united in marriage to Theresa E. Spencer, daughter of
Capt. Horace A. Spencer, of Bloomfield, Iowa. To this union three
children have been born: James M., Emma and Maude. In
politics Mr. Gray is a stanch Republican, and has served as justice of the peace and county judge. He has been a member
of the Masonic order twenty-five years. In the I. O. O. F.
fraternity he has filled every office in the Grand Encampment
except those of grand secretary and treasurer. He is past post
commander of David Robert's Post, No. 25, G. A. R.

Spencer Greer, farmer and stock raiser, was born in Grayson
County, Va., in 1825, and is a son of George and Nancy (Isom)
Greer. The father was born in Virginia in 1799, and was a
blacksmith, which trade he followed in youth and middle life, but
in later years cultivated land for a livelihood. He was married in
1824, and in 1836 moved to Lawrence County, Ind., where he purchased a farm and spent the remainder of his days, his death
occurring in November, 1864. His wife was born in Virginia in
1803, and died in 1884. She was the mother of nine children,
of whom Spencer is the eldest. When eleven years old he
moved with his parents to Indiana, and remained with them until
twenty-four years of age. In October, 1849, he married Miss
Serene Edwards, daughter of Edward and Mary (Cox) Edwards.
Mrs. Greer was born in Lawrence County, Ind., in 1832, and to
her union with our subject nine children were born, all dead
except two—Edward M. and William H. In 1852 Mr. Greer

left Lawrence County and went to Lancaster, Schuyler Co., Mo., and carried on the mercantile business until 1857, when he sold out and began to farm. In 1862 he purchased 160 acres of land, where he now resides. By economy, industry and good management Mr. Greer has added acre after acre to his possessions, until he now owns 520 acres of first-class land, and is an extensive dealer in fine stock, and keeps on an average 100 cattle, 300 sheep, 50 hogs and 10 horses. He is a Democrat, and cast his first presidential vote for James K. Polk, in 1844. He is a highly esteemed farmer citizen, and a member of the I. O. O. F.

George Groseclose, a prominent farmer and stock raiser of Fabius Township, was born September 12, 1825, in Tazewell County, Va., and is the third of eight children born to Joseph and Barbara Groseclose, natives of Wythe County, Va. Upon leaving there they moved to Indiana, and subsequently to Schuyler County, Mo., where they died, aged fifty-eight and seventy-three, respectively. The father was of German descent; the mother was a daughter of Christopher Foglesong, who died in Indiana. George Groseclose accompanied his parents to Johnson County, Ind., when two years old, and at the age of twelve became located in Schuyler County, which he has since made his home. He began life when twenty-one with eighty acres of land, which by good management has been increased, until he is now the owner of 200 acres, a fact which stamps him one of the energetic farmers of the county. In 1845 he was married to Miss Odyssey Lloyd, a daughter of Lemuel F. Lloyd, whose parents were of Virginian nativity. He was Indian agent under Gen. Jackson, and was also Secretary of the Treasury. His wife was a daughter of Elias Davis, who was also originally from Virginia. Mr. and Mrs. Groseclose have a family of fifteen children: Maryland J., Cena L., Joseph W., Susan D., Eliza C., Mary F., George, William, McGuffy W., Tillman, Melcena, Lee Price, Edwin L., Sarah Ellen and an infant, unnamed. Mr. Groseclose in politics is a Democrat.

William B. Groseclose, farmer and stock raiser, was born in 1842, upon the farm of which he is now a resident, in Fabius Township, Schuyler Co., Mo. He was the youngest child of Joseph and Barbara (Foglesong) Groseclose [see sketch of George Groseclose], and when fifteen years old, upon the death of his father, started in life for himself. He had no property to begin life with, but is now the possessor of a well-improved farm of 190 acres in the home place, and 160 acres in another tract, and is one of the enterprising and well-to-do farmers of the county. He served a short time during the Rebellion, and on March 20, 1869, was united in marriage to Miss Hannah E. Webster, daughter of Joseph and Margaret (Waddle) Webster. To Mr. and Mrs. Groseclose ten children have been born: Joseph L., Elizabeth, Sarah, David F., George E., Mary A., Reese, Roy B., Frank and Margaret. In politics Mr. Groseclose is a Democrat. He is a Master Mason, and a man highly respected in the community in which he lives.

James T. Guinn (deceased), was a prominent farmer and stock raiser of Chariton Township, and a son of Hardin Guinn. He was born in Kentucky, in the year 1837, and during his youth came to Schuyler County, Mo., where he married Unity Locher, by whom he became the father of three children, only one daughter, Jennie, now living. Mr. Guinn was divorced in 1871, and the year following married Miss N. C. Dameron, a native of Randolph County, Mo., born in 1840. This lady is a daughter of Benjamin and Matilda (Mathis) Dameron, early settlers of Randolph County, where they passed their lives. The second marriage of Mr. Guinn was blessed with two children, Mann and Kate. Mrs. Guinn is a worthy member of the Cumberland Presbyterian Church, as was also her husband. With the exception of some four or five years spent in Coatsville, as a business man, Mr. Guinn made farming and stock raising his sole occupation, although he also bought and shipped stock extensively with great success. He was a self-made man, but by hard work, industry and good management, became the owner of 700 acres of fine land. He was a member of the Masonic fraternity, and a highly respected man in the vicinity in which he lived on account of his integrity and high moral character. In politics he was a Democrat, but never sought or held offices of public trust, as he chose rather to perform the duties of a private citizen.

Enoch E. Hale. Judge Charles Hale was born in Sullivan County, Tenn., in 1819, and moved to Shelby County, Mo., in 1843, and two years later removed to a farm in Fabius Township, Schuyler County, Mo., where he has since resided. He was reared upon a farm and educated at a college in Greene County, Tenn. At the age of twenty-one he began life for himself with no capital, but is now the owner of a finely improved farm of 280 acres. October 1, 1840, he married Miss Melvina Lightner, daughter of Christian and Nancy (Glass) Lightner, and to this union eleven children were born: Sarah A., John M., Nancy E., Enoch E., Montraville F., Dora B., Martha F. and Mary M. (twins), James P., and two who died in infancy. The father of Mrs. Hale lived first in Pennsylvania, then in Virginia, then in Tennessee, where he was married; then in Schuyler County, Mo., and finally died in Hickory County, Mo. Mr. Hale is a member of the Baptist Church, and in politics is a Democrat.

He was appointed county judge by the Governor of the State,
served two years, and was twice re-elected, but resigned during
the second term of his office.   He was the third of a family of
thirteen children, all of whom lived to maturity.   His parents,
Lewis and Elizabeth (Bragg) Hale, were natives of Greene
and Sullivan Counties, Tenn., respectively.   The father was
a farmer, and during the War of 1812 was the commander
of a company.   He was a son of Meshach and Mollie Hale.
The former was of English descent, and a native of Virginia, the
latter of Irish descent.   Mrs. Elizabeth Hale was a daughter of
David and Elizabeth Bragge, early settlers of North Carolina,
and pioneer settlers of Sullivan County, Tenn., where they located
about 1775.   The immediate subject of this sketch, Enoch E.
Hale, is a son of Judge Charles Hale and Melvina (Lightner)
Hale, and was born in Schuyler County, Mo., in 1851.   He was
reared upon the farm and sent to the common schools of the
neighborhood, and afterward spent two years at schools in La
Grange.   He lived with his parents until twenty-four years of
age, and then began to clerk for Forsha & Irvin, for whom his
brother, John M., had been working for some time.   He and his
brother bought out the above named firm in 1876.   Four years
later Enoch gave up business life, and purchased a farm upon
which he engaged in stock raising, in connection with farming,
for four years.   He then returned to mercantile life with his
brother, James P., as a partner, and is now the senior member of
E. E. Hale & Bro., and a leading merchant of Glenwood.   Mr.
Hale was married January 14, 1877, to Lucia V. England, who
was born March 31, 1853, in Quebec, Canada, and came to
Schuyler County, Mo., with her parents while young.   Mr. Hale
belongs to the Missionary Baptist Church, and his wife to the
Congregational.   In politics Mr. Hale is a Democrat.   He has
risen from a poor man to one of the most enterprising and prosperous business men of Glenwood, and owns a good stock and
the buildings in which his business is conducted.

G. W. Hall, farmer and stock raiser, was born in Bourbon
County, Ky., in 1820.   He is the third child of eleven, born to
James and Frankie (Rice) Hall, natives of Kentucky.   The
father was of German descent, and a blacksmith, which trade he
followed all his life.   The maternal grandfather was a soldier in
the Revolutionary War.   When a boy G. W. accompanied his
parents on their westward journey, finally settling in Scotland County, Mo., but in 1840 moved to Schuyler County, and
located upon a piece of land one and a quarter miles northwest
of Tippecanoe.   In the fall of 1852 he commenced to farm upon the
place where he has since resided.   Having learned the blacksmith's

trade when but a boy, Mr. Hall followed that trade until 1880, but since that time has been exclusively engaged in farming, and by industry and good management has become the owner of 185 acres of good land, which he has cultivated, and which is now highly improved. In 1844 he was united in marriage to Miss Elizabeth Groseclose, daughter of Joseph and Barbara (Foglesong) Groseclose [see sketch], and eleven children have blessed this union, viz: Mary Ann C., Barbara F. (deceased), William J., Ella O. (deceased), Sarah E., David F., George E., Squire J., Martha M., Lewis V. and Eliza E. Mr. and Mrs. Hall are worthy members of the Baptist Church, and the former is a member of the Blue Lodge in Masonry. In politics he is a Democrat, and has served his township satisfactorily in several different capacities.

Caleb F. Hargis, is a son of Joshua and Samantha J. (Partin) Hargis, born in Kentucky, in 1811 and 1821, respectively. When young they moved to Howard County, Mo., where they were married and lived until 1852. They then made their home in Schuyler County, one year, and then went to Adair County, where the father died in 1862. The mother now lives with our subject, and is a devout member of the Christian Church. The father was a well-to-do farmer, and a Democrat. Caleb F. had three sisters and one brother. The latter was a soldier during the late war in the Seventh Missouri Cavalry, United States army, and died in Macon City, Mo., from the effects of the measles. Caleb F. was born in Howard County, Mo., in 1843. He was reared upon the farm, and received but a limited education at one of the primitive school-houses of those days. After his father's death Mrs. Hargis became the wife of James Lucas, who lived but a short time, and then the care of his mother devolved upon the subject of this sketch. In 1868 he was united in marriage to Odessa Hamilton, daughter of John Hamilton. Mrs. Hargis was born in Schuyler County, in 1851, and is the mother of the following children: Susan E., Joshua F., John F., Ada A., Joseph F., Ella M. and Nicholas C., of whom but the last named three survive. When he came to Schuyler County from Adair County, in 1866, Mr. Hargis was a poor man, but is now the owner of 360 acres of good land, and one of the prosperous men of the county. In politics he is a strong Democrat, a believer in woman's rights, and an earnest advocate of the temperance cause. He and his wife are Universalists.

Elder William Hartley was born in Washington County, Ind., in 1823, and is a son of John and Jane (Fox) Hartley. The father was of English descent and born in Burke County, N. C., in 1795. He was a farmer and politician and was married in his native State, and in 1814 immigrated to Washington County, Ind., where he spent the remainder of his days. He was representative of that county two sessions, and his death occurred in 1873. His wife was born in East Tennessee, in 1803, and died in 1843. Our subject is the fourth of five children, and was educated in Salem, Ind., making his home with his parents until he became of age. When nineteen he entered the ministry, being a member of the Christian Church, and was ordained in Salem, in 1847. September 8 of that year he was united in marriage to Miss Minerva Wilson, who was born in Charleston, Clark Co., Ind., in June, 1828. This union was blessed with eight children: Louisa (wife of Sydney Brown), Byrod B., John, Tilman, Mack, Alfred, Minerva (wife of William Yates) and Belle (wife of Thomas Lewis). In 1857 Elder Hartley left his native State and went to Bloomfield, Iowa, where he resumed his ministerial duties, preaching half of his time in Bloomfield and half in Lancaster, Mo. It was at the former place that his success was very marked. In the spring of 1866 he preached forty-seven sermons in succession, at a meeting which lasted five weeks and two days, and in this time he had 178 accessions, and 103 people were immersed. In 1869 he moved to Lancaster, where he now resides, and for twenty-three years has regularly expounded the gospel to his hearers. From 1869 to 1874 he traveled for Mount Hope Nursery, New York, his work being continued in Missouri, and during this time made ten trips to the nursery. In 1875 he purchased a farm of 120 acres, adjoining Lancaster, where he now lives a more retired life, preaching at irregular intervals, when his service is desired, and is frequently called upon to perform the rites of baptism, matrimony, and to preach funeral sermons. He is a Republican and cast his first presidential vote for James K. Polk in 1844. He is a Christian gentleman, highly esteemed and honored by the community.

Joseph W. Hatfield, farmer and stock raiser, was born in Wayne County, Ky., in 1834, and is a son of Andrew and Mary A. (Miller) Hatfield. The father was of English descent, and born in 1801 in Wayne County, Ky. During early life he engaged in distilling, but during the latter part of his life was engaged in agricultural pursuits. His father, Ale Hatfield, was a native of Kentucky, and in 1838 moved to Indiana, and died in 1837, at the age of ninety. Andrew was married in 1820, and in 1837 immigrated to Randolph County, Mo., and the following year moved to Adair County, Mo., settling six miles southeast of Kirksville, and becoming the owner of 720 acres of fine land. In 1840 he moved to Putnam County, and located in Elm Township, buying 220 acres of land. He died in 1879. He was a volunteer in the Florida War, but did not serve, as he was not called out. His wife was born in South Carolina, in 1804, and died in 1876. Our subject is the third of five children, and at the age of seven came to Northeast Missouri, making his home with his parents until eighteen years old. In 1852 he went to California overland, six months being required to make the journey. He there engaged in mining, teaming and hotel-keeping, and in 1861 returned to Putnam County, Mo. In August of that year he married Miss Emily, daughter of James Cain, of Putnam County. This lady was born in Putnam County in 1844, and is the mother of ten living children: Louisa A. (wife of Dennis Riggle), David A., Celia A., Joseph W., Alexander S., Emma C., Benjamin F., Gracie M., Elmer C. and Bertie L. Mr. Hatfield remained in Putnam County until 1863, then went to Nevada, and in the fall of that year returned to Missouri on business. Again going to Nevada he made that and California his home until 1881, when he returned to the scenes of his boyhood and settled upon the land above described. In politics he is a conservative Democrat, and his first presidential vote was cast for Buchanan, in 1856. He is a member of the K. of P.

Leroy Hays (deceased) was born in Union County, Ohio, in 1830, and there spent his youthful days. He was united in marriage to Sarah Hobert, also a native of that county, where she was born in 1834. They remained in Union County until 1858, and then moved to Lucas County, Iowa, and from there in 1865 to Schuyler County, Mo., where they located upon the farm where Mrs. Hays now lives. Mr. Hays was an expert carpenter, and erected some of the finest buildings in Glenwood, such as the St. Nicholas Hotel, Glenwood Flour Mill, etc., but in later life engaged almost exclusively in agricultural pursuits. He was an active and ardent Democrat, and one of the leading spirits of that party in his county after the late war. He was a prominent member of the I. O. O. F. for more than twenty-five years, and upon his death, in 1877, the county lost one of its representative citizens. His widow is a worthy member of the Christian Church, and bore Mr. Hays six children, four sons and two daughters, of whom but four sons are living. The eldest son, Joseph W., was born in Union County, Ohio, in 1851, where he received a good common-school education, and became familiar with a farmer's life, to which he has always devoted his attention. In 1886 he was united in marriage to Clara E. Majors, a native of Schuyler County. Politically Mr. Joseph Hays is a Democrat. Marvel J., another son, was also born in Union County, Ohio, his birth occurring in 1855; he, too, availed himself of the advantages offered by the common schools of his vicinity, and acquired a good English education. He is an enterprising young farmer, and, in partnership with his brother, Joseph, is engaged in farming and stock raising upon 340 acres of well cultivated and improved land. In 1883 he married Susan E. Morris, who was born in Davis County, Iowa, in 1860, and by her had two children: Sibyl E. and Gladys C. Both brothers are honorable members of the I. O. O. F., Glenwood Lodge, No. 233. McClellan L. Hays, the fourth son, was born in Lucas County, Iowa, in 1862, received a good common-school education, and is now engaged as salesman in his brother's store, in Glenwood, Mo. For over twenty-two years the Hays family have been residents of Schuyler County, and that name has always been synonymous of honesty. and respectability. When Leroy Hays located here he had but little property, but at the time of his death owned 180 acres of choice land, and was regarded as one of the substantial farmers of the township, and his sons are now considered enterprising and well-to-do young farmers.

Charles A. Hays is a son of Leroy and Sarah (Hobert) Hays, both natives of Union County, Ohio, where they were reared and married. They afterward moved to Lucas County, Iowa, and from there to Schuyler County, Mo., and located in Glenwood, where the mother still lives and where the father died. He was a tanner and carpenter by trade, and worked at those employments most of his life. After coming to Missouri he did a good deal of carpentering, and built the H. Nicholas Hotel and Glenwood Flouring Mill. He was a charter member of the I. O. O. F. Lodge, No. 233, at Glenwood, and in politics was an active Democrat. The mother is a member of the Christian Church. Charles A. is the third son of a family of four sons and one daughter, and was born in Lucas County, Iowa. When at the age of four years his parents moved to Glenwood, Mo., where he was reared upon a farm, and received a common-school education. When nineteen he obtained a teacher's license, but accepted a position in a store at a salary of $15 per month, but before half of the first month had expired his salary was raised to $25 per month for the remainder of the year. After three years of work at that place he went into the grocery business, has since increased the variety of his stock, and now owns a good general store and does a prosperous business. In 1882 he married Carrie Hodges, a native of Illinois. In politics Mr. Hays is a stanch Democrat, and he is a member of the I. O. O. F. Besides his business property Mr. Hays owns the Opera Hall, a building 22x70 feet, which he built, and which is nicely fitted up.

Dr. Cary W. Hight, druggist and prescriptionist, was born in Georgia, in 1844, and is a son of Nathan and Eliza (Horton)

****

Hight. The father is of German ancestry, and born in Virginia about 1809. He afterward went to Georgia, where he married the mother of our subject, who was a native of that State. After her death, in 1859, Mr. Hight married her sister, Miss Harriet. He has for many years been a resident of Louisiana, where he owns a large plantation. Cary W. was reared under parental instruction, and received a good academic and business education. Being of Southern birth and rearing, at the time of the late war, he, with a majority of the people of his adopted State, took up arms in the Confederate cause, enlisting in Company C, Twelfth Louisiana Volunteer Infantry, and was afterward transferred to the cavalry, and was held in reserve at Shiloh. He was in the battle of Corinth and the siege of Vicksburg, after which his service ceased. In 1866 he went to Illinois, and soon after to Randolph County, Mo., where, in 1868, he wedded Miss Nannie E., daughter of Robert Adams. This lady is a native of Randolph County, and has borne the Doctor two children: Emma F. and William B. He then came to Schuyler County, and in 1870 established a drug store at Green Top, two years later removing to Queen City. In early boyhood he developed a taste for his chosen profession, and with his past experience is now a thorough master of his business, and the selection and quality of his stock is very fine. He carries a full line of drugs, chemicals, stationery, school books, etc. In 1872 he was elected justice of the peace, but after a short service resigned. He is a Democrat, but cast his first presidential vote for Gen. Grant, in 1872. He is a member of the I. O. O. F.

Gibson R. Hombs. William Hombs, father of the subject of this sketch, is a son of Silas and Elizabeth (Nickelson) Hombs, both of whom were born in Garrett County, Ky., where they were reared and married. In 1818 they moved to Boone County, Mo., where they died at an advanced age. Both had been members of the Baptist Church for many years. The father served in the War of 1812. His occupation was that of farming, and he obtained a land warrant, which William located for him in this county. William was the fifth child of a family of eleven, and born in Boone County, Mo., July 26, 1826. He was reared upon the farm, and his education necessarily limited, his entire school life not aggregating more than three months. When fifteen years old he began to work in a tanyard at $5 per month. In 1846 he was a volunteer in Ralls' Second Regiment, Missouri Volunteers, and served until the end of the Mexican War, participating in the battles of Chihuahua and Santa Cruz. After returning home he farmed a year, and then in 1850 went to California, where he mined successfully for some time, and then went into the mercantile business. By the turning of the Tualma River out of its course, in search of gold, the company of which he was a member lost over $12,000. In 1854 he returned home and began to collect stock with the intention of taking it to California, but his design was frustrated, and the following year he came to Schuyler County, and commenced to improve land. He now owns 1,200 acres of well cultivated land, and ranks among the substantial farmers of the county. In 1856 he married Mary A. Rippey, daughter of William V., a native of Monroe County, by whom he has had four children: Gibson R., John P., Willie D. and Mittie E. In politics he is a Democrat. He joined the Masonic order at Lancaster, thirty-one years ago, has filled all the chairs, and is now Master Mason of Glenwood Lodge, No. 427. Our immediate subject, Gibson R., was born January 1, 1857, in Glenwood Township, Schuyler Co., Mo. He was reared upon the farm, and during his early life received an education at the common schools of the neighborhood, which was afterward completed by two years' attendance at the State Normal School, at Kirksville. At the age of fifteen he began to clerk for Judge Logan, and, after remaining with him nine years, became his partner in the mercantile business. This partnership continued two years, and, in 1885, Mr Hombs and Mr. Blackwood formed a partnership, the firm being known as Blackwood & Hombs. In 1879 Mr. Hombs married Emma Case, a native of Ohio, and born April 1, 1860. Mrs. Hombs is a worthy member of the Methodist Episcopal Church. Mr. Hombs is a stanch Republican. He is a Master Mason, and has been senior warden of Glenwood Lodge, No. 427, four years. He also belongs to the K. of P., being a charter member at Kirksville. He is one of the prosperous business men of the community, and one who has the respect of his friends and associates.

Dr. W. M. Hunter was born in Brooke County, W. Va., in 1839, and is a son of John and Margaret (Hill) Hunter. The father was of Scotch descent, and was born in Scotland in 1803, where he was reared to manhood. He was married near Pittsburgh, after coming to the United States, settled in Brooke County, W. Va., in 1843, and afterward moved to Allegheny County, Penn. He was a farmer by occupation, and died in 1853. The mother was born in Ireland, in 1814, and came to the United States after arriving at her maturity. Her death occurred in 1855. Our subject was the eldest of five children. His education was commenced at the common schools of Pennsylvania, and he afterward attended Duff's College, taking the commercial course, and Mansfield Academy two terms. He went to Cooper County, Mo., and taught three terms, and in 1863 went to Fulton County, Ill., and November 1, of the following year, married Miss Angie S. Tuthill, who was born in Genesee County, N. Y., in 1843. They have three living children: William E., Robert and Mamie M. While teaching he began the study of medicine, and began to practice that profession in 1861. In 1867 he became a disciple of Blackstone, and engaged in that profession until 1882, when he came to Lancaster, Schuyler Co., Mo., and engaged in the mercantile business. In 1883 he bought *The Excelsior*, of which he has since been the sole manager. The paper is Democratic in politics, and has a circulation of about 1,500, being one of the leading weekly newspapers of Northeast Missouri. The Doctor has always been a Democrat, and while in Illinois was township clerk, supervisor and township treasurer twelve years. In 1883 he was elected mayor of Lancaster, serving one year. In 1885 he became a member of the board of education, which position he still holds, and in 1886 was elected a member of the town council. He is a Master Mason, and himself and wife belong to the Christian Church.

Andrew Jackson, farmer and stock raiser, is a native of Morgan County, Ind., and was born in 1838. He is a son of Samuel and Margaret (White) Jackson, and labored from home all the time from thirteen years of age, except in winter, when he cut wood for, and took care of his mother. Thus he received but a meager education, and that only through his own exertions. In 1857 he wedded Melissa J., daughter of William and Lavina Phipps, formerly of Kentucky. Mrs. Jackson was born in Macon County, Mo., and to her and our subject eight children have been born, all living: Sarah Marinda (wife of David O. Cripps), Benjamin Franklin (married to Elizabeth J. Singleton), Mary E., William T. S., James L., Fannie B., Maggie J. and Andrew O. Mr. Jackson remained in Macon County until 1866, and then came to Schuyler County, where he rented land for six years, and then purchased land three miles northwest of Queen City, which he has cultivated and improved, and which is now a fine farm of 320 acres. This property is the result of his own labor and good management, as he started in life a poor man. In 1862 he enlisted in Company M, Northeast Missouri Militia, and served two years, until the disbandment of his regiment. In 1864 he enlisted in Company H, Forty-second Missouri Infantry, and served in Tennessee, Missouri and Alabama, having been stationed at Fort Donelson, Nashville and Tullahoma, Tenn. He served as corporal until the close of the war, and then returned home, where he has made farming and stock raising his occupation, and is one of the most practical farmers of the county. Mr. Jackson is a Republican, although he cast his first presidential vote for Stephen A. Douglas, in 1860. Since then he has voted for the Republican nominees. He is a member of the Masonic fraternity, and is identified with the Christian Church. His father, Samuel Jackson, was a boatman upon the river for some years, and died, in 1840, while away from home. The family then removed to Macon County, Mo., and in 1866 came to Schuyler County, where the mother died in 1866, about sixty-four years of age. She was twice married, her first husband being a cousin of Andrew's father, and also a Mr. Jackson.

William F. James was born September 21, 1830, in Pike County, Mo., and is the second of a family of nine children born to Morris and Mary S. (Beasley) James. His paternal grandfather in company with a brother were the first representatives of the family who located in Missouri, and the land upon which they farmed is now Broadway, St. Louis. The father of William F. moved to Pike County when a young man, and there married Miss Beasley, who had come to that county when a little girl. After living in that county some time he moved to Randolph County, from there to Macon, and from there to Putnam; but the chills were so prevalent in that district that the family finally removed to Schuyler County, Mo., January 4, 1837. The father died in California, where he had gone in 1850 with a brother, whose death also occurred in that State. The father of the notorious Jesse James, who was a cousin of Mr. James, preached his funeral sermon. In politics Mr. James was a Democrat, and in religion himself and wife were worthy members of the Christian Church. Mrs. James survived her husband's death but four years. William F. was reared upon his father's farm, but, owing to the lack of schools in that region, his education was very limited. At the age of sixteen he began life for himself, often working for 25 cents a day, or making rails at 25 cents per hundred. His mother died when he was but nineteen, and then the care of four younger brothers fell upon him. Since then his life has been one of reverses, his chief occupations being farming and merchandising. In 1874 he opened a business house in Coatsville, which he still runs. Seventeen years ago he lost his all, but since that time has retrieved his fortunes, and, besides owning a good business, has 725 acres of land, 400 of which are coal land. In 1862 Mr. James enlisted in Company A, Seventh Missouri Militia, and served until the close of the war, when he was discharged at Hannibal, Mo. In 1851 he married Eliza Headley, who was born in Muskingum County, Ohio, in 1832, and by her had four children: Martha J., John W., Mary A. E. and William I. F. In 1869 Mrs. James died, and the following year he mar-

ried Mrs. Martha E. Locker (widow), who was born in Russell
County, Ky., in 1828. In politics Mr. James is a stanch Democrat. In Masonry he has taken all the degrees, extending to the
Palm and Shell in Oriental Masonry, and is also a member of
the I. O. O. F.

De. N. Jewett, clerk of the circuit court and *ex-officio* recorder
of Schuyler County, is a native of Union County, Ohio, and was
born September 9, 1849, and is a son of Jared O. and Harriet S.
(Butler) Jewett. The father traces his ancestry to two brothers,
who left England previous to the Revolution, on a man-of-war,
and came to America, one settling in Maine and one in Connecticut, the latter becoming the progenitor of the family of which
our subject is a descendant. The father of Jared O. Jewett was
born in Massachusetts, and served as major in the Revolutionary War. Jared O. was born in Franklin County, Vt., in
1813, and in 1854 removed to Union County, Ohio, two years
later coming to Schuyler County, Mo., where he located two
miles west of Lancaster. In 1863 he settled in the town where
he has since resided. He was married three times, and his
second wife (the mother of our subject) was born in Franklin
County, Vt., in 1815, and died in 1871. De. N. Jewett was the
youngest of a family of three children, and, when seven years
old, came to Schuyler County, and received his early education
at the common schools of that county. In 1863 he attended
Berkshire Seminary, in Franklin County, Vt., and after studying
there for three years returned home, and farmed. November 1,
1872, he was appointed deputy circuit clerk, and served until
October, 1878, when he was appointed circuit clerk, to fill the
vacancy caused by the death of Ward L. Munsell. In November, of the same year, he was elected to that office, and in 1882
and 1886 was re-elected, thus forcibly illustrating his ability as
an able and efficient officer. January 4, 1872, he married Miss
Allie C. Ballenger, daughter of Joshua and Henrietta Ballenger.
This lady was born in Richmond, Wayne Co., Ind., in 1852, and
has borne our subject two children: Carrie M. and Llewellyn
Lee. In politics Mr. Jewett is a Democrat, and cast his first
presidential vote for Horace Greeley, in 1872. He is a Master
Mason, and a member of the A. O. U. W. He is a substantial
and honored citizen, and owns five town lots and a building. His
wife belongs to the Methodist Episcopal Church, and he to the
Episcopal.

Abraham Johnson, farmer and stock raiser, is a son of Thomas
J. and Mary (Hull) Johnson, and was born in Franklin County,
Ohio, in 1827. His father was of English descent, and was born
in New Jersey, in 1793. When a boy he accompanied his parents

to Ohio, where he married and spent the remainder of his days, his death occurring in 1837. He was a volunteer in the navy of 1812, but did not enter the service. The mother was born in Germany, in 1797. Her death occurred in 1874. After her first husband's death, in 1837, she was again married two years later, after which event our subject made his home with his uncle, Alexander Johnson. Young Abraham received but a limited education in youth. In 1852 he took a trip through Iowa and Missouri, prospecting, and finally came to Schuyler County, of the latter State, and the same year (1852) married Mary Courrier, daughter of a Mr. Courrier, of Ohio, and to this marriage two children have been born: Sarah (wife of Logan Laurghty, and Frederick. Mrs. Johnson died in 1860, and the following year Mr. Johnson was married, in Washington County, Ohio, to Miss Catharine, daughter of Jacob and Margaret Mock, by whom he had ten children, all of whom save one are now living: Eli, Frank, Catharine, W. A., Newton, Riley, Julius, Clarence and Irvin. Mr. Johnson first located in Adair County, but soon returned to Schuyler County, and located three miles northeast of Queen City, where he has a fine farm of about 500 acres, all of which is the result of his industry and good management. He was formerly a Democrat, but cast his first presidential vote for Gen. Taylor, but since the Rebellion has been strictly conservative.

Dr. J. T. Jones was born in Woodford County, Ky., April 7, 1855. His father, Louis P., was a native of Virginia, and when a young man moved to Kentucky, where he married Miss Smith, by whom he had two sons and two daughters. Our subject was the youngest child, and, his parents having died when he was very young, he lived with his aunt upon the farm. His early education was received at the common schools, and at the age of twenty he came to Schuyler County, and attended the State Normal School at Kirksville two years. After completing his studies he began to teach school and to study medicine under Dr. W. B. Smith, of Downing, Schuyler County. He attended a course of lectures at the Keokuk College of Physicians and Surgeons, but graduated from the Medical College of Ohio, at Cincinnati, in 1884. He then opened a physician's office at Glenwood, and managed a drug store in the town. In 1886 he and his brother bought the stock of drugs, and have since conducted the business under the firm name of Jones Bros. In 1884 Dr. Jones married Jennie D. Cone, daughter of Hawley Cone. She is a native of Davis County, Iowa, born in 1863, her father having come originally from Ohio. By her he has had two children: Mamie R. (deceased) and Florence M. Dr. Jones is a member of the Glenwood Lodge, No. 427, in Masonry, and in politics is a Democrat. During his three years' practice in Glenwood he has been very successful, and enjoys a liberal and lucrative patronage.

Horace A. Jones is a son of Thomas B. and Ellen F. (Young) Jones, and was born in Wayne County, Iowa, February 22, 1861. The father was born in Indiana, and the mother was a native of Illinois, but both moved to Iowa during their youth. They were both teachers in the same school in that State, and formed a friendship which soon ripened into love. After their marriage Mr. Jones embarked in the drug business, in which he is still engaged. About 1866 he moved to Lancaster, Mo., but after residing there a number of years returned to Iowa, and is now doing business at Roland. He is a Republican. Mrs. Jones is a member of the Methodist Episcopal Church. To them four children have been born: Horace A., Lute (wife of Charles E. Sterret, train dispatcher), Paul W. and Benjamin. Horace A. was only nineteen years of age when he was chosen cashier of the Depositors' Bank at Glenwood, and, when that institution was transferred to Judge Logan, Mr. Jones' faithfulness and ability were rewarded by the same position under the new management. He received his education at the Lancaster schools, and is a young man of intelligence, ability and enterprise. He is the secretary of Glenwood Lodge, No. 427, of Masonry. In politics Mr. Jones is a Republican. He began life a poor boy, but, in connection with his banking interests, is also engaged in stock raising at the present time, and ranks among the prosperous young business men of the county.

Dr. Howard S. Justice was born December 13, 1836, in Columbus, Ohio, and is a son of Joseph and Jane Smith (Little) Justice. The father was born in Franklin County, Ohio, in 1806, and farming was his occupation. His father, Robert Justice, was a native of Virginia, and a soldier in the Revolutionary War. He settled in Franklin County, Ohio, in 1800, where he died in 1836, at the age of eighty-five. Joseph Justice was married in 1832, and lived in Franklin County, Ohio, until 1838, when he moved to Vermillion County, Ind. In 1840 he went to Scotland County, Mo., and there was engaged in farming until his death, in 1874. His wife was born in Weathersfield County, Conn., in 1812, and at the age of three accompanied her parents, Nathaniel and Hitty (Deming) Little, to Franklin County, Ohio. She is now living with Dr. Justice, and is the mother of nine children, five of whom are living: Joseph H. (of Keokuk, Iowa), Howard S., Ellen E. (widow of William Childers), Hetty A. (wife of George Clarkson), and William F. (a physician of Lancaster). Howard S., the subject of this sketch, went to Scotland County, Mo., with his parents when but four years old, where he passed his youth, and received his early education. At the age of nineteen he left the parental roof, and started out in life for himself, first working with his uncle at the brick mason's trade in Springfield, Ill. In 1859 he began the study of medicine, and in 1861 studied with Dr. O. George, of Bonaparte, Iowa. In 1862 he attended the State University, from the medical department of which he graduated February 15, 1865. He then pursued the practice of his profession, in Middle Fabius, Scotland County, until March, 1867, when he came to Lancaster, Mo., where he has since resided, with the exception of the spring of 1882, when he attended the practitioner course of the Chicago Medical College, Chicago, Ill., and the winter of 1884–85, which himself and wife spent in Los Angeles, Cal. The fall of 1877 he was appointed United States Examining Surgeon, and served as such eight years. During his residence in Lancaster Dr. Justice has established a good and lucrative practice, and has become one of the most successful physicians of the county. He owns a dwelling, in a desirable locality of the town, which is valued at $5,000. He is a self-made man, having made his own way in the world since nineteen years of age, and has also reared and educated his brother, William F., since the latter was fourteen years old. December 1, 1859, he was united in marriage with Miss Helen A. Smith, daughter of Horace and Nancy (Ferguson) Smith. This lady was born in Summit County, Ohio, March 21, 1844, and to her much of the Doctor's success may be attributed, as she has proved a faithful helpmate under all circumstances. She is a lady of rare artistic talent, and has executed some work of beauty and value. Dr. Justice is a Republican, and cast his first vote for S. A. Douglas in 1860. February 3, 1880, he was elected president of the Schuyler County Bank, which position he filled for four years, also acting as director. He is a member of the Masonic fraternity of the Knight Templar degree, and himself and wife are members of the Christian Church.

Conrad Kaster, a leading farmer and stock raiser of Prairie Township, was born in Hardin (now La Rue) County, Ky., in 1829, and is a son of Nathan and Nancy (Gray) Kaster, both natives of Kentucky. The father was born in 1792 and was of Dutch and Irish ancestry. He was married about 1814, and in 1855 removed to Adair County, Mo., where he died May 6, 1865. His father, Conrad Kaster, was a native of Pennsylvania, and an early settler of Kentucky, where he greatly assisted in driving the Indians from the State. The mother of Conrad, Jr., was two years her husband's senior, and died in 1842, after which her husband married a second time, in 1854, Mrs. Lear Gray becoming his wife. Conrad Kaster, our subject, received a limited common-school education while living at home, and in 1851 was married to Sarah J., daughter of Stephen and Elizabeth Castleman. To her union with Mr. Kaster thirteen children were born, all living with the exception of one, viz.: Elizabeth (wife of D. W. Starbuck), Nancy, Matilda (wife of Newton J. Dufer), Stephen, James and Ida (twins)—Ida is the wife of Sigel Coons—Nathan, Martha and Mary (twins)—Mary is the wife of Eli Johnson—Uretta and Henrietta (twins), Philip, and Florence J. (deceased). Mr. Kaster remained in Kentucky until 1855, and then removed to Schuyler County, and located four miles southeast of Queen City, where his home has since been. He now owns over 500 acres of choice land, which is under a fine state of cultivation and improvement, and is one of the most enterprising and prosperous farmers of the county. In politics he has always been united with the Democratic party, and cast his first presidential vote for Pierce, in 1852. Mrs. Kaster is a member of the Missionary Baptist Church.

J. W. Kelso, farmer and stock raiser, was born in Vermillion County, Ind., in 1836, and moved to Fulton County, Ill., when he was about five years old, where he grew to manhood. When fifteen he became an apprentice at the cooper's trade, and worked at that business, until 1862, at Rock Island, Peoria, and in Fulton County, Ill. He came to Schuyler County, Mo., in 1873, and there engaged in agricultural pursuits, at which occupation he has since been engaged, and is now the owner of a well improved and cultivated farm of 200 acres, which is the result of his frugality, industry and good management, as he has had no material assistance from friends or relatives. In 1857 he was united in marriage to Miss Emsy Pritchard, who was born in Licking County, Ohio, in 1841, and taken by her parents to Fulton County, Ill., when quite young. Her union with Mr. Kelso has been blessed with nine children: David V., Frank P., George McClellan, Wesley S., Faety S., Ida May, Athelston, Walter H. and Clarence. In politics Mr. Kelso is a Democrat, but has never sought nor held office. His parents had nine children, of whom he was the youngest. The father, Thomas, was a Scotchman. Archibald Kelso was born in Baltimore, Md., in 1761. His mother was Lucinda (Kendall) Kelso, a German lady, but born in Virginia, and she moved with her parents, Enoch and Sarah Kendall, to Licking County, Ohio, where the parents of the mother lived and died.

Arius King, a well-to-do farmer, is the eldest of a family of ten children born to John S. and Nancy (Hays) King, natives of Ohio, and afterward residents of Kosciusko County, Ind., from 1836 to 1865, when they went to Lucas County, Iowa. There the father died in 1855, at the age of seventy-five, but the mother still lives at the advanced age of seventy-two. In early life Mr. King was a hatter, but, as that was not a profitable business, he afterward engaged in farming. In politics he was formerly a Whig, but joined the Republican party after its organization. Mrs. King is a member of the Christian Church, but Mr. King was a Universalist. Arius King was born December 18, 1834, in Franklin County, Ohio, and during his youth received a common-school education. When nineteen he drove cattle to California, where he resided two years, but at the end of that time joined his parents in Iowa. In 1857 he was married to Nancy Hellier, a native of Morgan County, Ohio, and by her had four children: Vance A., John M., Frank and Eliza J. (wife of George Camden). When starting out in life for himself Mr. King had a capital of but $3, but now, after twenty-two years' residence in Schuyler County, is the owner of 180 acres of land adjoining Glenwood, under a good state of cultivation. In politics he is a Republican. He is an Odd Fellow, belonging to Glenwood Lodge, No. 233, and to Glenn Encampment.

Bennett Kratzer, ex-judge of Schuyler County, was born in Brown County, Ohio, in 1828, and is a son of Samuel and Elizabeth (Still) Kratzer. The former was of German descent, and born in Ohio, in 1806. He was a farmer by occupation, and was married in Brown County, where he spent the remainder of his life, his death occurring in 1883. He was twice married, his second wife being Mahala (Malott) Kratzer, who survives. The mother of our subject died in 1840, and was the mother of five children, of whom Bennett was the eldest. When sixteen years of age he began life for himself as an apprentice to a blacksmith, working three years for his board and clothes, and receiving three months' schooling. He then worked as a journeyman a year, after which he bought out his teacher, and began business on his own responsibility. In the fall of 1855 he came to Schuyler County, Mo., and a year later purchased 160 acres of land, where he now resides, and, in connection with farming, built a blacksmith shop, and worked at his trade many years. He now owns 288 acres of land in the county, and ranks as one of its highly respected and substantial farmer citizens. October 29, 1848, he married Miss Mary Heaton, daughter of James and Elizabeth Heaton, a native of Brown County, Ohio, where she was born in 1831. To this union seven children were born, viz.: Alonzo, Melissa (wife of Anderson York, of Davis County, Iowa), Leila F. (wife of Albert York), James D. (physician at Lancaster), Theresa (wife of Noah Butts), Charley F. (physician of Savannah, Iowa) and May. In politics he has long been a

Democrat, and cast his first presidential vote for Franklin Pierce. in 1852. He served as justice of the peace in 1865, and in 1880 was elected county judge, and served two years with great efficiency. Himself, wife and six children are members of the Christian Church.

Dr. James D. Kratzer was born in Brown County, Ohio, in 1855, and is a son of Judge Bennett and Mary (Heaton) Kratzer. [See sketch of Bennett Kratzer, Fabius Township.] Our subject received his early education at the home schools, and the State Normal at Kirksville. In 1880 he began to study medicine under Dr. D. N. Dooley, at Savannah, Iowa, and March 3, 1886, graduated as an M. D. from the College of Physicians and Surgeons, Keokuk, Iowa. He then went to Lancaster, and began the practice of his chosen profession, in which he has met with marked success, having a large practice, and being highly esteemed by the community. In 1875 he married Miss Jane Enlow, who was born in Schuyler County, Mo., in 1859. This lady died September 14, 1879, and in December, 1882, Mr. Kratzer was united in marriage to Miss Mattie, daughter of Dr. D. N. Dooley. Mrs. Kratzer was born in Davis County, Iowa, in 1866, and is a worthy and consistent member of the Christian Church, as is also her husband. In politics the Doctor is a Democrat, and cast his first presidential vote for S. J. Tilden, in 1876.

Thomas Pleasant Leedom, farmer and stock raiser, is a native of Lancaster, Mo., and was born October 28, 1853. He is a son of Asa and Susan (Woodson) Leedom. The father was born in Ohio, in 1832, is a tailor by trade, but now resides upon a farm. He is of English descent, and came to Schuyler County, in 1845, with his father, Thomas Leedom, a native of Ohio, who is now eighty-seven years old, and one of the oldest living settlers of Schuyler County. Asa was married in that county, and at the age of sixteen learned his trade, at which he worked twenty-five years in Lancaster. In 1877 he settled upon the place where he now lives, which consists of eighty acres of land. His wife is of English descent, and was born in Kentucky, near Harrisburg, in 1825. She is the mother of eight children: James L., Thomas P., William A., John M. (M. D.), Alonzo, Loretta (wife of C. L. Hounsom), Willard G. and Amos. Our subject attended school in Lancaster, at the State Normal at Kirksville, and in 1874 took the commercial course at the Business College in Keokuk, Iowa, of which institution he is a graduate. He was then appointed deputy county collector by W. A. Coffey, and, upon the death of the latter, in September, 1878, was appointed to fill his unexpired term. In 1879 he was appointed deputy collector by Frank A. Irvin, and served as such until 1882, when he was elected county collector, and in 1884 was re-elected without opposition in his party. He collected the highest per cent of taxes of any collector in the State, averaging from 95 to 97 per cent, and in all respects proved himself to be a worthy and efficient officer of public trust. He is a leading Democrat of his county, a member of the Masonic and I. O. O. F. orders, and a charter member of the A. O. U. W. lodge in Lancaster. He belongs to the Methodist Episcopal Church, and his wife to the Lutheran. By industry, economy and good management Mr. Leedom has accumulated 440 acres of land in one tract, which is well improved and cultivated, and upon which is a well-built house and good outbuildings. August 24, 1884, he married Miss Annie Elizabeth Fansler, who was born in Preston County, W. Va., October 19, 1860, and to this union one child has been born— Thomas P., Jr.

William Wallace Lucas, farmer and stock dealer, is a native of Highland County, Ohio, where he was born in 1830, and is a son of William and Nancy (Owen) Lucas. The father was born in Pennsylvania, was of English descent, and a farmer by occupation. His death occurred in 1832. His wife was born in Ohio, and of Irish descent. She died in 1841, at the age of forty-five. She was the mother of three sons: Elijah, John and our subject. William was only two years of age at the death of his father, and ten at the death of his mother. He was educated at South Salem, Ohio, making his home with his uncle, Samuel Lucas, after the death of his mother. At the age of nineteen he left his uncle's house, and when of age began to teach, and continued occupied at that profession five years, his labors being in Highland, Ross and Pike Counties. In the spring of 1856 he left his native State, and went to Van Buren County, Iowa, and in August of the same year he married Miss Lucy Jane Oldaker, who was born in Highland County, Ohio, in 1829. To them seven children have been born, these now living: Armetheus, Cromwell, Sarah Florelen and John Elsworth. Immediately after his marriage Mr. Lucas came to Schuyler County, Mo., and settled upon the Chariton River, and in 1860 located where he now resides, his home place being upon his original purchase of 160 acres. He was but a penniless youth when starting in life for himself, and has endured all the hardships incident to poverty and pioneer life, but by industry, economy and good management, is now the owner of 1,000 acres of good land, and a well-stocked farm, keeping on an average from 100 to 150 head of cattle, 300 to 500 head of sheep, ten to fifteen horses, and from forty to sixty hogs. He is one of the largest landholders in the county, and considered one of its most substantial and prominent citizens.   He lost his wife March 14, 1886, and his daughter Sarah now keeps house for him.   He is a Democrat, and cast his first presidential vote for Pierce, in 1852.

Henry A. Lehye, farmer and stock raiser, is a native of Hesse-Darmstadt, Germany, and was born in 1833.   His father, John, was also a native of that place, and born in 1798.   He was a farmer, and immigrated to the United States, where he bought 160 acres of land in Hancock County, Ill.   He died in 1863. The mother of our subject, Anna Margaret (Wisserman) Leyhe, was born in 1797 in Hesse-Kassel, Germany, and is the mother of three children, Henry A. being the second.   Henry was ten years of age when he came to America, and until the age of twenty lived with his parents.   In 1858 he married Miss Fredrica Schafer, whose birthplace was the same as his.   She was born in November, 1840, and has ten living children: Henry I., Mary C. (wife of Samuel Snowberger), Leonard F., William A., Louisa, Edward, Albert, Helen, Bertha and Franklin.   In 1865 Mr. Leyhe came to Schuyler County, Mo., and purchased 230 acres of land, where he now resides.   He now owns 447 acres, has one of the finest farms in Liberty Township, and keeps on an average about seventy-five head of stock.   He is a highly respected citizen, and in politics affiliates with the Democratic party, his first presidential vote having been cast for James Buchanan in 1856.   He is a Master Mason, and a member of the A. O. U. W., and himself and wife are members of the German Lutheran Church.

William Logan, banker, was born near the historic battle ground of the Brandywine, upon the anniversary of that battle, September 11, 1848, and is a son of Rev. William P. and Sarah J. (McComb) Logan, natives of Chester County, Penn., and born in 1822 and 1825, respectively.   They were reared and married in their native State where they lived until 1852, when they moved to Adams County, Ill.; in 1855 moved to Hancock County, Ill.; then in 1872 they removed to Atchison County, Mo., where they still reside.   Both are active members of the Methodist Protestant Church, of which the father has been a local minister for thirty years, although his chief occupation has been farming. In politics he has always been a Republican.   The father's ancestors came from England with William Penn, and settled in Pennsylvania.   The mother's paternal ancestors came from Ireland, and the maternal from Scotland.   Mrs. Logan is a distant relative of Gen. McComb, of Revolutionary fame.   William Logan, the subject of this sketch, is the second of ten children born to his parents.   The sixth child died September 10, 1887, which was the first death in the family. William was educated at the common schools of Illinois, and when eighteen years of age began life for himself. He farmed in Illinois until 1861, and in 1869 removed to Memphis, Mo., where he engaged in the saw-mill business until 1871, when he came to Schuyler County and conducted several saw-mills. He became a sub-contractor in a $40,000 railroad tie contract, but upon the failure of his superior contractors in 1872 he was left penniless. Then for five years he engaged in the mercantile business although he was still interested in the tie trade. In 1882 he and others organized a bank at Macon, Mo., and the following year reorganized it into a national bank, of which Mr. Logan became president; he also opened the Logan's Bank at Glenwood, in 1882. In connection with his banking interests he is largely engaged in farming, owns 3,200 acres of land well stocked and improved, and has large landed interests in Kansas and other Western States; is connected with various financial institutions in Kansas, notably, in the Kansas First Mortagage Company of Hutchinson, Kas.; his wealth is estimated at from $150,000 to $200,000. In 1871 he married Sarah J. Jackson, a native of Illinois, where she was born in 1849, and by her two children, William A. and Eva B., have been born. In politics Mr. Logan is a stanch Republican, in 1884 was elected associate county judge, and in 1886 was chosen chief county judge; he was elected by his party in a county that has a Democratic majority of 350. He is a member of the Masonic fraternity, and has been the Master of Lodge No. 427, at Glenwood, for seven successive years. He is also a member of the Royal Arch Chapter, No. 53, at Kirksville, Mo., and Ely Commandery, No. 22, at the same place. Mr. Logan is a self-made man, a prominent and respected citizen, and a prosperous and enterprising business man. The St. Louis *Globe Democrat*, in a recent issue, said the following concerning Mr. Logan: "William Logan, of Glenwood; estimated wealth, $150,000; owns 3,000 acres worth $75,000; $6,000 town property; $10,000 bank stock; 500 head of cattle and mules; has land in Kansas and Texas, and much money loaned out; all accumulated in last ten years; made a start dealing in railroad ties and timber; property highly improved; lands all in grain; cattle high graded; proprietor of Logan's Bank in Glenwood; native of Illinois; Republican; elected county judge in 1884; twelve years in county."

James P. Logan, farmer and stock dealer, was born in Jo Daviess County, Ill., in 1852, and is the second of six children of William M. and Elizabeth (Claypole) Logan. The father was of Irish and Scotch descent, and was born in Jackson

County, Ind. When seventeen years old he went to Illinois, and
when about thirty-two years of age married in Jo Daviess County,
where he spent the remainder of his life as a farmer and stock
dealer. He was a man of considerable property, and held various
township offices. His death occurred in 1885. The mother was
twice married, and is still living in Jo Daviess County, Ill. She
is a member of the Methodist Episcopal Church. Our subject
lived at home and received a common-school education during
his youth, which he completed at the German and English
Normal School, at Galena, Ill. In 1873 he came to Schuyler
County, and located two miles northeast of Green Top, where he
now owns 320 acres of the choice land of Schuyler County, which
he has finely cultivated and improved, making him one of the
most substantial farmers of the county. He was married in
1877 to Miss Drusilla, daughter of Moses and Mary Towles, a
native of Schuyler County, by whom he has had four children,
three living: Clarence, Myrtle, William Henry and Bessie. Mr.
Logan is an enterprising and respected citizen, a member of the
Masonic fraternity, and a Republican in politics, having cast his
first presidential vote for Gen. Grant.

M. H. McCloskey, farmer, stock raiser and carpenter, was
born July 24, 1844, in Hartford County, Md., and moved to
Wheeling, W. Va., when quite small. In 1846 he went to Lee
County, Iowa, and in August of 1855 came to Schuyler County,
Mo., where he has since resided, engaged in farming. He owns
a well improved farm of 256 acres, and is one of the well-to-do
farmer citizens of the county. April 8, 1875, he was married to
Miss Nancy E. Ashworth, a native of Schuyler County, Mo., by
whom he had one child—Matthew. This lady died April 16,
1876, and June 19, 1879 Mr. McCloskey was united in marriage
to Miss Susan M. Howard, a native of Schuyler County, Mo.,
this union being blessed with the following children: Mary J.,
Allen, Eddie F., Emma and John Henry. Mr. and Mrs. McCloskey are members of the Cumberland Presbyterian and Christian
Churches, respectively. In politics Mr. McCloskey is a Republican in principle, and has served his township in several official
capacities. February 14, 1865, he enlisted and served until the
close of the war, being mustered out at Benton Barracks, St.
Louis, Mo. He was the youngest child of three born to Paul
and Jane (McMillan) McCloskey, natives of Pennsylvania. The
father was born near Lancaster, Penn. Mrs. McCloskey was the
daughter of John McMillan, of Scotch descent, and born July
15, 1807. Her death occurred April 12, 1884.

Thomas McGoldrick was the fifth of a family of thirteen
children of Thomas and Jane (Leedom) McGoldrick, and was

born in Allegheny County, Penn., in 1830. His father was born in Pittsburgh, Penn., in 1793, where he was reared and engaged in making edged tools. After his marriage he lived upon a farm until 1832, and then moved to Hardin County, Ohio. In 1847 he sought a home in Schuyler County, where he died in 1850. He was a Democrat in politics, and for six years served as magistrate. Mr. and Mrs. McGoldrick were both members of the Christian Church. Mrs. McGoldrick died in 1872 at the age of sixty-nine. Our immediate subject was reared upon the farm, and received but a common-school education. After the death of his father the care of his mother and the family devolved upon him, and he remained at home until twenty-five years of age, when he began life as an independent farmer. In 1857 he was united to Anna Weldon, who was born in Lewis County, Mo., in 1836. This union has been blessed with nine children: Charley, Lemoine, Eugene, Cora, Fannie, William B., Howard, Mollie L. and Ota. In politics Mr. Goldrick is a Democrat, and during the late war served in the enrolled militia. He is a Mason of Glenwood Lodge, No. 427, and himself and wife belong to the Christian Church. Mr. McGoldrick is an old resident of Schuyler County, having made his home here over forty years. He is the owner of 300 acres of choice land, and is a successful farmer, at which occupation he has made all his wealth.

Robert J. Maize was born in Jackson County, Ala., in 1822, and is a son of David and Katie (Acre) Maize, natives of Virginia and Wayne County, Ky., respectively. After their marriage they moved to Jackson County, Ala., and after living there six years removed to Lawrence County, Ind., where the mother died. The father was a soldier in the War of 1812, and served in New Orleans under Gen. Jackson. He was a farmer by occupation. Mrs. Maize was a member of the Baptist Church. After the death of his father, in Illinois, Robert J. accompanied a widowed aunt to Randolph County, Mo., and from there, in 1837, went to Schuyler County, Mo. Being but a lad of fifteen, at the time, he was not very enterprising, but, nevertheless, took up a claim. Later his ambition was aroused, and he became one of the most stirring business men of the community, and at one time owned 520 acres of land which he later disposed of. He is now living a retired life upon the interest of his property. In 1844 he married Louisa Riggsby, who was born in Macon County, Mo., in 1826. This union has been blessed with twelve children, eight of whom still live: Sarah A., Mary E., Martha M., Perry T., Nancy K., Cindica A., George W., Matilda R., Louisa E., Charles R., Julia E. and Ephraim H. In politics Mr. Maize is a stanch

Democrat, and during the late war served as captain of Company C, Twenty-ninth Enrolled Militia. His first presidential vote was cast for James K. Polk. Mr. Maize served his county some years as magistrate, and in his fifty years' residence here has won the esteem and honor of all his fellow citizens. Himself and wife are members of the Missionary Baptist Church.

Henry A. Miller was born in Monroe County, Wis., January 16, 1854, and for a couple of years lived in Marquette County, that State, when the family moved to Iowa in 1858. He is the son of A. D. and J. B. M. Miller, who were natives of Eastern Ohio, in and near Ravenna, where some of their relatives still reside. A. D. Miller's father was a German, while his mother was of English descent. He followed farming principally in early life, although he tried several other branches of business at different times. He was born in 1821. He was married, about 1843, to Miss Julia George, who was of New England parentage, and whose great-great-grandmother, on her mother's side, was one of the Mayflower pilgrims. She (Miss George) was born in 1825. In 1848 A. D. Miller moved his family to Wisconsin, then a new country, their neighbors being chiefly the Chippewa Indians, and it was among these neighbors that the subject of our sketch first saw the light. A. D. Miller, his father, was one of the California gold seekers of 1851, going "across" in an ox wagon, and coming back, poor, by the Panama Isthmus and New York. He was also one of the early settlers of Kansas, putting together the saw-mill and sawing out the cottonwood lumber for the first house in Eureka, the county seat of Greenwood County, where he died in 1881. Mrs. J. B. M. Miller died in Iowa in 1870. Henry, their son, was one of eight children, and in 1866, at the age of twelve, was apprenticed in the *Excelsior* printing office in Lancaster, Mo., where he worked, until in 1871 he and Mr. S. A. Dysart purchased the office. His educational advantages were very limited, being confined to the Iowa public schools till the age of twelve, and, after that time, such instruction as he could obtain from a private teacher, of evenings; he managed, however, to master the usual English branches, besides making considerable progress in German. In 1873 he purchased sole control of the *Excelsior*, which prospered very well under his management until 1883, when he traded it to W. M. Hunter for a stock of general merchandise, and has been engaged in the mercantile business ever since, having, however, associated himself as a partner with Mr. W. P. Murphy, in 1885. In all his business ventures Mr. Miller has been moderately successful, and the firm of Murphy & Miller does one of the most extensive businesses in the county. Mr. Miller was married, in

1875, to Miss Ella Potter, a native of Ohio, and a daughter of W S. Potter, one of the early settlers of the Buckeye State, and who still survives at the age of eighty-one. Three children have been born to Mr. and Mrs. Miller: Anna, Frank and Charles. In politics Mr. Miller is a Democrat, having been elected by that party to the office of county treasurer, in 1882, which office he filled for two years. He is also a Master Mason and a member of the A. O. U. W.

Albert Minear, farmer, was born in Van Buren County, Iowa, in 1841, and is a son of Samuel and Thaney (Rhoads) Minear. When about five years of age he was brought by his parents to Schuyler County, where he was reared upon the farm, and received but a common-school education. In 1862 he enlisted in Company G, Second Missouri Cavalry, Union army, and veteranized in 1864 in Company G, Forty-second United States Infantry. For two years he served as corporal. At the close of the war he returned home, and has since successfully engaged in agricultural pursuits. In 1865 he was united in marriage to Rachel Thompson, a native of Putnam County, Mo., and by her has had seven children: Armada, Alzada, Vesper, Clara, Leafie, Albert and Isaac E. In politics Mr. Minear is in hearty sympathy with the Republican party. He is a member of the G. A. R. Post No. 25, Department of Missouri, and is also united with the A. O. U. W. He owns a good farm of 160 acres, and is one of the prosperous and enterprising farmers of the township.

H. F. Minium, farmer and stock raiser, was born January 28, 1838, in Crawford County, Penn., and is the eldest of six children born to Sampson P. and Julia Ann (Cole) Minium, natives of Crawford County, Penn. The father was a soldier during the Rebellion, and served part of the time as drum major, and the remainder had charge of the barracks at St. Joe, Mo. The mother was a daughter of Jacob and Christine (Rennor) Cole, natives of Westmoreland County, Penn. H. F. Minium went to Brown County, Ill., August 29, 1855, and September 24, 1867, came to Schuyler County, Mo., locating in Independence Township, where he has since resided. He received a common-school education, and at the age of twenty-two started in life for himself, with no capital save energy, perseverance and good business ability. He at first worked as a farm hand, but is now the owner of 150 acres of finely improved land. February 22, 1860, he was married to Miss Sarah E. Davis, a native of Brown County, Ill., who bore him two children: Alice A. and Allen L. Mrs. Minium died in September, 1863, at the age of twenty-two, and October 11, 1864, Mr. Minium married Miss Martha McConnel, a native of Scott County, Ill. This union was blessed with eight children: Quincy A., Marcellus, Rose, Homer (deceased), Ida, Laura (deceased), Florida and Wayne. This lady died December 29, 1883, having been a devoted Christian for twenty-five years. March 5, 1885, Mr. Minium was united in marriage to Miss Fannie E. Blodgett, a native of Indiana, but principally reared in Schuyler County, Mo. She was born about 1848, and is the mother of one child—Dora I. Mr. and Mrs. Minium are members of the Christian Church, of which the former has been ruling elder for twenty years. While living in Illinois he was ordained, in April, 1867, by the Union Baptist Church. He is independent in politics, and cast his first presidential vote for Stephen A. Douglas. He was elected justice of the peace in a strong Democratic township, and served four years. In 1886 he was a candidate on the Republican (with which party he has principally acted since 1862) ticket for the Legislature, but was defeated by 400 majority, on account of the county being so strongly Democratic. The paternal grandparents of the subject of this sketch, Henry and Elizabeth (Peiffer) Minium, were natives of Pennsylvania. Henry Minium was a soldier in the War of 1812, and was stationed at Fort Erie. He was a son of Henry Minium, a soldier in the Revolutionary War. He was born near the western line of Germany, and came to America with Gen. LaFayette.

Dr. William F. Mitchell was born in Schuyler County, Mo., September 22, 1842, and is a son of Isaac and Sarah (Underwood) Mitchell. The father was a farmer, and born in Harby, England, in 1815, and in 1837 came to the United States, and located in Green County, Ill. In 1841 he married and came to Schuyler County, Mo., and entered 280 acres of land in Liberty Township, three miles south of Lancaster, which has since remained in the family. In 1865 he removed to Alton, Ill., and in 1873 went to Girard, where he died in 1885. He was one of the early settlers of Schuyler County, and an active and influential man in the county, in the welfare of which he is greatly interested. His wife was born in Cynthiana, Ky., in 1812, and is now a resident of Girard, Ill. She is the mother of four children: William F., Robert J. (a physician of Girard, Ill., and a graduate of Shurtleff and Rush Medical Colleges), John M. (who died in service at Memphis, Tenn., in 1864), and Mary J. (a graduate of Monticello Seminary, Godfrey, Ill., and who resides with her mother). When nineteen our subject began to teach, and the following year entered Shurtleff College, having previously attended Mrs. Baird's school in Lancaster. He also taught two terms in Illinois, and in 1866 entered the medical department of the State University of Michigan, from which institution

he graduated March 25, 1868. He immediately began to practice at his birthplace, and his skill and fine character soon
gained him an extensive and lucrative practice, and placed him
among the leading physicians and surgeons of the county. In
1880 he joined the Missouri State Medical Association, and in
1885 the American Medical Association, of which he is the only
member from Schuyler County. He is greatly interested in all
advancement made in the medical world, and has done much for
the literary progress of Lancaster. July 26, 1863, Dr. Mitchell married Miss Lizzie T. Marshall, who was born in Greene
County, Ill., March 26, 1846. To this union ten children have
been born: Elmer L., Mary A., Elillian Maud, Sarah, William
F., Jr., Bertha, Robert J., George Herbert, Frederick and Oliver
Wendell Holmes. In politics the Doctor is a Democrat, and
cast his first presidential vote for U. S. Grant, in 1868. He is a
Noble Grand in Odd Fellowship, and Past Master Workman of
the A. O. U. W., and examining surgeon of the same. He is also
surgeon of the Keokuk & Western Railroad, and is the United
States Pension Examining Surgeon of Schuyler County. His
wife is a Methodist. Dr. Mitchell during the war of the Rebellion
was a strong Unionist, and in "the times that tried men's souls"
never hesitated to actively and urgently advocate the cause of
Union arms. He supported the election of Samuel J. Tilden, and
has acted with the Democratic party ever since.

Thomas J. Mock was born in Schuyler County, Mo., in 1849,
and is the youngest of seven children born to Elijah and Mary
(Shackelford) Mock. The father was born in Bourbon County,
Ky., and the mother was a native of the same State. During its
early history they moved to Missouri, and located first in Howard
County, then moved on to Scotland County, and afterward permanently located in Schuyler County, where they were among the
pioneer settlers. Mr. Mock was a cabinet-maker by trade, but
after coming to Missouri spent most of his time farming and coal
mining, being more extensively interested in the latter. He
opened the first mine in the county on the Chariton River. In
politics he was Democratic in his views. Both Mr. and Mrs.
Mock died in this county. Thomas J. was reared upon the farm.
His educational advantages were very limited, as there were but
few schools in the country in those days. At the age of eighteen
he became interested in coal mining, and for fourteen winters he
occupied his time in that manner. He is still engaged in the
same business with his brothers, A. J. and Alfred, and, in partnership with the former, operates a saw-mill. He also owns a fine
farm, and is considered one of the best and most enterprising
business men of the county, of which he has been a resident

thirty-eight years. In 1870 he was united in marriage to Eliza Pennington, who was born in Pennsylvania in 1852, and by her has had three children: Eugene, Lunia and Alfred. Both himself and wife are members of the Christian Church. In politics Mr. Mock is a Democrat, and in Masonry a member of Glenwood Lodge, No. 427.

William S. Morgan, a prominent farmer and stock raiser of Fabius Township, was born in Marion County, Mo., in 1852. and moved to Schuyler County, Mo., in 1856, where he since resided. He started in life for himself, at the age of seventeen, with no capital, but by energy, perseverance and economy, now owns a nicely improved farm of 140 acres, upon which he lives, engaged in farming and stock raising. In 1875 he was united in marriage to Miss Lorinda Cook, who was born in Texas, and reared in Missouri. To her union with Mr. Morgan five children have been born: Sarah E. (deceased); Mary E., Oscar, Homer and Lulu May. Both Mr. and Mrs. Morgan are worthy and prominent members of the Missionary Baptist Church, of which the former has been a deacon about ten years. Politically Mr. Morgan is a Democrat, and as such has served his county very acceptably as constable. He belongs to the I. O. O. F. He is the eldest of three children of John and Mary Ann (Hodges) Morgan, natives of England and Kentucky, respectively. The father accompanied his parents to America when nine years old, and settled first in Marion County, Mo., but now resides in Schuyler County, of that State. The mother was a daughter of John and Malinda (Stone) Hodges, of Kentucky, and died in 1865. One year later Mr. Morgan was again married, to Miss Nancy Mullinix, and that union was blessed with two children, now deceased. Mr. Morgan was a son of Emanuel and Martha (Giutus) Morgan, natives of Southwest England. The former went to California in 1849, and, on returning home, died of cholera at Cairo, Ill.

W. P. Murphy, of the firm of Murphy & Miller, was born in Clark County, Mo., in 1846, and is a son of Ruel and Elizabeth Murphy. The father was born in Virginia in 1799, and in his youth went to Kentucky, where he married. In 1836 he removed to Clark County, Mo., and lived there until his removal to Memphis, Mo., in 1881. He was one of the pioneer settlers of Northeast Missouri, and died in 1885. Mrs. Murphy was born in Virginia in 1804, and died in 1880. She was the mother of eleven children, our subject being the youngest. W. P. was educated at the common schools of his native county, and in 1869 came to Lancaster, established a grocery store for himself, and has since been constantly engaged in business at Lancaster, with the exception of the year 1884, which he spent in Eldorado, Kas., in the grocery business. From 1875 to 1879 Mr. C. W. Bunch and Mr. Murphy were partners, and in 1885 the present firm of Murphy & Miller was established. They are energetic business men, and carry a fine stock of goods, and do the largest business in their line in Lancaster. In May, 1868, Mr. Murphy married Miss Dora Board, a native of Lewis County, Mo., and by her had one child—Ruel. Mrs. Murphy died in 1870, and three years later Mr. M. married Miss Ida Walker, daughter of James Walker. Mrs. Murphy was born in Ohio, and is the mother of three children: Guy, Earl and Paul. He is a Master Mason, and a member of the I. O. O. F. In politics Mr. Murphy is a Democrat.

T. G. Neeley, judge, farmer and stock raiser, is a native of Schuyler County, Mo., was born in 1849, and is a son of Robert S. and Julia D. (Jones) Neeley. The father was born in Ohio, near Lancaster, in 1821, and about 1844 came to Schuyler County, and settled upon the farm now owned by Russell Jones. He was married in this county in 1879, and then sold out and moved to Alamosa, Colo., where he now resides. He came to Schuyler County during the early history of that section of the country, and the first county court held in that vicinity was held at his house. He assisted in laying out the town of Lancaster, which he named in honor of the county seat in his native State and county. The mother of our subject was of German descent, born in Indiana, and died in 1854. T. G. is the eldest of a family of four children, and lived with his father until eighteen years of age, being educated in schools at Lancaster. In 1867 he went to Colorado and Wyoming, being absent about eighteen months, most of the time having been spent in hunting. In 1869 he returned to his birth-place, and in January, 1870, married Miss Hannah Elizabeth, daughter of John Fincher, a native of Greene County, Tenn., and born in 1849. She came to Schuyler County, Mo., when two years of age, and is the mother of six children: Martha C., Ida M., Minnie E., Ollie M., Robert Lee and Bertha I. In 1872 Mr. Neeley located where he now resides, and is the owner of 202 acres of fine land, and keeps an average of seventy-five head of cattle per annum. In politics he is a Democrat, and cast his first presidential vote in 1872 for Horace Greeley. He was elected county judge of the Northern District of Schuyler County for a term of two years, in 1886, and is now discharging the duties of that office with fidelity and zeal, and has won the esteem of the entire community.

William D. O'Briant, retired farmer, is a son of Zachariah and Elizabeth (Javoiden) O'Briant, natives of Virginia, born in 1792 and 1787, respectively. They were married in 1816, and lived in their native State until 1839. They then lived in Kentucky until 1852, and came to Schuyler County, Mo., where they spent the remainder of their days, dying in 1867, their deaths occurring four months apart. Both were active members of the Methodist Episcopal Church. The father was a soldier in the War of 1812, and, while erecting a fort at Camp Holly, was crippled for life by the falling of a log. In early life he was an overseer, but later turned his attention to farming. In politics he was a Democrat. Of a family of seven children, William D. and the youngest were born in Prince Edward County, Va. William was reared upon the farm, and attended school about a year at a primitive log school-house. In 1852 he married Elizabeth Foglesong, daughter of Charles Foglesong. Mrs. O'Briant was born in Wythe County, Va., and to her union with Mr. O'Briant six children have been born: Henry W., Harriet J. (deceased wife of W. L. Stacy), Zachariah, James E., William C. and an infant (deceased.) In politics Mr. O'Briant and all his sons are Democrats. He began life a poor man, but by industry and the assistance of his faithful wife he became the owner of 275 acres of land, of which he now owns 168. He has been a resident of Schuyler County for thirty-five years.

Henry W. O'Briant, farmer and stock raiser, was born in Schuyler County, June 26, 1853, and is a son of William D. and Elizabeth (Foglesong) O'Briant. He was reared upon a farm, and his educational opportunities were limited to the advantages offered by the common schools of his neighborhood. When twenty-one years of age he began life as an independent farmer, and in 1875 was united in marriage to Margaret W. Gosser, daughter of Jacob and Margaret (Walthour) Gosser. Mrs. O'Briant was born July 9, 1850, in Westmoreland County, Penn., and when about seven years old was brought by her parents to Schuyler County. Her union with the subject of this sketch has been blessed with seven children: William E., Charles H., Lewis I., Sarah E., Ida K., Hattie J. and Henry M. Both Mr. and Mrs. O'Briant are worthy members of the Methodist Episcopal Church South. At the time of their marriage Mr. and Mrs. O'Briant had enough money to purchase a nice little farm of forty acres, and by industry, economy and good management, they have increased their possessions to 214 acres of good, improved land, and are considered prosperous and enterprising citizens. Mr. O'Briant is a Democrat, and a member of the A. O. U. W. He takes especial pains in the rearing of fine stock as is well attested by his fine Short-horn cattle, Berkshire hogs and poultry.

Leonard A. Parker, junior member of the firm of Tice & Parker, is a native of Sangamon County, Ill., and was born in

1836. His father, Jacob, was a native of Kentucky, and of English descent. After his marriage to our subject's mother, Sarah (Bray) Parker, he moved to Sangamon County, Ill., and there died about 1849. He was a lieutenant in the War of 1812, and fought in the battle of New Orleans. He was a farmer by occupation. The mother was about five years her husband's junior, and a native of North Carolina. She died in 1841. When Leonard A. was but five years old he was bound out to Peter Gates, with whom he remained about nine years, attending school some two months of each year. When fifteen years old he began life for himself as an employe on a farm, and attended school during the winter months, and afterward taught school for four years. In 1857 he came to Schuyler County, where, in 1861, he married Miss Sarah, daughter of Benjamin and Charlotte Brown, formerly of North Carolina, but early settlers of Schuyler County, where Mrs. Parker was born. To this union seven children were born, of whom five are living: Albert (of Milan), Elias F. (of Kansas), Amice B., Ellen B. and Clara. Mr. Parker soon rented land and farmed about four years, then entered the mercantile business with William Gatlin, which he conducted five years, and then purchased a farm, and farmed fifteen years. In 1884 he purchased an interest in a general store, and is now a member of the firm as above stated. He is a Republican, and cast his first presidential vote for Douglas. He is a member of the I. O. O. F. Mrs. Palmer died October 1, 1881.

Hon. Mark B. Patterson is a native of Searsport, Me., and was born in 1827. His parents, John and Hannah (Lancaster) Patterson, were also natives of that State, where they spent their entire lives. Mr. Patterson's father was of Scotch-Irish ancestry, born in Belfast, Me. He was a shipbuilder and master mariner, and spent many years upon the sea. His death occurred in 1856. His widow died in 1861, at the age of seventy-six. Our subject received a common-school education, and at the age of fourteen went to sea, and for some years engaged in coasting from Bangor, Me., to Charleston, S. C., and other points, during the summer months, and during the winter attended school. He afterward made voyages to New Orleans, West Indies, and other places, and lived the life of a sailor, about nine years in all. In January, 1850, he went to California, and engaged in mining until the winters' rains set in. Becoming convinced that it would not be profitable nor expedient to remain in the mines during the rainy season, he determined to return home, but, on the eve of his departure, accepted a position upon a vessel running between Sacramento City and San Francisco, receiving $100 a month, for five months; then he returned to the mines again, and remained in same

five years; had reasonable success, and in 1856 he returned to
his native home, and in the fall of the same year went to Iowa,
purchasing a section of land near Grinnell. After a year and a
half's residence there he went to Pike's Peak, and spent about four
years. He then returned to Iowa, and in 1867 married Amanda
Crosby, and reared three children, all now dead. Soon after his
marriage he came to Schuyler County, Mo., where Mrs. Patterson
died in 1872, and a year later our subject wedded Mrs. Addie
Brower, widow of Elias Brower, and daughter of John and Bethany Mikel, formerly of North Carolina, where Mrs. Patterson was
born. She accompanied her parents to Schuyler County when
but two years old, where her father died in 1864 at the age of
sixty-four. He was of German ancestry. The mother is still
living in Adair County. When Mr. Patterson came to Schuyler
County he located two and one-half miles west of Queen City,
where he has a fine farm of 360 acres, on which he remained until
1873. In 1882 he removed to Queen City, where he has since
lived in retirement. He was a justice of the peace four years, and
in 1878 was elected to represent Schuyler County in the Lower
House of the General Assembly, and served two years very satisfactorily. His occupation in early life naturally led him to iden-
tify himself with the Democratic party, on account of its low
tariff and unrestricted commerce policy, which necessarily en-
hances a sailor's interests, and later, as an agriculturist, he advo-
cated the same political principles as he belongs to a class whose
interests are bettered by free commerce. His first presidential
vote was cast for Buchanan. He is a member of the Masonic
fraternity, and his wife has been united with the Methodist Episcopal Church South since twenty years of age.

Judge Yelverton W. Payton was born in Madison County,
Ky., in 1815, and is the second of a family of eight children.
His parents, Yelverton and Mildred (White) Payton, were
natives of Madison County, Ky., and the father was of English
ancestry. In 1843 he removed to Randolph County, Mo., where
he died in 1858, when sixty-four years old. His occupation was
that of farming, and he was a volunteer in the War of 1812,
serving under Gen. Harrison at the battle of Tippecanoe.
The grandfather of our subject, Yelverton Payton, was a native
of Virginia, and born in 1755. His wife, Anna (Guffey) Payton, was born at the same place in 1762. Mr. Payton was a soldier
in the War for Independence, and, as he was an early settler of
Kentucky, was in all the Indian Wars in that section. The mother
of Yelverton died December 25, 1885, at the age of ninety-two,
and had for many years been a member of the Baptist Church.
Yelverton W. was reared by his grandparents, and received but

****

a limited education. When sixteen years old he began to learn the tanner's trade, at which he served three years. In 1836 he wedded Miss Sallie Ann, daughter of William and Hannah Geery, formerly of Pennsylvania. Mrs. Payton was born in Madison County, Ky., in 1820, and has borne her husband nine children, eight now living, and all residents of Schuyler County: Henry Guffey, Elizabeth (deceased), Frances Ann (wife of Andrew Mills), Josephus, Susan (wife of Monroe Fugate), Emily, Lura (wife of David Easten), Laura (wife of James Fugate) and John C. In 1848 Mr. Payton removed to Schuyler County, and located at Lancaster, where he engaged in the tanning business some years. He then settled three miles east of that town, and there remained until 1865, when he removed to Iowa, but in the fall of the same year returned, and the next spring accompanied a colony to Carthage and remained during the summer, then went to Randolph County, and there remained two years. Returning to Schuyler County he located two miles southwest of Queen City, where he has a farm of over 300 acres, after having given about 100 acres to his children. He has always been an active and industrious man, and is regarded as one of the substantial and respected citizens of the county. He was a Whig during the days of that party, but is now a Democrat, and as such efficiently filled the office of county judge two years. His first presidential vote was cast for Harrison. He is a worthy and long standing member of the Masonic fraternity, and is greatly interested in the general welfare and prosperity of his country. Mrs. Payton died January 29, 1886.

Hon. Edwin F. Payton, attorney, is a native of Schuyler County, Mo., was born March 2, 1858, and is a son of Benjamin and Susan (Burford) Payton. The father is of Irish descent, and was born in Anderson County, Ky., in 1820. In 1857 he came to Schuyler County, Mo., and settled one and one-half miles north of Lancaster, where he owns 160 acres of land, but for the past eight months he has been a resident of Lancaster. The mother was also born in Anderson County, Ky., in 1818, and died in 1885. She was the mother of twelve children, ten of whom are living: John (a farmer), W. M. (a farmer), Amanda J. (wife of Josiah Beasley), Joseph B. (a farmer), Benjamin L. (a farmer), Sisie, James P. (farmer and stock dealer), Martha E. (wife of Lewis Van Aken), Edwin F. and Elmer E. (a farmer). Our subject was educated in Lancaster, and at the age of twenty began to teach, his last term of school being spent as principal of a Lancaster school. Later Mr. Payton began the study of law, under the Hon. C. C. Fogle, in November, 1880, was admitted to the bar, and in 1884 began to practice in partnership with the Hon. C. C. Fogle. In September, 1886, he established an office by himself, and is now practicing alone. In politics he is a Democrat, and in the spring of 1883 was made school commissioner of Schuyler County, which position he filled two years. In November, 1884, he was elected prosecuting attorney of Schuyler County, which position he filled two years, and so efficiently that in 1886 he was re-elected, and is now discharging the duties of that office. He is master Mason of Lodge No. 259, at Lancaster, and is a member of the A. O. U. W. December 14, 1886, he married Miss Annie Stokes, daughter of Daniel Stokes, a native of Wisconsin, and both are members of the Christian Church.

Otto Plessner, carriage and wagon manufacturer, was born in Berlin, Germany, in 1846, and when three years of age accompanied his mother to America. His father, Dr. M. C. T. Plessner, was born in Striegau, Prussia, in 1813, and was a son of Prof. Henry Plessner, of the University of Breslau. M. C. T. Plessner received a fine literary education at the gymnasium, and a medical education at the University of Berlin. He became so prominent in his chosen profession that he was chosen physician of the king, but on account of his sympathy with the people, during their revolt in 1848, was banished from the empire and his property confiscated. After the war he was pardoned by Emperor William, and given $40,000 for his lost property. In 1849 he came to America, and located at Saginaw, Mich., where his ability was soon recognized, and he became one of the foremost of his profession. He took an active interest in public affairs, and was for ten years president of the board of education in Saginaw. In 1868 he was a presidential elector upon the Republican ticket. In Masonry he took all the degrees. He died at the age of seventy-two. His wife who is nine years his junior is still a resident of Saginaw. Otto Plessner is one of a family of fourteen children, and was reared at Saginaw, where at the age of fourteen he learned the blacksmith's trade. When sixteen years of age he volunteered in Company H, of the Second Ohio Heavy Artillery, in which he served twenty-eight months. He accompanied Gen. Sherman from Chattanooga to Atlanta, and after that served under Gen. Stoneman. After the war he went to Indianapolis and learned the wagon-maker's trade. In 1869 he went to Saginaw, and established a carriage factory, but in 1873 was called to Danville, Ky., and offered a position as foreman of a factory at a salary of $1,500 per annum. Two years later he opened a factory at Sigourney, Iowa, and in 1883 came to Coatsville, Mo., and now owns the largest carriage factory in the county, and as a workman is unsurpassed in skill. While in Indiana, in 1868, he was married to Maggie Coy, and by her has had seven children: Mollie, Ettie, William, Daniel, Ida, Louis and Matilda. He is a Republican, and a member of the G. A. R., Glenwood Post, No. 25.

William D. Powell was born in Greene County, Va., December 15, 1834, and is a son of Jackson T. and Mandana (Yowell) Powell, natives of the same State. The father was of Welsh, and the mother of English ancestry. They were reared and married in Virginia, and that was also the native State of two of their children. In 1835 they moved to Cass County, Ill., where the father helped build and lay out the town of Virginia and served as sheriff several years. Two children were born to them while in that State. In 1842 they moved to Randolph County, Mo., where the father died in 1861. The mother still lives. Their family of children was increased to five while in the latter State. The father was a cabinet-maker by trade, but a farmer by occupation. The mother belongs to the Missionary Baptist Church. William D. was chiefly reared in Missouri, and received his education at the district schools. At the age of twenty-one he began to teach and farm, and after that engaged in mercantile business. In 1872 he came to Schuyler County, and engaged in cattle trading quite unsuccessfully. From there he went to Macon County, and in 1878 represented his county in the State Legislature. In 1881 he went to Clarence, Shelby County, and edited the Clarence *Courier*. In 1884 he moved to Moulton, Iowa, and took charge of the Moulton *Tribune*, which is ably edited by his wife, Mrs. Matilda F. Powell. In 1887 he gained control of the Glenwood *Criterion*, which he now conducts. In 1858 he married Matilda F. Dameron, daughter of Benjamin Dameron, sheriff of Randolph County, in which county Mrs. Powell was born in 1842. To this union three children have been born: Annie K., Ida M. and Effie J. During the late war Mr. Powell served as second lieutenant in the State Militia. He is a member of the A. O. U. W., and himself and wife belong to the Christian Church.

Sylvanus Purdy, farmer, is a son of Sylvanus and Julia (Hull) Purdy, both natives of the State of New York, where they were reared, married and spent their lives. The father was an extensive farmer in that State, and in politics a Democrat. Mrs. Purdy was the mother of three sons and five daughters, and a Christian lady, being a worthy member of the Baptist Church. Her death occurred in 1837, and Mr. Purdy married a Quaker, Mary Frost, by whom he had five children. The subject of this sketch was the youngest child of the first marriage, and was born in New York City, but, as his parents lived there but a short time, his youth was spent upon a farm on the Hudson. When about nineteen years of age he evinced a taste for the life of a sailor, and took passage on a vessel as a roustabout. He afterward became captain of a vessel, but, after filling this office a short time, went upon the ocean as fireman of the steamer "Georgia," captain, Admiral Porter, which ran from New York to Panama, stopping at Cuba. In 1851 he sailed from New York for San Francisco via Cape Horn, stopping at Rio Janeiro four weeks, and at Chili, and arriving at his destination after a voyage of six months. He worked a short time in the mines, and then went to Sacramento, and engaged in gardening four years. In 1856 he returned to New York, and married Ruth L. Coe, daughter of John H. and Maria (Lake) Coe, natives of New York, where their lives were spent in agricultural pursuits. Both were members of the Presbyterian Church. Mrs. Purdy was born in Ulster County, N. Y., in 1830, and to her marriage with Mr. Purdy four children have been born: Wells C., Amanda, Addison W. and John S. The three sons are engaged upon the railroad. After having merchandised, operated a mill, farmed, and kept a restaurant until about 1867, Mr. Purdy and his family moved to Iowa, where he engaged in farming and shipping grain. In 1874 he came to Glenwood, and has since dealt in grain and pressed hay, and has the credit of being the first man to run a hay press in the county. In politics Mr. Purdy is, and always has been, a Democrat, and cast his first presidential vote for Pierce. He was a Master Mason while living East. He now owns a nice dairy farm of eighty acres, adjoining Glenwood, and is one of the well-to-do farmers of the township. Mrs. Purdy is a Presbyterian.

John H. Rambo, M. D., is the oldest practitioner in Glenwood, His parents were George W. and Liza J. (Far) Rambo, natives of Ohio, where they were reared and married. They left their native State in 1856, and removed to Van Buren County, Iowa, where they still live. By trade Mr. Rambo is a potter, but for many years has engaged exclusively in farming. He is a member of the Dunkard Church. John H. Rambo is the third of a family of thirteen children, and was born in Muskingum County, Ohio, in 1851. His first work was grinding potter's clay, but he disliked the work so heartily that his one thought was, how to escape such drudgery. Seeing a physician pass, he became possessed of a desire to study the profession of medicine. To that end he was educated at the common schools of the neighborhood and then spent two years at a Normal School. He then taught school, and studied medicine in his leisure hours. Then for five years he clerked in a drug store and read medicine under Dr. Samuel L. Bergen. In 1879–80 he attended a course of lectures at the College of Physicians and Surgeons, at Keokuk, and graduated from that institution in 1882, having previously practiced to some extent in Glenwood. For the last seven years he has continued his practice at the last mentioned place, and enjoys a large and lucrative practice and the esteem and good will of the community. In 1874 he wedded Phidelia L. Gray, daughter of Jonas H. Gray, and by her has had two children—Mont E. and Maude. Mrs. Rambo was born in Perry County, Ohio, in 1848. Although his father is a Democrat, and he was reared under Democratic influence, Dr. Rambo is a stanch Republican. He is an Odd Fellow and a deputy in the order of A. O. U. W.

James A. Rector is a native of Lawrence County, Ind., his birth occurring in 1838, and is a son of Bennett and Elizabeth (Neal) Rector. The father is of Irish descent and a native of Grayson County, Va., where he was born in 1812. He was a farmer and cabinet-maker, and during his youth went to Lawrence County, Ind., where he was married in 1837, and in the spring of 1854, immigrated to Appanoose County, Iowa, and the following year came to Schuyler County, Mo., locating in Lancaster and engaging in the mercantile business. In 1861 he returned to Iowa and located at Eddyville, and engaged in the same business. In 1883, he sold out and returned to Schuyler County, Mo., where he now resides, four miles northeast of the county seat. His wife, our subject's mother, was born in North Carolina, March 17, 1807, and at the time of her marriage to Mr. Rector was the widow of Levi Melvin, who died in 1834, and by whom she had six children; and six children were born to the last marriage, of whom our subject is the oldest. When sixteen years of age James A. came to Missouri, and made his home with his parents until he was past twenty-one years of age. March 17, 1864, he married Miss Mary McGehond, a native of Pennsylvania, and then settled in Lancaster, where he engaged in mercantile pursuits for two years. Mrs. Rector died November 29, 1864, and October 11, 1868, Mr. Rector was united in marriage to Nancy B., daughter of George Moore. This lady was born in Virginia in 1847, and has borne the following children: Tillie E., Schuyler N., Nellie M., George B. and Bessie G. In 1868 Mr. Rector began to farm, purchasing eighty acres of land in Prairie Township. In 1883 he located where he now resides, a half mile south of Lancaster, and has increased his possessions to 120 acres. In politics he is a Republican, and his first presidential vote was cast for Bell and Everett. His wife is a member of the Methodist Episcopal Church. After the death of his first wife Mr. Rector went to Eddyville and became his father's partner in the grocery business, but, in 1868, returned to Lancaster, where he has since resided.

J. B. Riley was born June 3, 1836, in Fauquier County, Va.; moved to Scotland County, Mo., October 30, 1854, and to Schuyler County, Mo., April 16, 1865, where he has since resided. He has been engaged in farming and stock raising ever since his boyhood, and started in life dependent upon his own resources for a livelihood when but eighteen years old. He now owns 184 acres of land upon which he resides. April 23, 1863, he married Miss Mary Z., daughter of David and Margaret (York) Carney, natives of North Carolina, and Clermont County, Ohio, respectively, and the former, a Revolutionary War soldier. Mr. Carney was a son of Thomas and Mary (Hunt) Carney, natives of Iredell County, Va., who afterward removed to Pendleton County, Ky., where Mr. Carney died. The mother died in Johnson County, Mo. To Mr. and Mrs. Riley ten children have been born, viz.: William F., Emma S., John Thomas, Jesse Van Buren, Abba May, Carrie M., Charley, James A., Marietta and Evalyn. Mrs. Riley is a member of the Methodist Episcopal Church. Mr. Riley is a Democrat, and is the third of five children born to Willis and Elizabeth (Dean) Riley. The mother having died in 1852 Mr. Riley was again married, Miss Sarah Jett becoming his wife, by whom he had four children. His first wife was the daughter of John and Susan (Pullum) Dean. Mrs. Margaret Carney, the mother-in-law of the subject of this sketch, was a daughter of Jesse and Nancy (Gibson) York. Mrs. York was a daughter of Alexander Gibson, who was a soldier in the Revolution and the War of 1812. Mr. David Carney, the father-in-law of our subject, was a prosperous farmer and served in the Revolutionary War.

John Rice Rippey, a prominent farmer and stock raiser, is of Scotch-Irish and German parentage, and was born in Schuyler County, Mo., November 25, 1843. He is the seventh of nine children born to William V. and Nancy R. (Crim) Rippey, natives of Virginia, born in 1806 and 1808, respectively. When young they moved to Lexington, Ky., and there married and lived until about 1830, when they went to Howard County, Mo., and some time after to Monroe County. About 1837 they removed to Schuyler County, where the father died in 1866. William V. Rippey was a Whig until the dissolution of that party, and afterward became a Democrat. By occupation he was a farmer, and ranked among the most enterprising men of the county. He was a member of the Missionary Baptist Church, to which his widow belongs. Mrs. Rippey now lives with the subject of this sketch, who was reared upon the farm, and received a good education at the common schools of the neighborhood, and the Lancaster High School. At the age of seventeen he took charge of his father's farm, and after the death of his father, purchased the old homestead upon which he now lives, and by good management has increased his possessions to 700 acres of land. He is one of the most prominent farmers and stock raisers of the county, and makes a specialty of fine blooded stock, and has taken great pride in improving the quality of stock in the county. He owns two fine standard bred stallions—Royal Clay and Green Bush Warrior; two full blooded Clydesdale—Blooming Heather and Duke of Ottawa; two Mammoth Jacks—Thomas Moore, Jr., and Don Juan. Of cattle he has a herd of twenty registered Short-horns, and also owns some fine Poland-China hogs and poultry. In 1867 he married Mary E. Dickerson, a native of Monroe County, Mo., born in 1845, and by her has had four children: Jessie Maud, Lillian Clare, John Rice, Jr., and William Lyons. Mr. Rippey is a member of the Missionary Baptist Church, and his wife of the Cumberland Presbyterian. In politics Mr. Rippey is a Democrat, and cast his first presidential vote for Seymour. In 1880 he was chosen representative of Schuyler County to the Thirty-first General Assembly, and had previously served in the State Constitutional Convention of 1875. He is a member of the Masonic fraternity, and belonged to Glenwood Lodge, No. 427.

Nicholas T. Roberts, county collector, was born in Howard County, Mo., in 1839, and is a son of David A. and Rachel (Lee) Roberts. The father was of Scotch and German descent and born in Madison County, Ky., in 1815. When five years old he accompanied his father, Nicholas Roberts, to Howard County, Mo., where he was married in 1838. In February, 1840, he came to Schuyler County, Mo., and located four miles south of Lancaster, in Prairie Township, where he owned 240 acres of land. In 1846 he was elected justice of the peace and served four years. In 1854 he was elected county judge and served six years. He was a Union man during the war, and in the fall of 1862 enlisted in Company K, Tenth Missouri Infantry, and served nearly a year. He was discharged on account of disability and died ten days after returning home. He was a prominent and influential citizen, and a leading Democrat of the community in which he lived. His wife was of English descent, and born in Howard County, Mo., in 1822. She was the mother of ten children, of whom our subject is the eldest, and died in 1885. Seven of the children are now living. Nicholas T. was but an infant when he was brought to Schuyler County, and the entire northeast Missouri was an unbroken wilderness; he received a common-school education, and also attended the private school of Mrs. Baird in Lancaster, who was a highly cultured lady. At the age of twenty he began to teach school during the winter months, and farmed during the summer months, continuing this mode of life until 1875. His teaching was confined to Schuyler County with the exception of one summer, in 1860, he taught in his native county. In the summer of 1861 he enlisted in the Missouri State Militia and in the fall was captured at Hilltown, Iowa, but was soon released. In 1874 he was elected county assessor, and two years later re-elected; in 1878 was elected sheriff and re-elected in 1880, and in 1886 was elected county collector. October 14, 1860, he married Miss Nancy M. Fulcher, born in Schuyler County, Mo., in December, 1842. This union has been blessed with six children: Ida (wife of Samuel A. Dysart, attorney-at-law at Lancaster), Edson H. (lumber merchant and ex-deputy county clerk, deputy sheriff and deputy circuit clerk), Rachel, Nevada, Fannie and John A. In politics Mr. Roberts has always been a Democrat, and cast his first vote for Douglas in 1860; he is a Master Mason and a member of the A. O. U. W. His wife belongs to the Methodist Episcopal Church South. His uncle, Thomas Roberts, came to Schuyler County in 1840, and afterward became one of its prominent citizens and served as probate judge, sheriff, county collector and representative.

M. T. Rogers, farmer and stock raiser, was born January 31, 1841, in Schuyler County, Mo., and is the fifth child of eleven born to John and Anna (Beasley) Rogers. The father was born near Franklin, Ky., and the mother was a native of Georgia. The paternal grandfather of our subject was a minister of the gospel in the Baptist Church. M. T. Rogers has been engaged in farming and stock raising since his early boyhood, and when twenty years of age began life for himself with a capital of $400, and by good investment and economy has become the owner of 230 acres of nicely improved land, and is now one of the substantial farmers of the county. In 1861 he wedded Miss Jane Snider, who bore him one child—George Andrew. His first wife having died in 1871, a year later Mr. Rogers was united in marriage to Miss Malissa C. Snider, daughter of Edwin and Eliza (Groseclose) Snider, and to this union seven children have been born: Joseph E. (deceased), Howard L., Lewis T. (deceased), Walter E., William L., Thelan H. and Anna E. Mrs. Rogers is a member of the Missionary Baptist Church. Mr. Rogers is a Democrat, and during the war served about three months in the C. S. A., Missouri State Militia. In Masonry he is a member of the Blue Lodge.

George W. Rolston was born in Pennsylvania in 1839, and when ten years old went with his parents to Ritchie County,

Va., where he received a common-school education. At the breaking out of the Rebellion he enlisted in Company K, Sixth West Virginia Cavalry, Union Army, and served three years. He was in the battles of Second Bull Run, Gettysburg, Cedar Mountain, Drop Mountain and Rocky Gap, and a great many minor engagements. His service was most of the time under Gen. Averill and he received his discharge at Wheeling, W. Va., in 1864. In 1866 he was married to Miss Louisa L., daughter of Isaac and Sarah Spears, formerly of Ohio, where Mrs. Rolston was born, and to this union three children have been born, viz.: Alice, William and Nellie. Two years after his marriage Mr. Rolston removed to Schuyler County, and located one and one-half miles northwest of Green Top, where he now has a fine and well improved farm of 120 acres, which is the result of his labor and good management, as he started in life a poor man. He has made farming his chief occupation, although early in life he spent some time teaching school. He makes horse breeding a specialty, having raised on his farm some of the finest Percheron and Clydesdale horses in Northern Missouri. He is a son of Jeremiah and Elizabeth (Ross) Rolston, natives of Pennsylvania, and of Scotch descent, and born in 1810 and 1813. The father died in 1876, in Schuyler County, and the mother in 1861, in Virginia. Our subject is a Republican and cast his first presidential vote for John Bell in 1860.

W. D. Ross, farmer and stock raiser, was born in Brown County, Ohio, where he lived until 1880, and then moved to Schuyler County, Mo. Since boyhood farming has been his occupation, and after receiving an academical education he started out in life for himself at the age of twenty-two. He then had no property, but is now the owner of a nicely improved farm of eighty acres, upon which he resides. In 1857 he was united in marriage to Miss Martha Moyers, daughter of Joseph and Lena Ellen (Carter) Moyers, and to this union seven children were born: George A., Mollie E., and five who died in infancy. Mrs. Ross was a member of the Christian Church and died in January, 1886, aged fifty years and thirteen days. Mr. Ross is also united with the Christian Church, and in politics is a Democrat. His first presidential vote was cast for James Buchanan. He has served his township in several different capacities very acceptably, and is one of the respected and prosperous citizens of the county. He was the eldest of four children of Abner and Mary (Day) Ross, natives of Brown County, Ohio, but now residents of Schuyler County, Mo., where they moved in 1881. Abner Ross is a son of William and Catherine (Harper) Ross. The father was a soldier in the War of 1812, and served as lieutenant of his company. The mother is a daughter of Mark and Lena (Carter) Day, natives of Virginia and Ohio, respectively. Mr. Day was a soldier in the War of 1812, in which he was wounded. His parents were Asa and Isabelle Day. The paternal great-grand parents of the subject of this sketch, Isaiah and Mary (Harper) Ross, were natives of Virginia. Isaiah served during the entire Revolutionary War, was taken prisoner, and held for one year, at the end of which time he was released.

P. S. Sagerty was born in Cincinnati, Ohio, in 1836, and is a son of Thomas and Mary Ann (Sidles) Sagerty. The father is a descendant of a Dutch family, and was born in Ohio, in 1809, and is a carpenter and joiner by trade. His father, Jacob, was born in New York and officiated as a subordinate officer in the War of 1812, under Gen. Wayne. Thomas lived in Warren County and Cincinnati, Ohio, until 1836, and then went to Van Buren County, Iowa, where he now resides. His wife was born in Hamilton County, Ohio, in 1808, and died in 1865. She was of German descent, and her father, Peter Sidles, was a fife major in the war of the Revolution. She was the mother of nine children, of whom our subject is the fourth. He was educated at Lebanon, Ohio, and for two winters taught a select night school. When fourteen, he began to work in a printing office as an apprentice, for 50 cents per week, and remained there three years. The paper published was the *Western Star of Lebanon*, which had a wide circulation. He afterward worked as journeyman, and the last four years was foreman and editor of the same establishment. June 19, 1856, he married Miss Frances A. Whitaker, daughter of D. H. and Anna Whitaker, who was born in Hamilton County, Ohio, in 1838, and has borne our subject ten children: Alfred E., Mary F., Annie L. (wife of J. W. Cooksey), James F., Ida, Horace, George T., Myrtle, Harry, Chester. Mr. Sagerty farmed one year in Van Buren County, Iowa, and then went to Bentonsport, Iowa, and took charge of the Bentonsport *Signal*, but in fourteen months moved the paper to Albia, where the name was changed to the Albia *Republic*. Eight months later he abandoned newspaper work and went to Scotland County, Mo., and engaged in mercantile business two years, and in 1873 moved to Downing, Schuyler County, where he built the present large warehouse and bought and sold grain and kept a drug and grocery store for five years, during which time he erected eight houses. In 1882 he was appointed superintendent of the poor farm, of which he has since had control, treating the unfortunate ones with kindly consideration. He is a Democrat, and served as assessor of Scotland County two years, and also served as assessor of Schuyler County for two years and as justice of the peace of Schuyler

County for four years. He was chairman of the Democratic Central Committee of Schuyler County six years, and is Mason of the Royal Arch Degree.

Hon. Lucius Sanderson, attorney-at-law and notary public, was born in Vermont, in 1820, and is a son of Levi and Sallie (Bean) Sanderson. The father was born in Massachusetts in 1783, and died in 1869. He is of English ancestry and can trace his lineage directly back to the Puritan fathers. When of age he went to Vermont, married there in 1806, and spent the remainder of his days in that State, engaged in farming. He was a justice of the peace, and served as militiaman in the War of 1812. His father, John Sanderson, was a native of Massachusetts, and a soldier in the Revolutionary War. The mother of our subject was born in Nova Scotia about 1786, and died at the age of sixty-four. She was a daughter of John Bean, formerly a resident of the Hampshire grant of land, but during the War of Independence he accepted the offer, made by the British Governor, to grant large tracts of land to colonists who would settle in Nova Scotia. The tract upon which he settled now includes the city of Halifax, N. S. Lucius was reared at home and received an English academical education, and was also a student of the French language. He taught school while quite young and before his majority began to study law, which he has made his life profession and in which he has been very successful, being a fluent and eloquent speaker and a good reasoner. In March, 1843, he wedded Miss Lucretia M., daughter of Joseph and Rhoda Prentiss, of Vermont, and to them ten children have been born, of whom five are living: Joseph E. P. (of Ray County), Agnes L. (wife of William A. Lafler (of Brunswick, Mo.), Carrie E., (wife of H. O. Benton, of Brunswick, Mo.), Lucia M. (wife of Joseph G. Sickles of Centerville, Iowa), and Florence E. (widow of John W. Walker). In 1855 Mr. Sanderson removed to Kingston, Waushara Co., Wis., and about ten years later removed to Erie County, N. Y., and while living there accepted a position on the Wabash Railroad. In 1869 he removed to Missouri and lived for a time in Kansas City and Macon City, but in 1873 located at Queen City, where he has since made his home, practicing his profession with great success. Being of an active temperament, he in his early days preferred a more active life and gave more attention to outside business than to his profession. Later in life he has devoted more time to his profession, but confined it chiefly to office work. He was formerly a Whig, and cast his first presidential vote for Henry Clay in 1844, but since the war has been a Republican. Despite the earnest solicitations of his friends that he accept the nomination for the office of representative of Schuyler

County, he refused, preferring to devote his entire attention to his profession. Mrs. Sanderson was born in 1825, and has for many years been a member of the Congregational Church.

H. D. Satterfield, surveyor, was born in Pike County, Ohio, in 1838, and is a son of John and Mary (Copas) Satterfield, natives of Virginia, and born near Harper's Ferry in 1812 and 1813, respectively. When small they were brought to Pike County, Ohio, and were married in that State and county. In 1878 they removed to Schuyler County, Mo., where the mother died in 1882, and where the father is still living. Both had united with the Methodist Episcopal Church. Our subject was reared at home on the farm, and received but a common-school education. In 1863 he married Miss Rebecca, daughter of John and Nancy Johnson, all natives of Pike County, Ohio. This union was blessed with nine children, of whom six are living: Mary A., Susan, Cassie, Anna Florence, Lillie and Rosy (twins). Our subject remained in Pike County until 1874, and then located five miles west of Queen City, in Schuyler County, Mo., where he lived until 1883, and then removed to Queen City, where he now resides. He has made farming his principal occupation, and has taught school twenty-five years, during the winter. In 1884 he was elected surveyor of the county, and has since filled that position very efficiently. He has always been interested in all educational projects, and his children are receiving good educations, and fitting themselves for teachers. He is a Democrat, and cast his first presidential vote for Douglas. He is a member of the Christian Church, his wife of the United Brethren, and his three daughters of the Methodist Episcopal Church South. He is of Irish descent. His grandfather, James Satterfield, was born in Virginia, and was a soldier in the Revolutionary War.

William Schafer was born in Prussia in 1824, and is a son of Adam and Elizabeth Schafer, also natives of that country, and born in 1778 and 1790, respectively. The father died in 1828, and the mother in 1872. Adam was a farmer, distiller and butcher by occupation, and served as first lieutenant under Napoleon Bonaparte. He was also collector and treasurer of his town for some years. The mother came to the United States in 1855, and her death occurred at the residence of our subject, at Lancaster. William was one of a family of four children, and while in his native country complied with the law of that land, and attended school from the age of six until he became fourteen years of age. At the age of twenty he began to learn the wagon-maker's trade, at which he worked five years. In 1845 he immigrated to America, and located at Palmyra, Marion Co., Mo., where he resumed work at his trade. April 18, 1847, he married Miss Mary C. Kuthe, who was born in Germany in 1824, and came to America in 1845. Of this union there are six living children: William, Mary (wife of Louis Schmit), George, Catherine, Susan and Adam. In 1852 Mr. Schafer removed to Lancaster, working at his trade until 1855, when he engaged in the mercantile trade. He sold his store in 1857, and built a mill at a cost of $4,500, which he ran until 1874, and then erected his present building, which is a five-story brick, 36x46 feet, has ten sets of rollers, and is equipped with all the latest improvements. The building cost $17,000, and has a capacity of sixty barrels per day. Mr. Schafer does a large business, and makes several brands of flour, among them—"Extra Fancy," "Family," "Patent" and "Fancy Patent"—both for home and foreign trade. In politics he is a Democrat, and cast his first presidential vote for Taylor in 1848. In religion he and his wife are Catholics. They are among the prosperous and well-to-do citizens of the town, and reside in a house nicely situated, which cost about $3,000.

Peter F. Schwartz, merchant, was born in Germany, in 1836, and is a son of Andrew and Annie Schwartz, also natives of Germany, where they were reared and married. They came to the United States in 1842, and located in Centreville, St. Clair Co., Ill., where they both died in the same week, of cholera, in the year 1848. After the death of his parents, Peter F. lived in Illinois four years, with a family of the same name, and then went with them to St. Louis, Mo., staying there one summer, then moved back to Illinois, and in 1861 enlisted in Company C, Twenty-sixth Illinois Volunteer Infantry, and served through Tennessee, the battles of Vicksburg, Island No. 10, New Madrid, Corinth, Iuka, Missionary Ridge, and the entire Georgia and Atlanta campaign to the sea, then on to the grand review, at Washington. He was mustered out at Louisville, Ky. In September, 1865, after four years of active and faithful service for his adopted country, he was honorably discharged at Springfield, Ill. In 1867 he married Miss Apalonia Bellm, also a German, and to them the three following children have been born: Emma, Louisa and Frank. The year of his marriage he came to Schuyler County, and located at Glenwood. He established a harness shop, having learned that business when a young man, and remained there until about 1874, when he purchased a farm three-and-a-half miles west of Glenwood, and farmed until 1877, when he removed to Queen City, and resumed the harness business. In 1879 he purchased a stock of general hardware and agricultural implements, and has handled that in connection with the above named business since. He has been a prominent Mason for a long time, and is one of the most public spirited men of the community, and is giving his children a good college education. Formerly Mr. Schwartz was a Democrat and cast his first presidential vote for Buchanan, but since the war has become a Republican.

Reuben L. Scurlock was born in Jackson County, Ohio, in 1823, and is a son of Joshua and Martha (Long) Scurlock. The father was a native of Stokes County, N. C., and the mother of Botetourt County, Va. When young they went to Jackson County, Ohio, where they were married, and raised a family of thirteen children. In 1853 they came to Schuyler County. The father died while visiting in Iowa. The mother returned, and made her home with a daughter. In 1882, while returning home from a visit, Mrs. Scurlock fell in stepping from the train, and sustained injuries which proved fatal. She was a member of the Christian Church. Mr. Scurlock was a Whig in politics, and at one time served as lieutenant of a militia company. His chief occupation was farming, but he was also a good shoemaker, cooper, gunsmith, etc. Reuben L. was reared upon a farm, and received but limited educational advantages, but afterward increased his knowledge by reading and observation. He remained at home until 1850, and then married Lucy A. Aleshire, a native of Jackson County, Ohio, and born in 1828. To this union three children were born: Jugirtha T., Nelson J. and Reuben P. Mrs. Scurlock is a member of the Baptist Church. Mr. Scurlock is a stanch Republican, and during the war served as a militiaman. He has served his township as magistrate, and has also filled several minor offices. He lived in Ohio until 1856, and then moved to Schuyler County, locating upon the farm where he now lives, which consists of 160 acres of land under a good state of cultivation. Mr. Scurlock is a self-made man, and his property is the result of his own industry. He is a Master Mason, and a member of the I. O. O. F. Scotch, Dutch, and Irish blood flow in his veins. His paternal grandfather was a soldier during the entire Revolutionary War.

John G. Shattuck, liveryman, was born in the Province of Quebec, Canada, in 1834. His parents, Chester and Alma (Guy) Shattuck, were born in Canada, in 1810 and 1809, respectively. They were married in Canada, whither their parents had immigrated while they were young, and in 1845 came to Ohio, and in 1852 to Schuyler County, Mo., where they settled upon what is now Glenwood. The father was a carpenter by trade, but engaged in other employments such as hotel keeping, livery business, etc. In politics he was once a Whig, but afterward became an active worker in the Republican party. He died in 1887, but the mother still lives with the subject of this sketch, who is the only living child of a family of two children. During his youth John G. received a good common-school education. He has always lived upon the home place, and as his father was otherwise engaged, John became the manager of the farm, and gave evidence of considerable ability in stock raising and dealing. In 1887 he became engaged in the livery business where he is now located, having his son-in-law for partner. In 1856 he married Ann Chattin, who was born in England in 1849, and by her one child was born, Vinnie A. (wife of A. N. Davis). In politics Mr. Shattuck is a Republican, and during the late war offered his services to the country three times, but each time was rejected on account of disability. In business he is moderately successful, and owns a nice stable newly fitted.

Robert Shaw, farmer and stock raiser, was born in Licking County, Ohio, in 1812, and moved to Fulton County, Ill., in 1836, and in March, 1869, began to farm in Schuyler County, where he has since resided. He began life for himself when twenty-one years of age, and from a poor man has become the owner of 663 acres of choice land in Schuyler County, and 160 acres in Scotland County, Mo., and also has 350 acres in Fulton County, Ill., which is good evidence of his business ability and good management. In 1833, he was united in marriage to Miss Catherine Boadner, a native of Pennsylvania, and by her thirteen children have been born: Alexander, Minerva (deceased), Sarah, Peter (deceased), Emaline, Mary Ann, Isaac, Henry, Jasper Newton, Rebecca, John W., Amanda E. and James M. Mr. Shaw is a Democrat, and when in Illinois served two years as tax collector. He is the seventh of a family of thirteen children of Alexander and Mary (Bartley) Shaw, natives of Virginia, who moved to Licking County, Ohio, at an early day, at which place they lived and died. The father was a soldier in the War of 1812, and a son of Charles Shaw.

Dr. George A. Shirley, physician and surgeon, was born January 25, 1845, in Franklin County, Mo., and is the third of four children. His parents, Carter T. and Elizabeth (Cook) Shirley, were natives of Kentucky, the former born January 2, 1816, and the latter November 28, 1819. They were married in 1835, and four years later removed to Macon County, where they lived until 1872, with the exception of a few years spent in Franklin County. They then removed to Saline County, where they have since lived. Mr. Shirley is a mechanic. He served as sergeant major in the Second Missouri State Militia during the late war. Both himself and wife have been members of the

Methodist Episcopal Church since their youth. The Doctor was
reared at home and received a limited common-school education.
In 1864 he enlisted in Company B, Forty-second Missouri
Infantry, and was on duty in Tennessee and Missouri, and went
on a scouting expedition of twenty-six days. He remained in
service until the close of the war, and received his discharge at
St. Louis, in July, 1865. The same year he was united in
marriage to Miss Mattie J., daughter of Amos and Elizabeth
(Brannock) Barnett, formerly of Pendleton County, Ky., where
Mrs. Shirley was born. To this union five children have been
born of whom but two are living—William E. and Clarence E.
Our subject farmed in Knox County until 1869, and then embarked in the mercantile business at Kirksville, and the next
year began to study medicine with Dr. P. G. H. Barnett. In
1871-72 he attended the Keokuk Medical College, and then
began to practice at Willmathsville, in Adair County, where he
remained until 1879, and then came to Green Top, where he has
established a large and lucrative practice. He owns a comfortable home and forty acres of land just northeast of the town
where he resides. He is a genial gentleman and enjoys the
esteem of the entire community. He is greatly interested in all
educational projects, and his children are enjoying the best
educational advantages which he is able to give them. He is a
Republican, and cast his first presidential vote for Lincoln while
in the service. He is a member of the I. O. O. F., and himself
and wife belong to the Christian Church.

John M. Shoemake, butcher, was born in Ripley County, Ind.,
in 1843, and is a son of Levi and Louisa (Horton) Shoemake.
The father was of French descent, and born in 1801 in North
Carolina. He was a farmer by occupation, and while young
went to Hamilton County, Ohio, where he was married. In 1840
he moved to Ripley County, Ind. His death occurred in 1843.
His wife was born in Jackson County, Tenn., in 1803, and was
also of French descent. She went to Davis County, Iowa, in 1855,
and there died in 1865. Our subject, John M., was the youngest
of five children, and received his education at the common
schools of Indiana and Iowa, having gone to the latter State
when twelve years old. At the age of seventeen he began to
teach penmanship, at which occupation he was engaged five
years. During the late war his sympathies were with the Union,
and in August, 1862, he enlisted in the Third Iowa Cavalry for
three years, or during the war. He participated in the siege of
Vicksburg, and the battles of La Grange, Ark., Jackson, Miss.,
Selma, Ala., Columbus, Ga., and several other engagements and
several skirmishes, and at one time was slightly wounded in a

hand-to-hand sabre contest with an enemy. He received his discharge June 19, 1865, at Nashville, and then returned home. In February, 1866, he married Miss Mary K. Weldon, daughter of James Weldon. This lady was born in Lewis County, Mo., in 1847, and is the mother of five living children: Luna, Alvin A., Clarence W., Justice H. and Effie. After his marriage Mr. Shoemake located in Liberty Township, Putnam County, and commenced to farm. At the expiration of three years he removed to Chariton County, and located near Bynumville, where he engaged in the mercantile business, which he was soon compelled to abandon on account of his poor health. After selling his stock he removed to Schuyler County, and located in Glenwood Township, where he purchased a farm of 200 acres. In 1872 he moved to Glenwood, and worked at various occupations, and was a confidential employe of William Logan for several years. In 1880 he returned to his farm, and the same year he and Mr. Logan engaged in the railway timber business, at which they continued two years. In the summer of 1887 Mr. Shoemake came to Lancaster, and became a butcher, and at this business is quite successful. In politics he is a conservative Republican, and in 1872 was elected county assessor, and served two years. He is a Master Mason.

Simmons & Holbert, general merchants at Coatsville, is the oldest and leading firm in that business in the city, and although young in years, are very successful and enterprising business men, and have a stock of goods occupying a room 24x62 feet, and a large wareroom. The senior member, William D. Simmons, was born in Davis County, Iowa, in 1858, reared upon a farm, and educated at the common schools of the neighborhood. When nineteen years of age he began life for himself by clerking in a general store, and after following that vocation about eleven years, purchased a stock of goods, and began life as an independent merchant in Coatsville in 1885. In the fall of the same year, George R. Holbert, his brother-in-law, became his partner, and they have since been doing business under the firm name of Simmons & Holbert. In 1884 Mr. Simmons was united in marriage to Miss Arintha S. Holbert, a native of Davis County, Iowa. Mrs. Simmons is a devout member of the Missionary Baptist Church. Mr. Holbert, the junior member of the above firm, was born in Davis County, Iowa, in 1859, and spent his youth upon a farm. After receiving a good education at the common schools of the vicinity in which he lived, he attended the Ottumwa Business College, and fitted himself for mercantile life, and as the result of his labor, is now enjoying the life of a successful merchant. During the time between January 1, 1887, and October

1, the firm shipped over 29,790 dozen eggs, and as that is but one item of merchandise, some little estimate can be formed of the amount of business the firm does. Both partners are Democrats in politics.

John Sloop, a merchant, was born in Prairie Township, Schuyler Co., Mo., in 1847, and is the fifth of ten children of Nicholas and Elizabeth (Stauffer) Sloop, natives of Switzerland, and born in 1808 and 1811, respectively. When grown they emigrated to the United States and were married at Pittsburg, Pa., in 1832, and soon after settled in Marion County, Mo., where they remained until about 1843 and then came to what is now Schuyler County, where the father died in Feburary, 1862, the mother surviving until 1885. Mr. Sloop was an early pioneer settler of Schuyler Township, and at the time of his location there it required all the inhabitants within a radius of twenty or thirty miles to raise an ordinary log house. Himself and wife were both members of the Lutheran Church. Our subject was reared at home and received a meagre education at the primitive log school-house. In 1873 he left the farm and went to Queen City and engaged in the stock and grain trade. In 1876 he was married to Miss Minnie, daughter of George Eiffert. Mrs. Sloop is a native of Missouri, and has borne her husband four children, all living: Edward Clarence, Erma G., Ellison N. and Augusta. In 1879 Mr. Sloop embarked in the hardware business in which he has been very successful, owning the best establishment of that kind in town. He is a Democrat, and cast his first presidential vote for Seymour in 1868. He is a member of the Farmers and Mechanics Mutual Aid Association and of the Triple Alliance Life Insurance Company, and is one of the most energetic and enterprising business men of the city.

Daniel D. Smith was born in Henry County, Va., August 25, 1816, and is a son of John and Frances (Smith) Smith. The former was born August 22, 1781, in Bucks County, Pa., and when twelve years old went to Henry County, Va., where he married, and in 1837 moved to Lawrence County, Ind. In 1846 he came to Schuyler County, Mo., and his death occurred January 15, 1850. The mother was born in Henry County, Va., May 17, 1784, and died September 12, 1838. Two of the five children born to them are living: Daniel D. and John F., of Saline County, Mo. Daniel D. lived with his parents until of age, and March 2, 1837, was married to Miss Lucy B. Minter, who was born in Henry County, Va., October 18, 1816. To this union nine children have been born: Martin V. B., Henry C. (deceased), Joyce (wife of Joel W. Johnson), Frances, Jane (wife of John M. Searcy), Samuel H., Elizabeth (wife of J. T. Seunlock), John O. J. and

Margaret W. Soon after his marriage Mr. Smith removed to Lawrence County, Ind., as did his parents, and in 1846 all came to Schuyler County, Mo., and settled in Liberty Township. In 1851 he moved to Glenwood Township and there remained until 1874, when our subject was elected county clerk of Schuyler County, and filled that office so efficiently that he was re-elected in 1878 and 1882. He has always been identified with the Democratic party and cast his first presidential vote for Martin Van Buren in 1840. He is a man highly esteemed and honored by his neighbors and friends, and himself and wife are members of the Missionary Baptist Church.

Miles Smith, farmer and stock raiser, was born in Upper Canada, near Hamilton, in 1836, and when nine years old accompanied his parents to Whiteside County, Ill. He went to Boulder County, Colo., in 1860, and then to Schuyler County, Mo., in the fall of 1867, where he has since resided, with the exception of some time spent in Colorado, engaged in mining. He has followed the occupation of farming and stock raising since his boyhood, and, although he started in life when sixteen with no means, has a well improved farm of 110 acres. In 1858 he married Miss Nancy F. Jillson, daughter of George and Rhoda (McCapers) Jillson, natives of Genesee and Cattaraugus Counties, N. Y., respectively. The father was of English and the mother of Scotch-English descent. Mr. and Mrs. Smith have had eight children: Etta M., George C., William S., Louisa L., Henry H., Walter S., Mary A. and Charles C. Mr. Smith served under Col. Shoop during the Indian trouble in Colorado, and in politics is independent. He was the fourth child of ten. His parents, Harry and Hannah (Foman) Smith, were natives of Vermont and Germany, respectively. The father moved from Canada when twenty years of age, and died in Whiteside County, Ill., at the age of seventy-five. His father was born in England, and came to the United States at the age of twenty. The mother of Mrs. Smith was a daughter of Maj. McCapers, who came from England with his father when four years old, and settled in Cattaraugus County, N. Y.

J. M. Smith, general merchant, was born in Lewis County, Mo., in 1840, and moved to Schuyler County in 1854. He then returned to his native county, but in 1860 came to Schuyler County again, where he has since resided. He began life for himself when twenty-six years of age, a poor man with no capital, and is now the owner of a general store, his business property, and a residence in Downing, all of which are the result of his own labor and good management. In 1861 he enlisted in the army and served six months, after which he farmed until 1880, when he purchased a stock of goods from William Barbee, in partnership with N. A. Lane, and two years later became the owner of the entire stock. In 1866 he was married to Miss Phœbe Hook, a native of Pendleton County, Ky. Mrs. Smith was principally reared in Scotland County, Mo., and is a daughter of James H. and Sarah Ann (Morris) Hook, natives of Pendleton County, Ky. Mrs. Hook was a daughter of Richard and Phœbe (Caster) Morris, and her husband a son of Kimmith and Nancy Hook. Richard Morris was a soldier in the War of 1812. J. M. Smith, the subject of this sketch, is a Democrat in politics, and a Master Mason. He is the seventh of a family of ten children born to John C. and Marrilla (Martin) Smith, natives of Fairfax County, Va., who, in 1826, moved to Pennsylvania, and three years later to Missouri, where they died in Schuyler County at an advanced age. They were of German-Irish and French-English descent, respectively. Mr. J. M. Smith is a member of the Christian Church.

A. H. F. Smith, hardware merchant, was born in County Kilkenny, Ireland, in 1844, and is a son of Rev. Ambrose and Letitia (Rawlins) Smith, both natives of Dublin, Ireland, and of French-Huguenot descent. The father was a graduate of Trinity College, Dublin, and an ordained minister in the Episcopalian Church. He went to England in 1845, but after a residence of four years in that country he returned to Ireland. In 1849 he came to America, and located at San Antonio, Texas, being the first Episcopal minister of the place. About 1852 he went to New Orleans, and retiring from the ministry, became a private teacher of Latin and Greek. In 1858 he returned to his native land. He died in Wales. The mother lived in New Orleans until 1873, in which year she died at the residence of a daughter living in Southwestern Missouri. Our subject was the eldest son of a family of three sons and two daughters. He received a good English education, and at the age of thirteen began to clerk in New Orleans. In 1862 he was a volunteer in Company F, Crescent Regiment, Confederate Army, and served as second junior lieutenant. He participated in the battles of Shiloh, Texana Road, Franklin, Camp Bisland, and was in the Red River Campaign, under Gen. Taylor. After the close of the war, he became interested in mercantile pursuits in New Orleans until 1872. Four years later he located at Glenwood, and embarked in the hardware business, at which he still continues. In 1880 he married Celest O'Day, a native of Wisconsin, and a sister of the president of the San Francisco Railroad. To this union three children have been born: Ambrose, Thomas K. O. and Mary. Mr. Smith is an Episcopalian, and his wife belongs to the Catholic Church. In politics he is a Democrat. He is a member of Glenwood Lodge No. 427, in Masonry, and one of the respected and honored business men of the town.

Mathias Speer is a native of Overton County, Tenn., and was born in 1817, and is a son of George and Mary (Dougherty) Speer. The father was of Irish and Dutch descent, and was born in Virginia about 1822. He moved from Tennessee to Morgan County, Ill., and in 1836 went to Burlington, Iowa, and from there to Illinois, where he died. He was twice married. The mother of our subject died when he was a small child. He was reared at home, and received his education at Burlington, Iowa, bearing the expenses himself. When twenty-four years old he was married to Miss Lucy Ann Hill, a native of Illinois, and to this union four children were born, of whom two are living: Charles P. (of Atchison County, Mo.), and America J. (wife of George W. Pryor, of Harrison County). In 1853 Miss Helen M., daughter of H. D. and Susan Thorp, of Iowa, became his wife, and this union was blessed with six children, four of whom are living: Nathan T. (postmaster at Green Top), Emma S. (wife of J. Dyer, of Adair County), George B. M. and Alletta Catherine. About 1848 Mr. Speer removed to Schuyler County, and located nine miles northeast of Lancaster, and in 1853 went to Adair County. During the war he removed to Green Top, where he has since made his home, with the exception of the year 1884, which he spent in Kansas, where he owns 107 acres of land, well improved and cultivated, and he has 200 acres in Adair County, Mo. His son, Charles Porter, served in the Union Army during the late war. In politics Mr. Speer is a Democrat, and cast his first presidential vote for Van Buren in 1840. He is a member of the I. O. O. F. and the Rebecca Lodge at Glenwood. His wife is a Methodist.

Orland Byron Spencer, druggist, was born in Erie County, Penn., in 1837. His father, H. A., was born in Canada, where his parents had gone previous to the War of 1812. From there he moved to New Hampshire, and from there to Pennsylvania, where he married and lived until about 1840. After a short residence in Clay County, Mo., he moved to Illinois, and from there to Iowa where he died in 1883. The mother still lives there, and is about seventy years of age. She is a member of the Christian Church, of which Mr. Spencer was a minister. In politics H. A. Spencer was respectively a Whig, Know-nothing, Republican and Greenbacker. In 1861 he served as second lieutenant in Company E, of the Iowa Volunteer Cavalry, and the following year was made captain of the same, but in 1864 resigned on account of poor health. By trade he was a carriage and wagon-maker and blacksmith, and in the latter trade his father and four brothers were also proficient. Orland Byron was the eldest of eight children, and was chiefly reared and educated in Iowa. At the age of fifteen he began to learn the blacksmith's trade, at which he worked in all about twenty years. In 1864 he enlisted in Company D, Forty-fifth Iowa Infantry, and served a short time as company clerk. For twelve years he was in partnership with his father, but in 1876 opened a hardware store, which he ran until 1879. He then came to Schuyler County, and located in Glenwood Township, and went into business with G. D. Gray, who in 1886 was succeeded by his son. The present firm of Spencer & Gray is known as one of the first drug houses of the State, and does a thriving business. In 1882 Mr. Spencer was married to Emma Cullen, a native of Ohio, by whom two children have been born: James Clarence and William Horace. In politics Mr. Spencer is a Republican, and in Masonry belongs to the Commandery.

Isaac W. Stanley was born in Trumbull County, Ohio, in 1831, and is a son of John and Betsey (Hubble) Stanley, both natives of Pennsylvania. In early life they moved to Trumbull County; in 1849 they moved to Wapello County, Iowa, and afterward to Cass County, where both died. They were both members of the Congregational Church. The father was a strong Whig during the days of that party, but after the organization of the Republican party became a member of its ranks. His occupation was that of farming. Isaac W. was the youngest but one of a family of five children, and spent his early days upon the farm. His early education was confined to the district schools, but at the age of seventeen he attended Allegheny College a short time. He then taught school about four terms, and after engaging in farming to some extent, opened a store at Glenwood, which he conducted about two years. He then traded it for a mill, which in 1885 he converted into a roller mill of fifty barrel capacity. This being the best mill in Northeast Missouri, his patrons came from a distance of thirty and thirty-five miles to trade with him. In 1879 he bought the St. Nicholas Hotel, and is now the proprietor of the best hotel in the county, although he began life with but few advantages. In 1854 he married Eveline Campbell, who was born in New Hampshire in 1832, and accompanied her parents to Iowa when quite young. This union has been blessed with the following children: Edward F., Jessie and Harry L. The eldest child was a conductor on the Atchison, Topeka & Sante Fe Railroad, and in 1885 met his death while on a run-away engine. In politics Mr. Stanley is a Republican.

****

Elder Ennis Starbuck, minister and farmer, was born in Perry County, Tenn., in 1833, and is the second of twelve children born to Daniel and Nancy (Shelton) Starbuck. He came to Schuyler County with his parents, in 1852, and two years later was married to Miss Julia Ann, daughter of J. H. and Julia Hathaway, formerly of Vermont. Mrs. Starbuck was born in Ohio, and to her union with our subject eight children were born, six now living: Alma (wife of G. W. Smith), Lutheria A. (wife of J. C. De Armond of Colorado), Cary E., Lelia N., Dwight D. and Seth H. Mr. Starbuck has been a resident of this neighborhood over thirty-five years and owns 102 acres of land in the home place five miles east of Queen City, and fifty acres of land in timber. When in Tennessee and at the age of eighteen he united with the Missionary Baptist Church, and in 1854 was verbally licensed to preach, and was ordained in May, 1859. He is now in charge of the Baptist Church at Lancaster, and out of twenty annual sessions of the North Missouri Baptist Association he has presided at eleven, and is the present chairman of the executive board of that association. For over thirty years he has been a devout and zealous worker in the cause of religion and has baptized over seventy-five people, four of whom are his brothers and sister. Mrs. Starbuck and all but one of the children are members of the same church. When seventeen years of age Mr. Starbuck voluntarily resolved that intoxicating liquors should never pass his lips and has firmly adhered to this resolution throughout his lifetime.

Francis Marion Starbuck, farmer and stock raiser, was born in Perry County, Tenn., in 1843, and is a son of Daniel and Nancy (Shelton) Starbuck. Daniel Starbuck descended from an old Quaker family of Nantucket Island, and was born in North Carolina in 1799, but was mostly reared in Indiana by his grandfather, Gear Starbuck, a native of England, but an early settler of Nantucket Island. He afterward moved to North Carolina, and from there to Indiana, where Daniel was first married. After his removal to Perry County, Tenn., he was married to the mother of our subject, in 1831, and lived in Perry County until 1852, when he came to Schuyler County, locating five miles southeast of Queen City, spending the remainder of his life as a farmer and carpenter. He died in 1870, the county then losing one of its earliest settlers. The mother was born in Virginia in 1808. She is a member of the Baptist Church. When but nine years of age Francis Marion was brought to Schuyler County, where he was reared, his opportunities for attending school being very meager. Of Southern nativity and reared under Southern influence, his sympathies were naturally with the South at the breaking out of the war, and in August, 1861, he enlisted in Company C, of a Missouri regiment, doing gallant service under Gen. Sterling Price for over three years in a cause which he thought was right. Among the numerous engagements in which he participated were those of Pea Ridge and Corinth, after which he returned to Arkansas, and was discharged at Grand Prairie, in the latter part of 1863 on account of disability. Subsequently he was captured and confined as a prisoner for ten days in St. Louis. October 24, 1869, Mr. Starbuck was married to Miss Eliza J. Pruett, daughter of B. M. and Virginia Pruett, natives of Virginia, from which State they removed to Illinois, and thence to Schuyler County, at an early date. Mrs. Starbuck was born in Marion County, Ill., September 12, 1851. They have six children: Eleanor, born in 1872; Minnie, in 1873; Ettie, in 1875; Della, in 1879; Luretta, in 1882, and Sophronia, in 1885. Following his marriage Mr. Starbuck immediately located where he has since made his home, six miles southeast of Queen City, in Prairie Township. This is an excellent farm of 200 acres, substantially improved, the possession of which speaks well for one whose early opportunities and advantges were so limited. His entire life has been one of industry and frugality, his character above reproach and suspicion, and his business transactions strictly honest. He is a steadfast worker for the cause of education and the general upbuilding of the community, and spares no pains in the education of his children. He has been a life-long and consistent Democrat, and cast his first presidential vote for Tilden in 1876. He is a prominent member of the Masonic fraternity and of the Grange order. Himself and wife are members in good standing of the Missionary Baptist Church.

W. H. Starret, liveryman, is a native of Madison County, Ohio, and was born in 1842. His parents, John and Mary (Weaver) Starret, were born in Champaign County, Ohio, in 1811 and Clark County, Ohio, in 1817, respectively. The father was a farmer by occupation, and when a youth went to Madison County, Ohio. He was married in 1856, and moved to DeWitt County, Ill. In the spring of 1858 he came to Schuyler County, Mo., settled at Tippecanoe, and became the owner of 225 acres of land. His death occurred in 1887. Mrs. Starret is now seventy-one years of age, and is the mother of seven children, of whom our subject is the second. He came to Missouri when a boy, and lived with his parents until twenty years of age, receiving his education at the common schools. In August, 1862, he enlisted in Company D, One Hundred and Seventh Regiment, Illinois Volunteer Infantry, and served nearly three years, and was in the Atlanta campaign. He was discharged at Camp Butler, Ill., and returned to Schuyler County, Mo.   In 1868 he married Miss Angeline E. Walker, a native of Ohio, and the mother of three children: Fay (eighteen years old), May (ten years old), and an infant.   In 1866 Mr. Starret established a grocery store in Lancaster, and in 1869 secured the mail route between Lancaster and Glenwood, making two trips each day.   He has since been in the business on the present route,   In 1875 he built a livery stable, and has since been successful in that business, and owns ten horses, eight conveyances and an omnibus, being well prepared to supply the wants of the traveling public.   He is a Republican and cast his first presidential vote for Lincoln, in 1864.   He formerly belonged to the I. O. O. F., and his wife is a member of the Methodist Episcopal Church.

Thomas J. Threlkeld is a son of William G. and Mary (Churchill) Thelkeld, natives of Shelby County Ky., where they passed their lives,   Both were members of the Missionary Baptist Church.   The father was a saddler and farmer by occupation and served in Col. Dick Johnson's regiment, in the War of 1812, and was badly wounded at the battle of the Thames.   In politics he was a Whig.   Thomas J. was the third of a family of ten children and born in Shelby County in 1819.   He was left an orphan while very young and was cared for by an uncle.   He received a good English education during his youth, and at the age of sixteen began to learn the tailor's trade, at which he worked until twenty years of age, and then turned his attention to farming. In 1842 he came to Schuyler County, and located at the place whsre he now resides.   In 1844 he married Elizabeth J. Fulcher, a native of Boone County, Mo., and daughter of Jefferson Fulcher. This union has been blessed with ten children: William O., John H., Mary A., Susie E., Martha A., Henry C., Ella M., Thomas J., James M. and Minnie B.   John H. is a physician and preacher of Indiana.   Thomas J. is principal of the Glenwood schools.   Mrs. Trelkeld was a member of the Methodist Church South.   Her death occurred in 1874.   Mr. Threlkeld was a Whig during the days of that party, but is now a Democrat. He is a well-to-do and prosperous farmer, and the owner of 100 acres of good land.

Adoniram J. Tisdale was born near Springfield, Ohio, in 1834, December 15, and is the fourth of a family of seven children born to Robert D. and Minerva (Forsythe) Tisdale, natives of Virginia and Pennsylvania, respectively.   When young both moved to Ohio, where Mr. Tisdale studied medicine and practiced that profession successfully for about forty years.   He remained in Ohio until about 1836, and then moved to Adams County, Ind.   While there he served as county judge some time, and also was elected representative of Adams and Jay Counties, but as these duties interfered with his profession, he refused a re-election. The mother of our subject died in Adams County, a member of the Missionary Baptist Chnrch, to which church Mr. Tisdale belongs. The father is now living with his fourth wife, in Madison County, Iowa, where he moved in 1856. He was engaged in farming in Iowa some time, but is now living a retired life. Adoniram laid the foundation of his education at the village school, and afterward attended Franklin College. He also spent a large portion of his time in his father's apothecary shop, and studied under his guidance. After coming to Iowa with his parents he engaged in farming, but finding that the country needed his services, enlisted in 1861, in Company F, Fourth Iowa Infantry, U. S. A., as private, and from that position became successively corporal, sergeant, second lieutenant and captain. He participated in the battles of Pea Ridge, Vicksburg, Port Gibson, Jackson, Champion's Hill, Baker's Creek, Lookout Mountain, Missionary Ridge and Taylorsville. He afterward accompanied his regiment on the Atlanta Campaign, and was in the battles of Resaca, Dallas, Kenesaw Mountain, Atlanta, Jonesboro, and Griffin's Station, and from there marched on to the sea aad participated in the engagement at Savannah. He also marched through the Carolinas and fought at the battle of Bentonville. During his service of four years and three months, he was in every battle (thirty-six in all) in which his regiment was engaged, and at the battle of Dallas, Ga., received a severe injury, from which he has never recovered, and, on account of which, he now draws a pension. He received his discharge at Davenport, Iowa, in August, 1865. In 1863 he married Caroline Parker, a native of Coshocton County, O., born in 1842, and a daughter of Rev. Leonard and Mary (Hill) Parker, natives of New York and Vermont, respectively. They moved to Ohio when young, and there were married. The father was a minister of the Methodist Episcopal Church for many years, and while a resident of Ohio wrote a work on "Baptism" and "Universalism Against Itself." In 1855 he moved to Iowa, and engaged in farming in connection with his ministerial duties. Mrs. Parker was also a Methodist, and the mother of three sons and eleven daughters. After her death Mr. Parker was married to Rachel Peach. In early life he was a Whig, but afterward became a Republican. The union of Mr. Tisdale and Miss Parker has been blessed with four children: Albert M., Nellie F., Robert L. and an infant. In 1865 the family moved to Schuyler County, Mo., where they have since resided. Mr. Tisdale now owns a good farm of 280 acres of land, which he devotes to stock raising and farming.

In politics he has always been a Republican, and cast his first presidential vote for Abraham Lincoln. He was brought out by his party for circuit clerk of Schuyler County, in 1870, and for State Senator some years later. He belongs to the secret societies of Masonry, A. O. U. W. and G. A. R. Mrs. Tisdale is a member of the Methodist Church.

Wesley D. Trimble, farmer, was born in Morgan County, Ohio, in 1848, and is a son of Daniel and Nancy (Miner) Trimble, natives of Ohio, where they were reared and married. They moved to Illinois when Wesley was seven years old, taking him with them. In 1856 the family moved to Appanoose County, Iowa, where Mr. and Mrs. Trimble spent their latter days. The father was a farmer by occupation, and in politics a Democrat. Our subject was the third child of a family of eight sons and two daughters. He was reared under the parental roof, making himself useful upon the farm, and received but a very limited school education. At the age of twenty he began life for himself by working upon the railroad. In 1872 he went to southwestern Kansas, but after living there four years, and suffering greatly from chills, spent a year in travelling through Texas, Arizona and New Mexico. He then returned to Iowa, and in 1879 married Miss Julia A., daughter of Alexander and Hannah (Noggle) Wills, natives of Macon County, Mo., and Ohio, respectively. Mr. and Mrs. Wills were married in Illinois, and afterward became early settlers in Schuyler County, locating upon a farm from which they never moved, and upon which Mr. Trimble now resides. This farm now consists of 167 acres of well cultivated land, upon which is a comfortable house and good outbuildings. Mrs. Trimble was born in Schuyler County, in 1857, is a worthy member of the Christian Church, and the mother of four children: James E., Clarence F., Mary N. and Effie L.

Stephen S. Vittetoe, farmer and stock raiser, is a native of Grainger County, Tenn., and was born in 1818. His parents, Thomas and Susannah (Dodson) Vittetoe, were early settlers of his native county, and the father died there in 1880. The mother is still a resident of the same county. Our subject remained at home until fifteen years of age, and then worked out until twenty-one years old, when he started in life for himself. In 1840 he married Miss Emeline, daughter of William Proctor and Margaret (Yaden) Proctor, formerly of Grainger County, Tenn., where Mrs. Vittetoe was born. To Mr. and Mrs. Vittetoe twelve children have been born, all save one now living: Frankie (wife of Isaiah Capps, of Cedar County), Thomas, William Proctor (of Cedar County), Silas, Joseph, John R., Levandie, Minnie (wife

of James Coleman, of Adams County, Ill.), Mollie (wife of John
Van Meter), Rhoda (wife of Henry C. Patterson), and Florence.
In 1842 Mr. Vittetoe removed to Adair County, where he lived
about thirty years, and then went to Des Moines County, Iowa,
where he remained until 1871, when he came to Schuyler County
and located just west of Queen City, where he now has a fine
farm of 120 acres and thirty acres of timber. Mr. Vittetoe has
always been a hard working and industrious man, and his property is the result of his hard labor and good management. He
was one of the early settlers of Adair County, Mo. Politically
he is a Democrat, and cast his first presidential vote for Van
Buren, in 1840. His wife is a member of the old Baptist
Church.

William Wayman, farmer and stock raiser, was born in Michigan in 1840, and is a son of William and Mary (Price) Wayman, natives of Bucks County, Penn., where they were reared
and married. They afterward lived in Indiana and Michigan,
and in 1840 removed to Jo Daviess County, Ill., where the father
died in 1846. The mother was married a second time about
1856 to George Byers, who is also deceased. Mrs. Byers lives
in Illinois, and is a member of the Methodist Episcopal Church.
Our subject was reared by his mother, and in 1862 married Miss
Sarah Ellen, daughter of Amos and Elizabeth Scott, natives of
Pennsylvania and Kentucky, respectively. Mrs. Wayman was
born in Illinois, and to her union with our subject eight children
have been born, all save one living: Henry E., William Ira,
Mary E., Amos Scott, Jesse E., Thomas W. and James. Mr.
Wayman remained in Jo Daviess County until 1876 and then
came to Schuyler County, and located one mile north of Green
Top, where he has 486 acres of land under good cultivation. He
has made farming his sole occupation, and is now one of the
prosperous and substantial farmers of the county. In politics he
is a Republican, and cast his first presidential vote for Lincoln.
He is a member of the I. O. O. F. and is a public spirited citizen,
greatly interested in the education of the future generation.

William Welsh, farmer and stock raiser, is a native of Scotland, and was born in 1815. He is a son of William and Margaret (Derby) Welsh, also natives of Scotland, where they
were reared and married, and where the father died when our
subject was an infant. His widow was again married in 1852,
emigrated to the United States, and soon after died in Illinois.
William availed himself of the advantages offered by the
best schools of his native country, and soon acquired proficiency
in his studies, being especially advanced in mathematics. When
eighteen years of age he came to the United States, and spent

several years working on a canal, and then went to Illinois where he superintended the construction of a railroad being built in that State. He was married in New York City, in 1833, to Miss Jane Chissolm, a native of Scotland, by whom he had twelve children, six of whom are now living: Joseph (of Kansas), Alexander (of Kansas), Isabella (wife of William Birney), George, Jane (wife of William Farr) and Thomas. Mrs. Welsh died in 1863 and the following year Mr. Welsh married Mrs. Nancy Reduian, by whom he had five children, three now living: John, Charley and Newton. In 1865, he located two and one-half miles north of Queen City, where he has a fine farm of 760 acres, after having given his children 800 acres. His farm is one of the finely improved and cultivated tracts of land in this section of the country, and is the result of industry and good management. He is also an extensive stock dealer. In politics he was once a Whig, but is now a Republican. He is a member of the Methodist Episcopal Church, and one of the substantial and worthy men of the county.

William J. Williams, proprietor of the Glenwood Woolen Mills, was born in Wales, in 1838, where he was reared and educated at the common schools of the country. During his youth he became proficient in the millwright and carpenter trades, which he learned of his father. When eighteen years of age he left his native country and came alone to the United States, and after arriving in Des Moines County, Iowa, near Burlington, where an uncle of his was residing, he decided to remain and work on his uncle's farm for a while, but his uncle died suddenly and left him to shift for himself again, and he began to build and repair mills, but by working on river mills, got the fever and ague so bad that he was not fit to live or die. He purchased a saw-mill and timber, and engaged in the manufacture of lumber and also added woolen machinery for the manufacture of woolen goods. Later he gave his whole attention to the latter business, and, in partnership with two others, ran a large factory, but on account of mismanagement and debts contracted without his knowledge, by his partners, the business was soon ruined. In 1881 he came to Glenwood and purchased the Glenwood Woolen Mills, which he has since run, and to which he has attached a saw-mill. September 15, 1870, he married Amanda J. Johnson, a native of Iowa, and born October 20, 1852. To this union five children have been born: John Albert, George Thomas, Annie May, Walter Greenleaf and Howard Percy. Mr. Williams is a member of the Congregational Church. In politics he is conservative and votes for the man he thinks best without regard to political affiliation. For twenty-three years he has been a Mason and is a member of Glenwood Lodge No. 427; was initiated in 1864 at Adoniram Lodge No. 120, Iowa.

Dr. James A. Wilson, physician and surgeon, was born in Virginia in 1845, and is the son of Dr. Joseph and Rachel L. (Bell) Wilson, also natives of Virginia, where they spent their entire lives. The father was a graduate of Jefferson Medical College, of Philadelphia, Penn., and made the medical profession his life-long occupation. He was for some time physician and surgeon of the insane asylum of his State, and died at the age of seventy-three, full of professional honors. The mother died in 1853. Our subject was reared at home, and his early school life was spent at the common schools of his county. He took two courses at the Washington and Lee University at Lexington, Va., and read medicine one year with his father. In 1866–67 he attended the medical department of the University of Virginia, at Charlottesville, Va., from which institution he graduated in 1867. A year later he graduated from the Bellevue Hospital Medical College of New York, and immediately commenced to practice his profession in Augusta County, Va., where for a number of years he was recognized as one of her leading physicians. In 1878 he came to Schuyler County, and located at Green Top, where he has built up an extensive and lucrative practice, and ranks among the foremost in his profession in the county. He also superintends his farm of over 500 acres. In December, 1864, he enlisted in McClannahan's battery, Confederate Army, and served six months during the Virginia campaign. The next six months he had charge of a signal line from Staunton to Huttonsville, Va., and then for three months was at Staunton in the topographical department, aiding in perfecting a description of the campaign of the valley, and also spent three months at the same occupation in Winchester and vicinity. In September, 1872, he was married to Martha T., daughter of Henry and Angeline Mish, a native of Virginia, by whom he has had six children, three of whom are living: Wallace, Maggie and Susie. Mrs. Wilson died June 15, 1886, and Dr. Wilson wedded Miss Sallie J. Dunlap, a native of Virginia, in March, 1887, and lost his last wife, in June, 1887. In politics Dr. Wilson is a Democrat, and he is a member of the I. O. O. F. He is a public spirited man, and is always interested in laudable public enterprises.

Charles Wirth, lumber merchant, is a native of Bavaria, Germany, and was born in 1842. His parents, Michael and Anna (Graser) Wirth, were natives of Germany, where the father was engaged in mercantile business. He was born in 1800, and died in 1868. The mother was born in 1805, and died in 1869.

Our subject is the only living child of his parents, and received his early education at the common schools of his native country until fourteen years of age, and then attended a business college for four years, and, after graduating from that institution, traveled for a match factory for three years, at the end of that time immigrating to the United States and locating in Burlington, Iowa, and worked in a lumber yard. His employers moving to Keokuk in 1870, Mr. Wirth accompanied them, and remained in their employ until 1875, when he came to Lancaster, and established a business for himself, in which he is still interested. He now owns the oldest and largest lumber yard in Lancaster, and deals in all kinds of pine lumber, shingles, doors, windows, etc., and is regarded as one of the best business men of the town. He is comfortably situated in a two-story frame dwelling, which he erected in 1883 at a cost of $3,000, and which is located in a desirable locality. In April, 1872, he married Miss Mary Maurer, daughter of Henry Maurer of Burlington, Iowa, in which Mrs. Wirth was born in 1857. This lady is the mother of three children: Minnie, Ida and an infant. Mr. Wirth is a Democrat, and cast his first presidential vote for S. J. Tilden in 1876. He is a member of the I. O. O. F., of the past-grand degree, and himself and wife are members of the Roman Catholic Church.

Jacob Wittmer was born in Switzerland, in 1828, where he received a common-school education. He left his native country in 1845, and came to the United States, locating in Ohio until 1858, and then coming to Schuyler County, Mo. In 1859 he located at Green Top, and engaged in shoemaking until 1880, since which time he has been a furniture dealer, cabinet-maker and undertaker at that place. He was married at Portsmouth, Ohio, to Miss Susan, daughter of John Reuder, a native of Bavaria, and to this union five children were born, viz:: Jacob (of Sullivan County), Elizabeth (wife of Samuel Walker, of Horton, Kas.), Charlotte (wife of Milton C. Asher, of Trenton), Deborah and Mary. In 1882 Mr. Wittmer was elected county judge of the Third District, and filled that office efficiently for a term of two years. He is a Democrat, and cast his first presidential vote for Pierce in 1852. He is a prominent member of the I. O. O. F., and has served as representative in the State lodge two years. His parents were George and Aster (Stirneman) Wittmer. The father was born in 1801, and the mother about ten years previous. In 1848 they immigrated to the United States, and located in Ohio, where they spent the remainder of their lives. In early life Mr. Wittmer was foreman of a silk factory, for twenty years.